Guide to:

CATSKILL TRAILS

Second Edition
The Forest Preserve Series (2nd ed.), Volume VIII

Editors, Carol and David White
Series Editor, Neal Burdick

The Adirondack Mountain Club, Inc.

Copyright © 1988, 1994 by
The Adirondack Mountain Club, Inc.
All rights reserved.
Photographs by Bruce C. Wadsworth except where noted otherwise.
Design by Idée Design, Diamond Point, NY

First edition, 1988
Second edition, 1994
   reprint with revisions, 1995, 1998, 2000, 2002

Published by the Adirondack Mountain Club, Inc.
814 Goggins Road, Lake George, NY 12845-4117
www.adk.org

Library of Congress Cataloging-in-Publication Data

   Guide to Catskill trails / editors, Carol and David White
Adirondack Mountain Club.
      —2nd ed.
         p. cm.—(The Forest preserve series. ; v. 8)
   Includes index.
   ISBN 1-931951-01-2 : $16.95
   1. Hiking – New York (State)—Catskill Mountains – Guidebooks.
2. Trails— New York (State)—Catskill Mountains—Guidebooks.
3. Catskill Mountains (N.Y.)—Guidebooks   I. Adirondack Mountain Club,
Schenectady Chapter.   II. Title.   III. Series : Forest preserve
series (2nd ed.) ; v. 8
GV199.42.N652C378   1994
796.5'1'0974738—dc20   2002105261
ISBN 0-935272-64-x (set)   CIP

Printed and bound in the
United States of America

Dedication

Sooner or later, every hiker meets a forest ranger. Helpful information may be exchanged in a friendly conversation on the trail. Or the ranger may be acting as an educator, speaking to your organization on a topic of common concern. Perhaps the ranger descends out of the sky from a helicopter to provide assistance to an injured hiker. The ranger may be on patrol, fighting a fire, catching up on paperwork in the office, or talking by telephone from his or her home at night when the conversation takes place.

In all cases, the hiker has come to expect a helpful attitude, a quiet professional competence, and a sense of dedication from the person wearing the Forest Ranger shoulder patch.

Let us remember the forest ranger. Since May 15, 1885, when the Forest Ranger force was created, rangers have protected both the forests of the state and the people who use them. It has been a job well done.

BRUCE C. WADSWORTH

Catskill Region

87 Interstate highway
17 State highway
47 County road

Margaretville

Pepacton Reservoir

Turnwood
Quaker Clearing

To Hancock

Lewbeach
Mongaup Pond

Roscoe

Claryville

Liberty

Neversink Reservoir

N

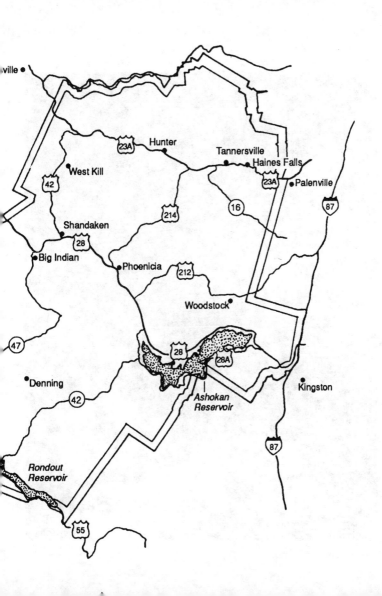

Spring mountain laurel, Willow Trail

Preface to the Second Edition

The four years since the first edition of this book have seen great changes in the Catskills. The region is entering a great struggle in reference to water rights and water purity. The Catskill Interpretive Center is about to become a reality. Perhaps the most significant factor in regard to hiking is the completion of many unit management plans by the Department of Environmental Conservation (DEC). DEC is now implementing those plans. This is particularly true in Sullivan and Ulster counties, where many new trails have opened in the Willowemoc–Long Pond Wild Forest and around Alder Lake. This edition of *Guide to Catskill Trails* reflects these changes. Many new trails have been added and other changes made to the book.

Another significant change has been in trail maintenance. The New York/New Jersey Trail Conference has assumed light trail maintenance responsibilities for many DEC trails. Trail work by the Appalachian Mountain Club has continued. The Adirondack Mountain Club has sent its professional and volunteer crews into this region. This combined interest has resulted in much improvement in trails.

This edition of *Guide to Catskill Trails* has new sections and appendices that will be of great use to the physically impaired and to those hiking with children.

Finally, the author is most thankful for the many hikers who helped in field work, offered suggestions or assisted in many other ways. The personnel of DEC, especially Bill Rudge, have been most helpful, and their assistance is very much appreciated.

BRUCE C. WADSWORTH
Guilderland, New York
May 1994

Preface to the First Edition

The Adirondack Mountain Club tried for many years to find someone to write a Catskill guidebook. Though there were many people eminently qualified to do the job, the club could find no one person willing to take on such an immense task. In 1985, the Schenectady Chapter of ADK proposed that it undertake the guide as a chapter effort. The club's Publications Committee was enthusiastic about the idea, and a four-year project was begun.

A coordinating committee consisting of myself, Gerhard Salinger, Betty Lou Bailey, John Wiley, Kathleen Gill and Kenneth Coulter determined the basic format of the book.

I had primary responsibility for the writing and for coordination of the effort. Before the book was finished, however, over 30 individuals, both from club and nonclub sources, had done field work, written rough drafts, and provided crucial information.

Particularly essential to the success of the venture was my wife, Betty, who spent most of three years walking trails with me, changing personal plans to accommodate the guidebook work schedule, and providing unending encouragement.

Chapter members who made especially significant contributions were Evelyn and Gerhard Salinger, Mary and Michael Bunch, John Wiley, Doris Quinn, and Kenneth Coulter. Other chapter and club members who participated in the project were Winifred Balz, Linda Laing, Larry Russ, Carl Kaplan, Marvin Weaver, Robert Barnhart, Alan Belensz, Virginia Plunkett, Patricia Mead, Inger Maeland, Elisse Kessler Wiley, Hans T. Kessler, Mildred and Clark Gittinger, Beryl Wolfe, Walter Herrod, Evelyn Johnson, Etto Von Zastrow, and Peter

Wadsworth.

DEC personnel who were unending in their willingness to provide current information were, Region 3, William Rudge; Region 4, Richard Weir and John Sencabaugh; and DEC Bureau of Environmental Education, Craig Thompson.

Communications with Halbe Brown (Frost Valley YMCA) and Howard Beye (Finger Lakes Trail Conference, Inc.) were very helpful.

Finally, many thanks go to the ADK Publications Committee for its encouragement and support, to ADK Publications Director Carmen Elliott for her quiet professionalism in making a manuscript into a book, and to the Forest Preserve Series editor, Neal Burdick, for his professional excellence.

To all who have helped, thank you.

BRUCE C. WADSWORTH
Guilderland, New York
August 1988

Attention All Hikers, Backpackers, and Canoeists!

Because trail and waterway conditions change, and new boundaries and easements are established, we revise and update our guidebooks regularly. If you have come across an error, discrepancy, or need for an update in this guidebook (be sure you are using the latest edition), we want to hear about it so a change can be made in the next edition.

Please address your comments to the publications director of the Adirondack Mountain Club, citing guidebook title, year of edition, section or trail described, page number, and date of your observation. Thanks for your help.

Note: ADK makes every effort to keep its guidebooks up to date. However, each printing can only be as current as the last press date; thus, use of this information is at the sole risk of the user.

Contents

Route Guides and Page Maps

Note: This guide can be used with the New York–New Jersey Trail Conference's 5-part topographic map set, *Trails of the Catskill Region.* The map set can be purchased by calling ADK at 1-800-395-8080 (M–S, 8:30–5), by visiting our Web site (www.adk.org), or from the New York–New Jersey Trail Conference, 232 Madison Avenue, New York, NY 10016 (tel. 212-685-9699). *Booksellers:* To obtain the map set, please contact the Trail Conference directly.

1885   1985

THIS TABLET COMMEMORATES
THE ONE HUNDREDTH ANNIVERSARY
OF NEW YORK STATE'S
FOREST PRESERVE.
THE SURROUNDING MOUNTAINS,
STREAMS AND WOODLANDS REMAIN
A LEGACY FROM THE PAST.
PROTECTED BY THE
CONSTITUTION OF NEW YORK STATE,
THEY REPRESENT A HERITAGE
FOR FUTURE GENERATIONS.

ERECTED 1985 BY
ENVIRONMENTAL
CONSERVATION DEPARTMENT
STATE OF NEW YORK

Introduction

The Adirondack Mountain Club
Forest Preserve Series

The Forest Preserve Series of trail guides covers myriad hiking opportunities within the Adirondack and Catskill Forest Preserve of New York State. The Adirondack Mountain Club (ADK) published the first guidebook in this series sixty years ago with the idea that its hiking guides would eventually cover all Forest Preserve lands; it is appropriate that the completion of this series coincided with the decade-long centennial celebration of the enactment of the Forest Preserve legislation. Each guide in this series, listed below, has been revised within the last few years.

Vol. I: *Guide to Adirondack Trails: High Peaks Region*
Vol. II: *Guide to Adirondack Trails: Northern Region*
Vol. III: *Guide to Adirondack Trails: Central Region*
Vol. IV: *Guide to Adirondack Trails: Northville–Placid Trail*
Vol. V: *Guide to Adirondack Trails: West-Central Region*
Vol. VI: *Guide to Adirondack Trails: Eastern Region*
Vol. VII: *Guide to Adirondack Trails: Southern Region*
Vol. VIII: *Guide to Catskill Trails*

The public lands that constitute the Forest Preserve (Adirondack and Catskill) are unique among all other wild public lands of the United States in that they enjoy constitutional protection against sale or development. Today, groups such as the Adirondack Mountain Club strive to guard this constitutional protection.

The protection of many of the scenic and aesthetic resources of the Forest Preserve also rests with the individual hiker, who has the responsibility not to degrade these resources in any way while enjoying their wonders. The Forest Preserve Series of trail guides seeks not only to show hikers where to hike but also to interpret the area's natural and social history and offer guidelines whereby users can minimize their impact on the land.

The Catskills

Aboard the *Half Moon* in September 1609, Hendrick Hudson must have been impressed as he watched the sun fall behind the mountains to the west. His vantage point on the Hudson River gave a commanding view. Gazing upward, he admired what Henry Rowe Schoolcraft called *Ontiora*, the "Mountains of the Sky."

To the Dutch, they became the Katts Kills, but nobody is quite sure why. In Dutch, the word "kill" means "stream". Popular explanation has it that a wildcat, the bay lynx, lived in the area, so Katts Kill could be Anglicized to become Wild Cat Creek. Others believe a creek was named after Jacob Cats, a well known poet, magistrate, and keeper of the Great Seal of Holland during that period. It is known that a Dutch ship, christened *The Kat*, voyaged up the Hudson shortly before the term appeared.

For a time, the mountains were known as the Blue (Blew) Mountains. John Burroughs thought it would be more fitting to call them the Birch Mountains, since this tree is so common there. Almost no one remembers they were once the Hooge Landt van Esopus, the Lothian Hills, the Blauwbergen, or the Katzbergs. Today, they are the Catskill Mountains, although geologically they are not mountains at all.

The Catskills are often said to be mountains with only one side. The Great Wall of Manitou, forming the eastern scarp of the region, rises 1600 feet above the valley; the slopes peter out to hills in the west. The Catskills are the eroded edge of the Allegheny Plateau, with rivers cutting into the plateau to form narrow valleys known as cloves. Between the cloves, the remaining plateau forms structures which outwardly resemble mountains. The almost horizontal rock layers, unlike the more tilted or folded rock of true mountain ranges, are proof that the uplift was uniform.

Springtime hikers immediately notice the difference between the Catskills and the Adirondacks. Catskill trails tend to be more firm and dry. The Catskill hiker often starts in a narrow clove and climbs steeply upward, whereas the Adirondacker eases up moderate beginning grades. The differences are due to the geology of the regions. The more easily eroded sedimentary shales and bluestones of the Catskills age differently from the hard massive metamorphic anorthosites and gneisses of the Adirondacks.

Geologists tell us that North America and Africa collided and parted several times in the last billion years. Each collision lasted millions of years. Centimeter by centimeter, mountain ranges were forced upwards by this tectonic process. Early collisions helped form the Adirondacks; later ones, beginning about 500 million years ago, formed the Appalachians.

The Taconic mountains (part of the early Appalachians) rose to the east. Plantless and bare, the earth rapidly eroded into the shallow sea to the west, where the Catskills and New York's Southern Tier are now found. In the late Silurian Period, red and green clays were deposited to form the shales now found in the lower stretches of the Plattekill and Katterskill cloves. By the Devonian Period, 395–345 million years ago, nearly 8000 feet of sediments had accumulated.

A final collision began the Acadian Orogeny in the Northeast; the mountains of New England emerged from the sea. A side effect of this relentless force created the Appalachian Plateau and Catskill

Delta. The large Catskill Delta included both today's Catskills and Pocono mountains. Erosion has since gouged out valleys between them, making them appear distinct from each other. To the east, the softer Catskill shales eroded faster than the harder limestones of the Taconics and the Hudson River valley formed, separating the Catskill Delta from its sediment source.

In the Catskills, a hard cap rock conglomerate (the Twilight Park conglomerate) protected the softer rock beneath, but cloves kept deepening wherever the conglomerate had worn through. Catskill ranges and valleys generally run southeast to northwest.

Over all this, Pleistocene Ice Age glaciers advanced several times in the last two million years. Adirondack and New England mountain ranges, running southwest to northeast, were affected far more significantly by glaciation than were the Catskills. Consequently there are few naturally formed lakes in the Catskills, and relatively few other glacial formations. The glacial meltwaters did cause rapid erosion of the shale layers, forming the many waterfalls seen today throughout the Catskill vales wherever more resistant sandstone or siltstone layers slowed the process.

The Catskill shales and sandstones readily accept water between or in their layers, resulting in underground aquifers rather than the lakes found lying on the impervious rocks of the Adirondacks and throughout New England.

Just as the origin of the name "Catskills" is a mystery, so the geographic area represented by the term is often unclear. The Forest Preserve was created on May 15, 1885, to protect the state's water resources. The Catskill portion of the Preserve included "all the lands now owned or which may hereafter be acquired by the State of New York ...," in Greene, Sullivan, and Ulster counties. Delaware County was added to the list in 1888.

The Catskill Park was created in 1904. Its "Blue Line" boundary encompassed the Forest Preserve land and some of the private lands in the four counties named above. Of its over 700,000 acres of both public and private lands, 280,000 acres, or 42% of the total, is Forest Preserve. That is not all of the Catskills, for when the Temporary State Commission to Study the Catskills was created by the legislature in 1971, the commission was charged to study over 6,000 square miles of Catskills, within its "Green Line." The Green Line encompasses the counties of Greene, Delaware, Otsego, Schoharie, Sullivan and Ulster, plus the townships of Berne, Coeymans, Knox, New Scotland, Rensselaerville, and Westerlo in Albany County.

Alf Evers, the noted Catskill historian, once asked an old man where the Catskills began. The answer was, you keep on going until "there are two stones for every dirt." Evers also quotes his son, Christopher, as saying, "They used to say that for six days the Lord labored at creating the Earth and on the seventh he threw rocks at the Catskills."

Rocks do dominate the Catskills. The imposing escarpment on its eastern edge seems a fortress. To the Indians it was the Great Wall of Manitou, behind which the evil spirit Mitchie Manitou lurked to defend against human spirits.

The region reminded the Dutch and Palatine Germans of the deep, forbidding forests of Europe. They, too, avoided going into it. Colonial land survey records show that 20% of the original Catskill forest was hemlock—dark hemlock whose shadows hid the wildcats that screamed in the night. Behind that steep wall lived the Devil. Hikers will find the Devil's Path, Devil's Kitchen, Devil's Chamber, Devil's Pulpit, Devil's Tombstone, and Hell Falls. Transforming old legends from Europe, blending in Indian stories and weaving their own tales, colonists developed a dread fear of these mountains.

The Dutch sought the rich bottomlands around the steeper slopes. The Palatine Germans left the Hudson and settled the Schoharie Valley in the west. When the English changed New Amsterdam to New York, a century after Hudson had explored the great river, they were after tall timbers for the masts of the king's navy ships.

A prosperous Kingston merchant, Johannis Hardenbergh, through means yet not fully understood, managed to be granted a 1.5-million-acre land patent in 1708. It essentially included the whole of the Catskill Mountains. Years of legal battles chipped off pieces as the Livingstons, Cornelius Cool, the Hurleys, and others gouged out their fiefdoms.

Gradually, homesteaders were enticed to rent the deeper valleys. The hated Colonial Whig absentee landlords found that English promises of free land made Tories of many of their Dutch tenants during the American Revolution. The Mohawk Chief, Joseph Brant, was quite selective in whom he ordered his tribesmen to kill or capture.

Once the American Revolution ended, the attack on the Catskills by outside interests began in earnest. The target was trees. Landlords reserved trees above a certain diameter for their own use. Tenants who arbitrarily cut them down lost their rights. Landlords required tenants to transport specific amounts of lumber to mills as part of their yearly obligations.

One species of tree, *Tsuga canadensis*, the Eastern hemlock, became more prized than all others. Tannin was needed for tanning leather, and the hemlock's bark had a rich supply. By 1816, when Colonel William Edwards came to the Catskills, there were at least 75 tanneries in the mountains.

These small tanneries wounded but did not slay the forest. Colonel Edwards, backed by New York City money, established in Hunter on the Schoharieskill a tannery of such scope that it soon not only drove the small tanners out of business, but also changed the character of the Catskills forever. Colonel Pratt did the same thing a few years later, in Prattsville. Whole hemlock groves disappeared, letting in the sunlight and drying out the earth to foster conditions more appropriate for birch, oak, and maple. Acids from the tanneries polluted the streams, but there was prosperity until the hemlock was gone. Over a century later, there is again pressure to cut these great slopes, now protected in the Forest Preserve, even though 85% of the forests within the Green Line are on private lands.

The 19th century brought the world to the Catskills. Several forces simultaneously converged to make the Catskills famous. In 1819, Washington Irving wrote *The Sketchbook of Geoffrey Crayon, Gent,* and the world was introduced to Rip Van Winkle. That delightful character from the Village of Falling Waters (Palenville) went off to South Mountain and, after bowling a bit with the ghosts of Henry Hudson's crew, slept for twenty years.

Then there was Thomas Cole. There had been other painters of the Catskills before Cole—notably Van Berganin in the 1730s, P. Lodet in the 1790s, John Vanderlyn in the early 1800s—but it was about Cole that John Trumbull, the recognized leader in Amencan art in this period, said, "This youth has done what I have all my life attempted in vain!" Said to be a romantic realist, Cole was the first of what eventually became known as the Hudson River School of Landscape Painting.

Steamboats now brought vacationers rapidly upriver from New York City. Railroads were soon to penetrate the valleys. Grand hotels such as the Overlook House, Catskill Mountain House, Laurel House, Grand Hotel, Tremper House, and Rexmere hosted the elite of the United States and Europe.

Then came World War I, automobiles, airplanes, and new vacation meccas around the world. Like Rip Van Winkle, the Catskills slept (except for the Sullivan County resorts such as Grossingers and the Concord, which are outside the Catskill Park). The best of the mountains was protected by the Forest Preserve, but little else developed in any organized manner until the Catskill

Center formed in 1969, the Temporary State Commission to Study the Catskills reported its findings in 1975, and the Catskill Park State Land Master Plan was released in 1985. The great resources and cultural heritage of the Catskill region are once again receiving the critical attention needed to preserve them for the future.

Using This Guidebook

The trails described in this book are, for the most part, within the Blue Line of the Catskill Park. All are within the greater Catskill region. Principal highways in the region are NY 30, NY 23 and 23A, NY 28, NY 42, NY 212, and NY 214. Interstate 87 in the east, Interstate 88 in the west, NY 17 in the south, and NY 32 in the north are used by motorists to reach the region. (See pp. iv and v.)

An extensive network of roads into the larger valleys and cloves makes day trips feasible for most Catskill outings. This book is designed to accommodate the day tripper. The organization of the book is built around major valleys and their road networks. Each section has one or more Route Guides for trunk roads and all laterals that lead to trailheads. Since one of the most difficult problems in the Catskills is determining trailhead access, this system will greatly simplify planning for hikers.

Like all books in the Adirondack Mountain Club's Forest Preserve Series, this book is intended to be both a reference tool for planning trips and a field guide to carry on the trail. All introductory material should be read carefully, for it contains important information regarding the use of this book as well as numerous suggestions for safe and proper travel on foot.

The introductions to each of the sections in this book will give hikers an idea of the varied opportunities available to them.

Maps

The maps designed to be used with this book are composites of USGS quadrangles with updated overlays of trails, shelters, and private land lines. They were developed by the New York-New Jersey Trail Conference and have been modified for use on Catskill trails. These maps are especially valuable because of the combination of contour lines from original base maps and recent trail information. Copies of the Catskill maps can be purchased from ADK by calling 1-800-395-8080 (M–S, 8:30–5) or from the New York-New Jersey Trail Conference, 232 Madison Ave., New York, NY 10016.

The trails described in this guide have been coded to the maps to make locating them on the maps easier. The reduction in map scale when making map composites necessarily reduces map detail. Trail descriptions fill in the essential information for outings on trails. Off-trail bushwhacks are another matter. It is always a good idea to purchase the larger-scale 7.5-minute series topographic maps for off-trail use. The greater topographic detail of these maps can add a significant degree of safety and enjoyment to bushwhack outings.

Unmaintained Trails and Bushwhack Routes

Some trails are routinely maintained by DEC crews, forest rangers, ADK or other designated groups and individuals. These trails are generally clear and otherwise in good condition, though seasonal blowdown, heavy storms or other short-term events may temporarily cause a problem. In this guide, such trails are numbered.

Other trails have no official designated maintainers and may indeed be illegally maintained. The hiker should not expect these trails to be in as good condition as the maintained trails. Some of these trails are described in the guide, but are not numbered. However, they are normally quite usable.

Some routes are defined as bushwhacks. A bushwhack is a route where there is no trail. In this book, bushwhack routes also are not numbered. Sometimes, frequent use of the bushwhack route results in one or more herd paths which may or may not lead to the desired destination. The participant in a bushwhack should have good map navigation skills and have done thorough planning before initiating the outing.

Reaching a trailless peak presents a different kind of challenge from following a marked trail to a mountain summit. Use USGS maps (for large scale) when route planning. The hiker must be able to read a map, use a compass, and possess that all too rare commodity, common sense. When you are picking your way through cripplebush, trying to set a steady course and swatting blackflies at the same time, there can be considerable psychological strain. It always seems you've walked farther than you actually have, so when a check point isn't hit at the estimated time, it's easy to second guess yourself. A significant mental error, an injury, a sudden change in the weather, or any of a dozen other unforeseen events can result in an unexpected night in the woods.

Consequently, while off-trail hiking is probably the most satisfying outdoor adventure, one should ease into it. Learn from experienced people, have planned escape routes in mind, and be sure someone at home knows where you are hiking and what to do to get help if you don't report in by a given time.

Trail access points and general routes of ascent for those trailless Catskill mountains over 3500 ft. in elevation are given in this guidebook. Estimated distances and specific routes have intentionally not been given. If you cannot determine a good line of ascent and make a fair estimate of the distance, you are not ready for off-trail hiking. Being able to set your own course and then demonstrate that you can successfully reach your destination is one of the primary satisfactions of bushwhack experiences.

The Catskill 3500 Club has placed bright orange canisters on the summits of those trailless peaks over 3500 ft. in elevation. The canisters mark the true summits and contain notebooks for the recording of ascents.

Select your party members carefully. The group should be small to reduce impact on the land. Be sure each individual is up to the challenges of the outing. Stick together on the mountain. Carry extra clothing and food. Determine your ascent and descent routes and write in compass bearings in the comfort of home rather than at the top of a windswept mountain in the rain.

Trail Signs and Markers

With normal alertness to one's surroundings, trails in the Catskills are easy to follow. In most cases, where a trail leaves a highway or comes to a junction there is a sign to direct the hiker. As much as possible, descriptions in this guidebook are detailed enough so the hiker can find the correct route even in the rare case where signs are temporarily down. The trails themselves are usually marked with plastic disks identifying the organization responsible for maintaining them. Trails maintained by the DEC are marked with blue, yellow, or red disks; the particular color for each trail is indicated on the signs and in the guidebook description.

Hikers must be aware that some trails are easier to follow than others due to level of use. Although this guidebook does mention particularly tricky turns in the trail descriptions, each hiker must remain alert at all times for changes of direction. Group leaders have a particular responsibility not to let inexperienced members of the party travel off by themselves. A trail that seems "obvious" to a more experienced person may not be that way at all to the neophyte.

In addition to a map, all hikers should carry a compass and know at least the basics of its use. In some descriptions, this guide uses compass bearings to differentiate the trail at a junction or to indicate the direction of travel above timberline. More importantly, a compass can be an indispensable aid in the unlikely event that you may lose your way.

Finally, it should go without saying that one should never remove any sign or marker. Hikers noticing damaged or missing signs should report this fact to the appropriate group: DEC, Region 3 Headquarters, 21 S. Putt Corners Rd., New Paltz NY 12561 for Sullivan or Ulster counties; and DEC, Region 4 Subregion Office, Jefferson Rd., Stamford NY 12167 for Delaware and Greene counties.

All trails described in this guide either are on public land or on private land where the public has permission to hike. However, there may be "posted" signs at some points. These are usually there to remind hikers that they are on private land over which the owner has kindly granted permission for hikers to pass. In most cases neither leaving the trail nor camping, fishing, or hunting are permitted on these lands, and hikers should respect the owner's wishes.

Winter Hiking

There's nothing quite like the first hint of dawn light on fresh snow in a snug mountain valley. One cannot adequately express the feelings one has when braced against a stiff wind above tree line with the view stretching seemingly to infinity. Mountains in winter are entirely different from the ones you've come to know in the summer.

Just as the visual world is vastly different in winter, the challenges that must be met are also greatly different. Winter hiking presents a different level of activity. Energy output is much higher and heat control becomes a major concern. The amount of daylight is shortened. Snowshoes and boots add greatly to the weight lifted with each step. Good planning is essential. The price for error is much higher in winter than in summer.

For many people, the Catskills can be reached by a fairly short drive from home. The steepness of the mountain slopes can be challenging, the time for ascents is generally not overly long. There are many snowshoe outings that permit the climber to have a nice day hike and still return home fairly early in the evening. Nordic skiing is also possible and to a greater extent than is generally recognized.

Your vehicle should be in good operating condition. Many Catskill trailheads are at isolated places where a breakdown is no joke in winter. Be sure you have a full tank of gas, a shovel and a well-charged battery. A sleeping bag and extra food are also good things to have available.

Many Catskill trails have steep, rocky ascents and ledges. Great care is needed. Instep crampons should always be in your pack after first frost. A good walking stick or ice axe is another essential piece of winter equipment.

Sudden weather changes can rapidly create hypothermic conditions for the unprepared. Good wind protection should be carried.

Finally, always have a good flashlight. Get an early start because nightfall comes early.

This guidebook is not a manual for winter hiking. Within the confines of this guide, it is only possible to stress that one should not attempt winter hiking without preparation and knowledge. There are some excellent books available on winter hiking and camping. ADK's *Winterwise: A Backpacker's Guide* by John Dunn is a good starting point. Go on trips with experienced winter hikers before heading your own party. The mountains are great in the winter, but you must know what you are doing.

Hiking with Children

Hiking with children can be one of the most interesting and meaningful events an adult can experience. The younger the child is when first pleasantly exposed to the out-of-doors, the more deeply will an appreciation of nature grow within that child. The key word in the last sentence is *pleasantly*.

It is essential for the supervising adult to realize that the child's innate curiosity will stimulate the youngster to do many things the adult may not have placed on the day's agenda. If the child is to develop a strong feeling for nature, the adult must allow the child time and opportunity to explore and become immersed in these activities, within the boundaries of safety.

Distances:

The very young should be carried. At rest breaks, let the child wander, while being closely monitered. The emphasis should be on letting the child's curiosity create the activity pattern; the adult should encourage, but not force, activity. When the child is old enough to walk easily, observe if the first few trips are too easy or too hard. In general, before the age of four, be careful to keep the trips quite short, unless it is obvious the child wants longer trips. By age six, most children can handle moderate day trips and some can do as much as some adults, if the pace and difficulty are reasonable. Young children are often seen in the mountains, but parents should not force these trips on the mentally unwilling or the physically unready.

Pace:

Children vary tremendously in their ability to hike. The younger the child, the longer the time that must be allowed for the trip. The joy of being with children is to have the time needed to participate in unplanned events that occur, without the nagging feeling that you are behind schedule.

Let the child lead the way occasionally and see how fast you are being led. There will come a time when you are the one moving too slowly for the group and the child will go ahead. *A good rule is to tell your child never to pass a trail junction without waiting for the rest of the group to catch up.* The key to pacing is to set reasonable speed for the child or the slowest member of the party.

Supplies:

Today, there are child carrier pack frames with special pockets for diapers, etc. However, if the child is big enough to walk along easily, then the child should be able to carry some of the needed supplies. Perhaps a small pack for snacks, bathing suit or some small toys might be a starter. As time goes on, the child can carry water and lunch. It won't be long before a compass or flashlight is added. The adult will be carrying the bulkier and heavier items for quite a few years. Remember, the emphasis is to interest the young. Do not over-exert them with too much gear to be comfortable. By age four or five, magnifying glasses can be fun to use. Later on, field binoculars, magnetic compasses and even simple mapwork can be introduced. Photography of flower identification may lead to collections and scrap books.

Attitude:

Often, when hiking parents find their children don't enjoy hiking, they fail to realize that it is their attitude, and not that of the child, that is at fault. The adult must realize the nature of the child and allow time for the desire to "rough it" to develop naturally. By starting slowly, the child soon will be asking for more; by overdoing it, the child will want less. Make things enjoyable. Provide opportunities and suggestions, but let the child select those things that are of interest. Build upon the child's interests.

For suggestions on suitable hikes for children in the Catskills, refer to Appendix III, *Table of Short Hikes*, found on page 294.

Hiking with the Physically Impaired

Everyone should have the opportunity to share the beauties of nature and the joy of testing one's skills in the out-of-doors. Physically impaired individuals have completed the 132-mile Northville–Placid Trail, paddled great rivers, camped in winter snows and participated in practically any outdoor activity that can be named. However, we all have limitations and it is necessary to stay within these parameters if we are to have a safe and enjoyable experience. It is important that each individual and each trip leader know the limitations of members of the group. Therefore, while there are really no trails that are off limits for *some* physically impaired individuals, each person must realistically determine the limitations that exist for him or her.

Trip Leader:

Before taking a physically impaired person on a particular trail, it is essential that the trip leader be extremely familiar with that trail and has taken into account the necessary actions that will be required to safely negotiate any rough spots with the physically impaired person. This person should be informed of difficulties to be met along the way and the expected demands.

The trip leader must also take into account the other members on the trip. Is the trip especially designed for the physically impaired person or is it one that happens to have a physically impaired person in the group? Will the rate of travel and general situation be a surprise to others in the group, completely changing the expected nature of the hike, or will the travel rate and situation be essentially as they would be in the absence of the physically impaired person? If the former is the case, then the other members of the group should be notified prior to the trip.

The Senses:

Part of the enjoyment of nature is exposure to heightened experiences of the senses. Take this into account when designing trips for the physically impaired. If the person has lost specific senses, try to explain activities that will increase use of the other senses. Night or pond sounds, the murmuring of a brook, star gazing, the smell of balsam fir, swimming, the sounds of moving birds, the feel and sound of falling rain or snow, the roaring of wind and many more sensations can have special meaning if they are new or infrequently experienced by the physically impaired person.

Attitude:

The physically impaired person, trip leader and friends should have a clear and mutual understanding of what outcomes are expected on trips. No desired activity should be considered impossible until detailed thought has taken place. Outings become failures only when problems have not been anticipated, when difficulties are not eagerly looked upon as desired challenges and when the limitations of the trip have not been accepted so the possibilities can be fully enjoyed. A "can do" attitude will result in many happy experiences.

For suggestions for some possible hikes and other outings for the physically impaired, refer to Appendix IV, *Opportunities in the Catskill Region for Physically Impaired Recreationists*, on page 297.

Distance and Time

Except for trailless mountain descriptions, mileage in this guidebook is generally accurate to within one-tenth of a mile. Short distances are expressed in yards.

In the beginning of each section of this guide is a listing of trails described in the section, the length of each trail, and the number of the page on which the trail description is found. All mileage distances are cumulative, the beginning of the trail being the 0.0 mi. point. A distance summary is given at the end of each description with a total distance expressed in kilometers as well as in miles. If a trail has climbed significantly over its course, its total ascent in both feet and meters is provided. To the inexperienced hiker, these distances may seem longer on the trail, but he or she will quickly learn that there is a great difference between "sidewalk" miles and "trail" miles.

Many Catskill trails were first described in a period when the beginning parts of trails were over dirt roads. Several current guides retain the original dirt road sections, although they are, today, actually paved roads. In this guide cumulative mileage begins at the trailhead, where actual walking usually begins. This makes some of the total distances given in this guide seem shorter than in some other guides. Logistical planning can more realistically be carried out, however, by using the actual walking distances expressed in this guide.

No attempt has been made to estimate travel times on these trails. A conservative rule to follow is to allow an hour for every 1.5 mi. plus one-half hour for each 1000 ft. of ascent, letting experience indicate how close the hiker actually is to this standard. Most day hikers will probably go a little faster than this, but backpackers will probably go somewhat slower as the weight of the pack increases. Some quickening of pace usually occurs when descending, although this may not be true on steep descents.

Abbreviations and Conventions

In each book in the Forest Preserve Series, R and L, with periods omitted, are used for right and left. The R and L banks of a stream are determined by looking downstream. Likewise, the R fork of a stream is on the R when one faces downstream. N, S, E and W, again without periods, are used for north, south, east and west. Compass directions are given in degrees, figuring from true N, with E as 90 degrees, etc. The following abbreviations are used in the text and on the maps:

ADK	Adirondack Mountain Club
DEC	New York State Department of Environmental Conservation
PBM	Permanent Bench Mark
USGS	United States Geological Survey
ft.	feet
jct.	junction
km	kilometer or kilometers
m	meter or meters
mi.	mile or miles
yds.	yards

Wilderness Camping

It is not the purpose of this series to teach one how to camp in the woods. There are many good books available on that subject which are more comprehensive and useful than any explanation that could be given in the space available here. The information below should, however, serve to make hikers aware of the peculiarities of the Catskills while giving strong emphasis to currently recommended procedures to reduce environmental damage—particularly in heavily used areas.

Lean-tos are often found at convenient locations along the trails; there are also many possibilities for tenting along the way. The regulations regarding tenting and use of shelters are simple and relatively unrestrictive when compared to those of other popular backpacking areas in the country; however, it is important that every backpacker know and obey the restrictions that do exist, since they are designed to promote the long-term enjoyment for the greatest number of people.

General Camping Guidelines:

Except for groups of ten or more, and smaller groups planning to stay in one place for three nights or longer (see "Groups" below), no camping or fire permits are required in the Catskills, but campers must obey all DEC regulations regarding camping. Listed below are some of the most important regulations. Complete regulations are available from the DEC and are usually posted at trail access points.

1) No camping within 150 ft. of a stream, other water source, or trail except at a designated campsite. Camping areas are designated with the following symbol:

An inappropriate campsite, or one that can no longer be used for camping, will be marked with a similar symbol, but will have a diagonal line through the teepee.

2) Except in an emergency, no camping is permitted above 3500 ft. in elevation. (This rule does not apply from December 21 to March 21.)

3) All washing of dishes must be done at least 150 ft. from any stream, pond, or other water source. No soap, even so-called "biodegradeable" soap, should ever get into the water. Use a pot to carry water at least 150 ft. away from your water source, wash items, and then dispose of the dirty water away from the water source. One can also take a surprisingly effective bath by taking a

quick dip and then using a pot for soaping and rinsing away from the stream or pond.

4) All human excrement must be buried under at least four inches of dirt at a spot at least 150 ft. away from any water source. All toilet paper should either be similarly burned or packed out. Use established privies or latrines when available.

5) No wood, except *dead and down* timber, may be used for fire building. Good wood is often scarce at popular campsites, so a portable stove for cooking is highly recommended.

6) No fire should be built near any flammable material. Much of the forest cover in the Catskills is composed of recently rotted twigs, leaves, or needles and is highly flammable. Build a fire at an established fireplace, on rocks, or on sand. Never leave a fire unattended. Before leaving, be sure the fire is extinguished and that all traces of any fireplace you built have been destroyed. Again, a portable stove is preferable to an open fire.

7) Paper or wooden refuse can be burned or carried out of the woods. Do not bury refuse. Be sure that no packaging to be burned contains metal foil—it will not burn no matter how hot the fire. Remember—if you carried it in, you can carry it out!

8) In general, leave no trace of your presence when leaving a campsite, and help by carrying out any litter left by those less thoughtful than you.

Lean-tos:

Lean-tos are available on a first-come, first-served basis up to the capacity of the shelter—usually about seven persons. A small party cannot therefore claim exclusive use of a shelter and must allow later arrivals equal use. Most lean-tos have a fireplace in front (sometimes with a primitive grill) and sometimes a privy. Most are located near some source of water, but each camper must use his own judgment as to whether or not the water supply needs water purification before using. (As older lean-tos are being replaced, they are often rebuilt farther from the water supply.)

It is in very poor taste—and is illegal—to carve or write one's initials in a shelter. Please try to keep these rustic shelters in good condition and appearance.

Since reservations cannot be made for any of these shelters, it is best to carry a tent or other alternate shelter. Many shelters away from the standard routes, however, are rarely used, and a small party can often find a shelter open in the more remote areas.

The following regulations apply specifically to lean-tos, in addition to the general camping regulations listed above:

1) No plastic may be used to close off the front of a shelter.

2) No nails or other permanent fastener may be used to affix a tarp in a lean-to, but it is permissible to use rope to tie canvas or nylon tarps across the front.

3) No tent may be pitched inside a lean-to.

Groups:

Any group of ten or more persons, and smaller groups planning to camp in one place for three nights or longer, must obtain a permit *before* camping on state land. This system is designed to prevent overuse of certain critical sites and to encourage groups to split into smaller parties more in keeping with the natural environment. Permits can be obtained from the DEC forest ranger closest to the actual starting point of one's proposed trip. The local forest ranger can be contacted by writing to him or her directly; if in doubt about whom to write, send a letter to the DEC office of the region in which you will be hiking (see page 12). Your letter will be forwarded to the correct ranger, but allow adequate time.

One can also make the initial contact with the forest ranger by telephone, but keep in mind that rangers' schedules during the busy summer season are unpredictable. Forest rangers are listed in the white pages of local telephone books under "New York, State of; Environmental Conservation, Dept. of; Forest Ranger." Remember when calling that most rangers operate out of their private homes. Observe normal courtesy, please. Contact by letter is much preferred, and, as one must realize, camping with a large group requires careful planning several weeks before the trip.

Drinking Water

For many years, hikers could trust practically any water source in the Catskills to be pure and safe to drink. Unfortunately, as in many other mountain areas, some water sources have become contaminated with a parasite known as *Giardia lamblia*. This intestinal parasite causes a disease known as *Giardiasis*—often called "Beaver Fever." It can be spread by any warm-blooded mammal when infected feces wash into the water; beavers are prime agents in transferring this parasite because they travel widely from waterway to waterway. Hikers can unknowingly become agents in spreading this disease if they happen to be unaffected carriers and use poor camping procedures by which giardia organisms are spread. Symptoms of the disease may not become apparent for a number of weeks, long after the hiker has returned home.

Prevention: Follow the guidelines for the disposal of human excrement as stated in the section "Wilderness Camping" (above). Equally important, make sure every member of your group is aware of the problem and follows the guidelines as well. The health of a fellow hiker may depend on your consideration.

Choosing a Water Source: While no water source can be guaranteed to be safe, smaller streams high in the mountains which have little possibility of a beaver dam or human presence upstream are usually safe to drink. Day hikers are advised to carry water from home. Treat any water that gives cause for concern.

Treatment: Boil all water for 2-3 minutes, administer an iodine-based chemical purifier (available at camping supply stores and drug stores), or use commercial filters designed specifically for Giardiasis prevention. If after returning from a trip you experience recurrent intestinal problems, consult your physician and explain your potential problem.

Lyme Disease

Hikers in New York State need to be familiar with Lyme disease. Named for an illness with arthritic-like symptoms that appeared in Lyme, Connecticut, in 1975, this disease has been a definite concern in Suffolk and Westchester counties. It is slowly moving up both sides of the Hudson River and has been detected in most counties.

The disease is caused by bacteria but is spread by ticks in various life-stages. It is particularly associated with the deer tick and over-populated deer herds. In 75% of documented cases, people with Lyme disease developed a skin rash resembling the bite of a large insect. The rash spreads outward from the bite in rings. Other early symptoms are fever, headache and fatigue. Later stages of the disease cause paralysis of facial muscles, arthritis, irregular heartbeat, heart blockage and meningitis.

While the disease is not in epidemic proportions (1993), it is something with which hikers should be familiar. If early symptoms are recognized, antibiotics can usually control it with good success. In later stages, treatment has been less successful. EARLY DETECTION IS IMPORTANT.

Hikers can reduce their chances of being bitten by ticks if they wear long pants and long-sleeved shirts, tuck pants bottoms into sock tops and use insect repellents having a high percentage of DEET. On returning from a wooded area, thoroughly inspect yourself and take a shower or bath. Wash your clothes immediately. Seek prompt medical attention if any of the early symptoms appear.

Rabies

For several years rabies has been moving northward from Pennsylvania. While it is most often associated with raccoons, any warm-blooded mammal can be a carrier.

It is essential that hikers do not feed or pet wild animals.

Avoid any wild animals that are behaving oddly. If bitten by a raccoon or other animal, go immediately for medical care. Rabies is a fatal disease and immediate care is essential to prevent death.

Campsite Cleanliness

Campsite cleanliness has several purposes, other than the obvious one of general comfort. You will find it rubs off, and others pick up the habit. This, in turn, can mean that you find a tidier campsite to occupy elsewhere, or when you return. There will be fewer animals getting into your gear and food. It will be a healthier campsite to occupy.

Bear Bags:

Bears are common to the Catskills. Some are ingenious in how they go about reaching your food; all are hungry. The camper should store food at least 10 ft. high and 5 ft. away from the main trunk of trees. The drawing on page 27 is one way to protect your food.

Tips on Bear-Proofing Your Campsite

Never store food in your tent.

Wrap odiferous foods well.

Wrap trash in sealed plastic bags or other sealed containers.

Hang clothes worn while cooking with your pack. They hold food odors and attract bears.

Keep a clean fire pit. Grease and food scraps will attract bears.

Hang packs from a high branch incapable of holding a bear's weight.

Report any bear encounters to the nearest forest ranger or ranger station.

Forest Safety

The Catskills are noted for their steep, rocky grades, which often lead up to relatively flat ridge trails. One must be prepared for sudden storms with accompanying sharp drops in temperature in all seasons. Hikers should carry extra clothing, including wind and rain gear.

The particular demands of each outing must be evaluated prior to the trip. While all rock requires caution, wet rock can be extremely hazardous. Almost anyone can climb the Slide Mt. Trail from near Winnisook Lake, but novices should probably gain experience before heading down the steep slopes from the Slide Mt. summit towards Cornell and Wittenberg. Rocks in the Catskills tend to be much slicker when wet than rocks in the Adirondacks.

Spring comes later and autumn comes earlier on the summits than in the valleys. Although true winter conditions generally won't be seen before November, they last into April on the upper slopes. Remember, too, that hypothermia is much more common in windy, warm months than in the colder months, when most people wear the proper clothing to combat it.

In winter conditions it is strongly suggested that persons travel in groups not less than four in number. Proper gear should include equipment needed for an overnight bivouac of an injured person. For more information on winter travel, see *Winterwise,* the Adirondack Mountain Club's guide to winter backpacking by John Dunn.

Hikers and Hunters

One marvelous aspect of publicly owned state land is that it is open to everyone for many recreational purposes. Since hunting is one very popular use, hikers should expect to encounter hunters in the woods occasionally. Much stress and displeasure can occur when either party is inconsiderate of the needs and/or rights of the other party. The occurrence of problems can be greatly reduced by careful planning.

It is advisable to avoid heavily hunted areas during big game seasons. Since it is difficult to carry a deer or bear long distances or over steep terrain, hikers will meet few hunters over a mile from a roadway or in rugged mountain country. Lower deciduous slopes of beech, maple, and hemlock have much more hunting pressure than cripplebush spruce and balsam fir on upper slopes. Motorized vehicles are not allowed in areas designated as Wilderness, so hike there; most areas designated as Wild Forest have woods roads where vehicles can be used, so avoid these areas. Hunters will be found in deep woods areas where there are roads. Try to avoid the opening and closing days of regular deer season. For safety purposes, wear a bright-colored jacket or shirt.

Big game seasons in the Catskills are as follows:

Archery Season (Deer and Bear): October 15 through the day preceding regular deer season and the five days following regular season.

Regular Season (Deer): First Monday after November 15 through the first Tuesday after December 7. (Bear): First Saturday of regular season through the first Tuesday after December 7.

Muzzle-loading Season: When a season is held, it may be the seven-day period ending on the day before the regular season or the seven days following the regular season.

The hiker should also be alert during spring turkey season.

Emergency Procedures

An ounce of prevention is always worth a pound of cure, but if one needs emergency assistance, the DEC forest rangers are the first people to contact for help. The names and telephone numbers of local rangers are often posted inside each trail register box. Forest rangers are listed in the white pages of local telephone books under "New York, State of; Environmental Conservation, Department of; Forest Ranger." If this fails, one should seek directory assistance for the nearest regional DEC office. A third source of help is the New York State Police. Tell the operator it is an emergency.

Be sure persons going for help have written down the information that will be given to the agency providing the rescue assistance. This must include the status of the injured person and a clear description of the location of the party needing assistance (preferably marked on a map).

The Adirondack Mountain Club

The Adirondack Mountain Club (or ADK, the initials AMC having been claimed by the previously formed Appalachian Mountain Club) was organized in 1922 for the purpose of bringing together in a working unit a large number of people interested in the mountains, trails, camping, and forest conservation. A permanent club headquarters was established, and with increasing membership, club chapters were organized. The chapters are as follows:

Adirondak Loj (North Elba), Albany, Algonquin (Plattsburgh), Black River (Watertown), Cold River (Long Lake), Finger Lakes (Ithaca–Elmira), Genesee Valley (Rochester), Glens Falls–Saratoga, Hurricane Mt. (Keene), Iroquois (Utica), Keene Valley, Knickerbocker (New York City area), Lake Placid, Laurentian (Canton–Potsdam), Long Island, Mid-Hudson (Poughkeepsie), Mohican (Westchester and Putnam Counties, NY), New York (metropolitan area), Niagara Frontier (Buffalo), North Jersey (Bergen County), North Woods (Saranac Lake–Tupper Lake), Onondaga (Syracuse), Ramapo (Rockland and

Orange counties), Schenectady, Shatagee Woods (Malone), and Susquehanna (Oneonta). In addition, there is an extensive membership-at-large.

Most chapters do not have qualifying requirements: a note to the Membership Director, Adirondack Mountain Club, 814 Goggins Road, Lake George, NY 12845-4117, will bring you information on membership in a local chapter (e.g., names and addresses of persons to be contacted) or details on membership-at-large. Persons joining a chapter, upon payment of their chapter dues, *ipso facto* become members of the club. Membership dues include a subscription to *Adirondac,* a bimonthly magazine; ADK's newsletter; and discounts on ADK books and at ADK lodges. An application for membership is in the back of this book.

Members of the Adirondack Mountain Club have formulated the following creed, which reflects the theme of the club and its membership:

> We, the Adirondack Mountain Club, believe that the lands of the State constituting the Forest Preserve should be forever kept as wild forest lands in accordance with Article XIV, Section 1, of the New York State Constitution. We favor a program under the administration of the Department of Environmental Conservation (in the Adirondacks, pursuant to the Adirondack Park Agency policy) that will provide ample opportunities for outdoor recreation in a manner consistent with the wild forest character of the Preserve. We favor acquisition of additional wild lands to meet the goals of the State Land Master Plans for watershed and wildlife protection and for recreation needs, and we support protection of the open-space character of appropriate private lands within the Adirondack and Catskill parks. We believe an informed public is essential to the well-being of the Preserve and the parks. We seek to accomplish measures that are

consistent with this policy, and we oppose measures that are contrary thereto.

In the 1990s, nearly 35,000 "ADKers" enjoy the full spectrum of outdoor activities, including hiking, backpacking, canoeing (from floating on a pond to whitewater racing), rock climbing, cross-country skiing and snowshoeing. Most chapters have an active year-round outings schedule as well as regular meetings, sometimes including a meal, and programs featuring individuals ranging from chapter members to local and state officials. Many ADKers are also active in service work ranging from participation in search-and-rescue organizations to involvement in the ongoing debate over the best use of our natural resources and forest or wilderness lands, not only in the Forest Preserve but also in their immediate localities.

ADK Information Center & Headquarters

At the southernmost corner of the Adirondack Park is the long log cabin that serves as the ADK Information Center and Headquarters. The building, located just off Exit 21 of I-87 ("the Northway") about 0.2 mi. S on Route 9N, is open year-round. Hours: Monday–Saturday, 8:30 A.M.–5 P.M.

ADK staff at this facility provide information about hiking, canoeing, cross-country skiing, climbing and camping in the Adirondack and Catskill Forest Preserve, and about ADK's lodges and facilities near Lake Placid. In addition, they host lectures, workshops, and exhibits; sell publications and ADK logo items; and provide membership information. Call or write ADK, 814 Goggins Road, Lake George, NY 12845-4117 (telephone: 518-668-4447) or visit our Web site at <www.adk.org>.

NEAL BURDICK, Forest Preserve Series Editor
BRUCE C. WADSWORTH

Black Dome Valley– North Point Section

The great horseshoe of mountains surrounding Black Dome Valley offers the hiker a large variety of options for day trips or backpack outings. The Blackhead Range on the S side of the horseshoe includes three of the highest mountains in the Catskills (Black Head, Black Dome, Thomas Cole). Windham High Peak, on the N side of the horseshoe, is also over 3500 ft. in elevation.

The N half of the Escarpment Trail from North Point is contained in this section. (This is also part of the Long Path.) The Escarpment Trail, from Blackhead Mt. to NY 23, composes the N part of the great horseshoe. All access routes to the Escarpment Trail and the Blackhead Range are included in the trail descriptions.

The Windham Peak access parking area for both the Escarpment Trail and the Long Path is found on the N side of NY 23, about halfway between Windham and East Windham. This can be used as a reference point for reaching the Big Hollow-Barnum Rd. access routes. Co. Rd. 65 to Maplecrest is found 1.2 mi. W of the Windham Peak access parking area.

Trail in winter: *Windham Peak is an easy winter climb and a good one for novices. Blackhead Mt. provides excellent views, but is more demanding. The loop from Blackhead Mt. to Acra Peak and back to the parking area is a good full-day outing. Doing Thomas Cole, Black Dome and Blackhead in one winter day requires an early start and good physical condition. The stretch W of Thomas Cole is quite open and often requires good wind protection. Descent off the E side of Black Dome is steep and requires care.*

Short Hikes:

Camel's Hump—*3.0 mi. round trip. A pleasant walk with a few short, challenging parts that can be done slowly. The reward is a sweeping view introducing one to the region.*

Dutcher Notch Trail—*4.0 mi. round trip. An ascending woods walk that is not difficult if not rushed. There are no sweeping views from the trail, but the forest is very attractive, especially in spring and autumn.*

Moderate Hikes:

Windham High Peak from NY 23—*6.6 mi. round trip. Generally gradual, moderate grades lead to a summit providing excellent views of the region.*

Acra Point Loop—*5.1 mi. point to point. This loop includes a short part of the Black Dome Trail to the Batavia Kill Trail to the Escarpment Trail to the Acra Point/Burnt Knob Access Trail. It begins and ends at the Big Hollow Rd. terminus parking area. Many open vistas of the region are available.*

Black Dome Mt. Trail—*4.0 mi. round trip. This trip, though short, requires some stiff climbing. The best view of this part of the Catskills is from Black Dome Mt.*

Harder Hikes:

North End of Escarpment Trail—*11.5 mi. point to point. From Big Hollow, climb to the Blackhead Mt. Spur Trail. Ascend to the summit of Blackhead Mt. and then N on the Escarpment Trail to Windham High Peak and NY 23. A rigorous hike with rewarding views.*

Blackhead Range Trail to Big Hollow Road—*5.4 mi. point to point. Though a relatively short trip, the cumulative vertical ascent and descent makes this a challenging but very interesting trip.*

Trail Described	Total Miles (one way)	Page
Long Path (NY 23 to Co. Rd. 10)	6.95	36
Windham High Peak	3.3	42
Elm Ridge	1.1	43
Acra Point/Burnt Knob Access	1.1	44
Batavia Kill	1.0	45
Escarpment (Northern Section)	15.9	45
Dutcher Notch	2.0	50
Colgate Lake to Dutcher Notch	4.3	51
Black Dome Mt.	2.0	53
Blackhead Mt. Spur	0.6	55
Blackhead Range	3.4	55

ROUTE GUIDE TO BIG HOLLOW RD.

Mileage W to E	Description	Mileage E to W
0.0	Windham High Peak trailhead parking area, 17 mi. W of I-87 (NYS Thruway) on NY 23. Continue W from this point.	8.5
1.2	Turn L on Co. Rd. 65 for Maplecrest.	7.3
2.0	Turn L, just before bridge, onto Co. Rd. 65A.	6.5
2.3	It becomes Co. Rd. 40, which continues to Maplecrest. R turn leads a short distance to Hensonville. (Good ice cream store.)	6.2
4.2	Maplecrest. Continue straight ahead on Co. Rd. 56, if going to Big Hollow. If going to	4.3

(1) Long Path: NY 23 to Co. Rd. 10

Map 41: M-1, N-1
NE Catskills

Some 94 mi. of the Long Path pass through the Catskill Park. This section of the trail is the northernmost part that is partially found in the park. It travels over three peaks and is deceptively strenuous. This is because the approximate ascents of 1690 ft. and descents of 1455 ft. give a cumulative total of 3145 ft. of elevation change over a 6.95 mi. distance.

Trailhead: The southern trailhead is on the N side of NY 23, 3 mi. E of Windham village at the intersection with Cross Rd. There is a large DEC parking area there. The N end of this section is reached from Windham village by taking Mitchell Hollow Rd. N about 5 mi. to Co. Rd. 10. Turn R (E) and after a short distance follow a curve L past Cunningham Rd. The Long Path crosses Co. Rd. 10, 0.3 mi. farther down the road. Parking must be at roadside near the trailhead.

From the S, the Long Path comes off Windham Peak (trail 2), crosses NY 23 and then follows Cross Rd. 150 ft. to a point 50 ft.

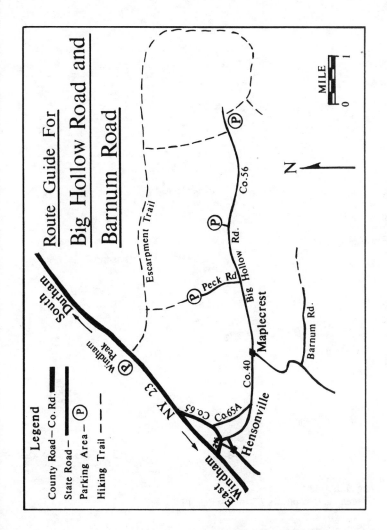

Route Guide For
Big Hollow Road and Barnum Road

Legend

County Road – Co. Rd. ▬▬▬
State Road – ▬▬
Parking Area – Ⓟ
Hiking Trail – – – –

MILE

N

Escarpment Trail

Co.56

Peck Rd

Ⓟ

Ⓟ

Big Hollow Rd.

Maplecrest

Barnum Rd.

Co.40

Hensonville

Co.65

Co.65A

NY 23

Windham Peak

Ⓟ

South Durham

East Windham

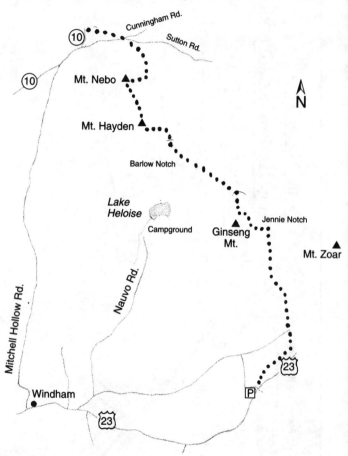

Long Path (trail 1)
Base map is Hensonville 7.5-min. series, 1945

beyond the entrance of the parking area. Here, it turns R, into the woods where a trail register is soon seen attached to a tree. The trail follows blue DEC trail markers, which must be carefully observed along most of this section. This is a walk through an open woods where there is not a well defined treadway.

The route is parallel to NY 23 and sound, but not sight, of vehicles is evident. A wet area is crossed on a log walkway at 0.1 mi. At 0.3 mi. the route turns NW. The slope climbs gradually, soon entering a hemlock stand. Old Rd. is reached at 0.75 mi. and the trail leaves state land. *Henceforth, trail markers on private property are aqua-colored paint blazes.* A double paint blaze means that a sharp change of direction will soon occur on the trail.

Turn L and walk 20 ft. to Jenne Notch Rd. Turn R and follow this pleasant country lane. At 1.0 mi., macadam ends and grades begin to climb gradually. There is a red metal gateway at 1.3 mi., just past a brick house. The trail proceeds past the gate, ascending a brief grade, where height of land at 1.4 mi. provides good views. Behind you across the valley is the ridge of the Escarpment Trail. Ahead at R front is Mt. Zoar, Ginseng Mt. is at L front, and Jenne Notch is between them.

The generally flat gravel road soon reaches a dip to the L and then begins a stiff climb toward the notch with moderate and steep grades. At 2.2 mi., the route makes a sharp turn L and another to the R, before ascending steeply to a second metal gate. Beyond the gate is a deep rock outcrop at L—perhaps an old quarry. Again, there are good views to the rear.

The trail is now nearly level on an older woods road. Height of land in Jenne Notch is reached at 2.35 mi. Here, the trail makes a sharp L and begins to climb another woods road of moderate grade on Ginseng Mt. The way soon becomes extremely steep for 500 ft. before making a sharp turn R, entering the woods as a path. Still climbing, but less steeply, the path begins to cross below the summit of Ginseng Mt. almost on contour. Heading NW, this short stretch has difficult footing, as leaves make walking the cross slope a bit challenging. (It is a short vertical ascent to the summit, where excellent viewing is possible in winter, but where summer leaves greatly limit observers at other times, except to the NE.)

The trail eventually merges with and follows a faint old woods road. It makes a sharp turn L off the woods road, and after about 200 ft., a much more clear woods road is joined at 2.85 mi. Bear R. From here, the ridgeline is followed generally NW all the way to Mt. Nebo.

A long gradual downgrade ensues. About 20 minutes later Lake Heloise can be seen far below at L. Mt. Hayden is close in at R front. Mt. Pisgah and, far away, Huntersfield Mt. can be seen on the horizon to the L of Mt. Hayden. Then, at 3.2 mi., the logging road makes a sharp drop L, but the trail bears R on the level and enters the woods. It winds along the rim of an escarpment to a point where the Ski Windham slopes can be seen beyond Lake Heloise on Cave Mt. Ginseng Mt. can now be seen easily.

At 3.6 mi., the trail makes a sharp R and follows some short switchbacks to a point very near the top of a ridge knob in an open field at 3.7 mi. Here, with confusing trail change of direction trail signs, the route makes a sharp L and descends. Part way down the slope, another set of confusing change of direction trail signs simply means a jog around a boulder with continued descent.

Beyond this, the trail becomes level at 4.0 mi. in Barlow Notch. Pass straight through a 4-way jct. and then almost immediately turn R at a T-jct. A flat stretch soon leads to the base of a steep, winding woods road up Mt. Hayden. (There is a nice lookout into the valley of the Manor Kill to the R, 100 yds. before climbing commences.)

The ascent up Mt. Hayden is a series of alternating steep and then level sections. After two steep sections another potentially confusing spot occurs on a long level zone at approximately 4.5 mi.

Here, the trail leaves the logging road, reentering the woods, where it follows an escarpment rim for a distance before rejoining the same logging road at approximately 4.7 mi. where steeper climbing begins up the mountain again.

The reason this is confusing is that aqua paint blazes occur not only along the rim trail, but also on rocks along the logging road. This presents a problem if the hiker follows the logging road markings because when the rim route reenters, visible markers can be seen leading the wrong way back to the rim edge, but none are present in the correct uphill direction. *Continue uphill, though no trail markers will be seen for a considerable distance.* The flat summit of Mt. Hayden is reached at 4.95 mi. No views are available.

The descent from Mt. Hayden is initially moderate in grade, but eventually becomes gradual along a faint woods road. Mt. Nebo appears a distinct mountain when seen from a distance but is really the end of the long continuing ridge off Mt. Hayden. Its "summit" is just a level spot on this ridge and is reached at 5.55 mi.

A sharp switchback R is the beginning of a steep descent off the side of the mountain that runs down to the valley below. Again the hiker must be careful for a short stretch. A woods road is joined at 6.2 mi. and the way becomes easier. The remains of a burned and collapsed home are passed just before Sutton Rd. is reached at 6.3 mi.

Immediately to the L is a fork jct. where Sutton Rd. merges with Cunningham Rd. Walk straight through this fork onto Cunningham Rd. Re-enter the woods just past the road fork on the N side of the road. The route gradually descends through a scraggly woods to the NW. Soon the quality of forest improves to mostly young maples and the trail gradually ascends W until it reaches Co. Rd. 10 at 6.95 mi. Across the road, the Long Path continues into the next section toward Mt. Pisgah.

Distances: *To Old Rd., 0.75 mi.; to first gate on Jenne Notch Rd., 1.3 mi.; to col of Jenny Notch, 2.35 mi.; to point directly below summit of Ginseng Mt., 2.6 mi. Summit elevation, 2810 ft.; to top of knob, 3.7 mi.; to col of Barlow Notch, 4.0 mi.; to summit of Mt. Hayden, 4.95 mi. Summit elevation, 2920 ft.; to summit of Mt. Nebo, 5.55 mi. Summit elevation, 2660 ft.; to Sutton Rd, 6.3 mi.; to Co. Rd. 10, 6.95 mi. (11.3 km).*

(2) Windham High Peak Trail

Map 41: N-1
NE Catskills

The route up Windham High Peak from the W follows a section of the Escarpment Trail to its summit. The grade varies from gradual to moderate, making a generally easy climb. This would be an excellent beginner snowshoer's winter ascent.

Trailhead: *A DEC sign marks the trailhead parking area, 3.0 mi. E of Windham on NY 23.*

From the trailhead (0.0 mi.), cross NY 23 and head E, following blue DEC trail markers. Almost immediately a picturesque bridge takes you over the outlet of Silver Lake to a flat, grassy route past old stone walls and apple trees that leads to a trail register at 0.1 mi.

From here, a gradual incline leads through deciduous forest. The trail becomes rockier as it steepens at 0.7 mi. The route turns L at 0.8 mi., leveling before turning back to the R, where it enters an old woods road. A switchback climbs moderately to the Elm Ridge Trail jct. at 1.1 mi. The Elm Ridge Trail leads S to Peck Rd.; see below. (A pipe spring is found 0.2 mi. down the Elm Ridge Trail.

Continuing on the blue trail, a side trail R at 1.15 mi. leads 100 yds. to the Elm Ridge Lean-to. The trail becomes moderate again.

Varying grades, never really difficult, guide you upward. The trail crosses several sections of split logs over a wet area at 1.8 mi. and passes a DEC 3500 ft. elevation sign at 3.1 mi. Then it levels and runs just below the actual summit of Windham High Peak at 3.3 mi.

Fine viewing is found to the N. Hikers who have spotted a second vehicle at the end of Big Hollow Rd. can extend their outing by continuing another 2.7 mi. over Burnt Knob to the Acra Point/Burnt Knob Access Trail (see below) and then walking another 1.1 mi. down it to their vehicle. This would make a through trip of 7.1 mi. A still longer day trip of 10.0 mi. is possible by continuing along the Escarpment Trail past the Acra Point/Burnt Knob Access Trail jct., over Acra Point, and then down to the parking area via the Batavia Kill and Black Dome Trails (see below).

Distances: *To Elm Ridge Trail jct., 1.1 mi.; to Elm Ridge lean-to, 1.15 mi.; to bog bridging, 1.8 mi.; to 3500 ft. elevation sign, 3.1 mi.; to summit, 3.3 mi. (5.3 km). Ascent, 1784 ft. (535 m). Summit elevation, 3524 ft. (1078 m).*

(3) Elm Ridge Trail

Map 41: N-2
NE Catskills

The Elm Ridge Trail connects into the Escarpment Trail (trail 6) and Peck Rd. (See Big Hollow–Barnum Rd. Access Routes above.)

Trailhead: *This short trail leaves the parking area at the terminus of Peck Rd. (0.0 mi.). It is marked both with yellow DEC trail markers and cross-country trail markers. A trail register is found 100 ft. along the trail.*

Heading N, the route is a nearly level old woods road and may be wet in early spring. Stone walls are on both sides of the trail at 0.4 mi., as a gradual grade begins to climb the ridge. A pipe spring (look sharp) is at 0.65 mi. The junction with the Escarpment Trail (trail 6) is reached at 0.85 mi. (Turning R, one can find a side trail R a short distance along the Escarpment Trail, leading 100 ft. to the Elm Ridge lean-to).

Distances: To stone walls, 0.4 mi.; to spring, 0.7 mi.; to Escarpment Trail jct., 0.9 mi. (1.4 km).

(4) Acra Point/Burnt Knob Access Trail

Map 41: O-2
NE Catskills

The Acra Point/Burnt Knob Access Trail provides a connection with the Escarpment Trail (trail 6) and thus permits a variety of loop options for day hikes in the region. This trail is sometimes included as a section of the Blackhead Range Trail or as part of the Black Dome Trail in other trail guides. Since it connects with the Escarpment Trail on the opposite side of the valley from the Blackhead Range, its designation as used in this guide is considered less confusing.

Trailhead: The trail begins on the N side of Big Hollow Rd. (0.0 mi.), 0.1 mi. W of the parking area at the end of the road. It follows red DEC trail markers. One hundred ft. after entering the woods, it crosses a bridge over the Batavia Kill to where a trail register is located. It then crosses a tributary, on rocks. (This second crossing can be difficult in times of high water.)

The route then follows the E side of the tributary and recrosses it at 0.34 mi., leaving the attractive creek climbing steadily for 0.45 mi. Bearing NW at 0.8 mi., the grade becomes nearly level to the jct. It reaches the Escarpment Trail at 1.0 mi. Burnt Knob is 1.0 mi. W. Acra Point is 0.7 mi. E.

Distances: *To bridge, 100 ft.; to last crossing of tributary, 0.5 mi.; to Escarpment Trail, 0.7 mi. (1.1 km).*

(5) Batavia Kill Trail

The Batavia Kill Trail provides access to the Escarpment Trail (see below), enabling the hiker to have several options for day hikes. It gains 500 ft. elevation before reaching the Escarpment Trail (trail 6).

Trailhead: *The trail originates at a jct. (0.0 mi.) with the Black Dome Mt. Trail, 0.5 mi. from the Big Hollow Rd. parking area.*

From the jct., cross the Batavia Kill and head SSE along the S stream bank, following yellow trail markers. The gradual upgrade route is generally in view of the stream as it ascends the valley. The trail makes a swing to the E just before it reaches the Batavia Kill lean-to at 0.65 mi.

Climbing soon becomes more difficult on a moderate grade beyond the lean-to. It levels just before reaching the jct. with the Escarpment Trail at 1.0 mi.

Distances: *To Batavia Kill lean-to, 0.65 mi.; to Escarpment Trail, 1.0 mi. (1.6 km.) (1.5 mi. from Big Hollow Rd.).*

(6) Escarpment Trail (Northern Section)

This section of the Escarpment Trail follows long grades. With full pack they are enjoyable when going downhill, but the hiker will find energy is sapped when going uphill. Day trippers biting off a section at a time with light packs will find the trail delightful. Vistas are frequent. Carry plenty of water, since it is sparsely distributed on the ridges.

The Long Path (see "Extended and Challenging Opportunities", p. 281) coincides with this entire portion of the Escarpment Trail. Since the Long Path is generally described from S to N, so must the Escarpment Trail. If day trippers use judicious selection of access trails, so as to hike the Escarpment Trail northward, the use of this guidebook will be facilitated. The Windham High Peak Trail (trail 2) description covers the northernmost part of the Escarpment Trail in a N to S direction.

General background on the Escarpment Trail can be found in the chapter "Extended and Challenging Opportunities." Refer to the Palenville–North Lake Section for a description of the first 7.2 mi. of the Escarpment Trail northward to North Point.

The portion from North Point to Blackhead Mt. is the least used part of the trail. Consequently it is very enjoyable. The forest traveler will see few others and should be prepared to be totally self-sufficient.

Trailhead: *This trail section description begins at the 7.2 mi. point of the Escarpment Trail. The trail leaves North Point from a DEC signpost (7.2 mi.), heading NE across nearly flat bedrock. There is good viewing at 7.3 mi. and some of the Blackhead Range can be seen to the N. The route follows rock cairns, paint blazes, and some trail markers L around a horseshoe-shaped bluff. North and South lakes can be seen nearly a thousand feet below. The thin ribbon of the Hudson River is in the distance.*

A gradual SW ascent takes you into the forest and over the tree-covered, 3180-ft. summit of North Mt. at 7.7 mi. A minor descent reaches a small saddle, where Winter Clove can be seen below to the

N. An ascent begins towards Stoppel Point, then the trail steepens to a moderate grade as it rises up the S slope.

A DEC signpost marks the summit of Stoppel Point at 8.9 mi. Elevation is 3420 ft. The summit offers modest views to the E.

The trail descends for over two mi. from here to the Dutcher Notch/Colgate Lake Trails jct. (trails 6 and 8). The walking is pleasant over generally gradual grades, which occasionally level or steepen.

A yellow spur trail L at 9.1 mi. does not offer particularly good views, but High Peak and Roundtop mts. can be seen from a second lookout at 9.2 mi. The remains of a downed airplane are located at the R side of the trail at 9.3 mi. The sharp-eyed hiker may find an informal trail R at 9.35 mi.; this leads down to Winter Clove House. A short, moderately steep trail section is found at 9.35 mi. The cliff edge called Milt's Lookout at 10.1 mi. presents excellent viewing NE directly over Cairo Roundtop Mt. to the distant Hudson River.

Varying grades take you to 11.0 mi., where a 300-ft. moderate descent of rocky trail ends in a col where the Dutcher Notch/Colgate Lake trails meet at a 4-way jct. in Dutcher Notch. Here there is a large grassy bowl partially surrounded by a rock wall. DEC signs note that camping is prohibited within 150 ft. of the trail. A spring is located 0.4 mi. downslope on the Dutcher Notch Trail; Floyd Hawver Rd. is 2.4 mi. farther along this trail.

The trail climbs out of Dutcher Notch (elev. 2550 ft.) at a moderate to steep grade. At 11.5 mi. the route becomes moderately steep. Variation in the sediments deposited in oceans many millions of years ago formed rocks of differing resistance to erosion. These rocks, over which this trail now passes, consist of a series of short, steep layers of harder rock interspersed with more moderate slopes of softer rock. The hiker will work until reaching a side trail at 12.2 mi., which cuts sharply back to the L at 150 ft. to an outstanding lookout point from which Lake Capra can be seen far below to the S.

Dutcher Notch and Stoppel Point are also visible. The height of land known as Arizona ("arid region") is reached at 12.6 mi. Once called Webster Mt. (also The Sentinel), at slightly over 3400 ft. elevation this is the highest point between Stoppel Point and Blackhead Mt.

The flat high ground soon gives way to a modest descent, after which the trail begins a gentle climb toward Blackhead Mt. A high point of land is followed by a dip at 12.7 mi. Avoid the unmarked footpath R, marked by a cairn at 12.9 mi. Steep grades, open views, and blueberries in season mark the final ascent to a 3-way jct. at the summit of Blackhead Mt. at 13.6 mi. Summit elevation is 3940 ft. Blackhead Mt. is the fourth highest peak in the Catskills.

(The yellow-marked trail heading W from the trail jct. passes several excellent lookouts as it descends 500 ft. into the col between Blackhead Mt. and Black Dome Mt. (Lockwood Gap). The hiker may well seek out one of these spots for lunch or a few minutes' respite before continuing on the trail.)

The Escarpment Trail turns R and follows blue trail markers NE from the 3-way jct. Though initially a gradual downslope, the trail loses 1100 ft. elevation in the next mile to the Batavia Kill Trail jct. The rate of descent soon steepens. The route levels briefly near the 3500 ft. elevation DEC sign and then resumes a moderate down-grade. Views are frequent through the trees. At Yellow Jacket Lookout at 14.1 mi., vistas as far N as Albany are sometimes possible. Finally, the trail flattens out when it reaches the Batavia Kill Trail (trail 5) jct. at 14.6 mi.

(The yellow-marked Batavia Kill Trail descends 0.25 mi. to the Batavia Kill lean-to, where abundant water is found. It then contin-ues to Big Hollow Rd., a total of 1.5 mi. from the jct. See above.)

The trail makes a sharp turn R around a large rock at 15.0 mi. It climbs gradual grades.

Acra Point is reached at 16.4 mi. Elevation is 3100 ft. An open area offering views is found here. A side trail L at 16.6 mi. presents excellent views of the Blackhead Range, Burnt Knob, and Windham High Peak. Loss of elevation continues to the Acra Point/Burnt Knob Access Trail (trail 4) at 17.1 mi. (The red-marked Acra Point/Burnt Knob Access Trail runs 1.1 mi. down to Big Hollow Rd.; see above. A good stream is found 0.2 mi. from the jct.)

The blue route soon leaves the level terrain found beyond the jct. and begins the long gradual upgrade to Windham High Peak. A side trail L at 17.4 mi. leads to a lookout toward Blackhead Mt. The trail bypasses the summit of Burnt Knob (3180 ft.). A downgrade at 18.0 mi. leads to an expansive view N and to Windham Mt., a few ft. R off-trail. Another side trail L at 18.4 mi. offers SW views.

A downgrade reaches a col at 19.0 mi. before the trail climbs around another knob and again drops into a dip. A cave can be seen R at 19.4 mi.

The route now climbs mixed grades over some open rock to the summit of Windham High Peak at 19.8 mi. Several spur trails offer vistas, particularly to the N. Summit elevation is 3524 ft.

The trail then begins a pleasant, final descent of over three mi. along Elm Ridge to NY 23. It crosses log bridges at 21.3 mi. A side trail L at 22.0 mi. takes you 100 yds. to the Elm Ridge lean-to.

The Elm Ridge Trail (trail 3) jct. is reached in another 90 yds. (This side trail leads 0.9 mi. to the end of Peck Rd. and another 1.2 mi. to Big Hollow Rd.; see above. At 0.2 mi. from the jct. a spring is found.)

The trail reaches a DEC trail register at 23.0 mi. Once through an open field it crosses a bridge over the outlet of Silver Lake and reaches NY 23 at 23.0 mi. A large parking area is on the opposite side of the highway.

Distances: *To North Mt., 0.5 mi.; to Stoppel Point, 1.7 mi.; to Dutcher Notch, 3.9 mi.; to summit Blackhead Mt., 6.4 mi.; to Batavia Kill Trail jct., 7.4 mi.; to Acra Point, 9.2 mi.; to Acra Point/Burnt Knob Access Trail jct., 9.9 mi.; to Burnt Knob, 11.2 mi.; to summit Windham High Peak, 12.6 mi.; to*

Elm Ridge lean-to, 14.75 mi.; to Elm Ridge Trail jct., 14.8 mi.; to NY 23, 15.9 mi. (25.8 km), 23.1 mi. (37.4 km) from beginning of Escarpment Trail.

(7) Dutcher Notch Trail

Map 41: O-3
NE Catskills

The Dutcher Notch Trail offers a little used route to the Escarpment Trail (see above). Its gradual but very steady grade makes an excellent woods walk, and a fine all-day outing can be made by taking the Escarpment Trail (trail 6) S to Stoppel Point or N to Blackhead Mt.

Trailhead: *Access to the trailhead is off NY 32, along Heart's Content Rd. This is the road to Roundtop and Purling, not far from the Catskill Game Farm turnoff. Follow Heart's Content Rd. 4.0 mi. to Maple Lawn Rd. Turn L and travel 1.1 mi. to Floyd Hawver Rd. Turn L and then immediately R at the DEC signpost at Stork Nest Rd. Travel 0.4 mi. along Stork Nest Rd. to a small parking area on the L side of the road, now dirt, just before it enters private property, where vehicles are not allowed.*

The yellow DEC marked trail heads SW past a large house, entering woods at 0.1 mi. It follows a woods road gradually upgrade to a trail register and small bridge across a brook at 0.3 mi.

Still gradual, but a little more inclined than before, the route becomes more rocky as the eroded cuts in the road deepen. State land markers, first seen at 0.8 mi., are followed by a large swing to the NW at 1.0 mi.

A grassy lane replaces the rocky passage as elevation increases. From the 1.5 mi. point, the trail slabs the slope, which drops off fairly sharply on the R and climbs steeply to the L of the trail. In summer, only occasional glimpses of the broad Hudson Valley can be seen through leaves of the trees, but a winter climb on snowshoes or skis would present marvelous views.

A well-tended, shallow spring is located at 1.65 mi., on the L side of the trail at the base of a large rock outcrop. The trail passes an attractive grove of hemlocks before crossing the Escarpment Trail at Dutcher Notch at 2.0 mi. Here, a large, flat area has several campsites and fire rings.

The Escarpment Trail continues 2.2 mi. S to Stoppel Point and 2.5 mi. N to the summit of Blackhead Mt.; see above. The unmarked 4.25 mi. trail W from the jct. is the Colgate Lake Trail (see below).

Distances: *To state land, 0.8 mi.; to spring, 1.65 mi.; to Escarpment Trail jct., 2.0 mi. (3.2 km) (2.4 mi. from Floyd Hawver Rd.).*

(8) Colgate Lake Trail to Dutcher Notch

Map 41: O-3
NE Catskills

This trail was the shortest way for farmers of the Jewett Valley in the 19th century to get to market in the village of Catskill. The name Colgate reflects the fact that much of the land the trail passes over was once owned by Robert Colgate of the Colgate Palmolive–Peet Co. The trail's very gradual grades lead up to Dutcher Notch, where the route intersects the Escarpment Trail (trail 6) (see above). The old woods road continues on to Floyd Hawver Rd. as the Dutcher Notch Trail (see above). During a pleasant walk along this trail, the hiker will see much interesting evidence of the historical past of the Catskills.

Trailhead: *Trailhead access is off Co. Rd. 78, E of the hamlet of East Jewett. Drive 1.7 mi. E from East Jewett to the third DEC parking area; it is on the L side of the road. The yellow DEC marked trail starts from the trail* *register (0.0 mi.) at the L rear of the grassy parking area. It then follows the edge of a field. Dutcher Notch can be seen to the R in the distance with the Blackhead Range visible to the N.*

At 0.2 mi. the wide, grassy trail enters a birch-maple forest before joining an old woods road. The trail weaves into and out of many such roads, so the hiker needs to keep a sharp eye out for the trail markers.

The trail swings NE from its original N direction at 0.5 mi. and begins a loop around the Camp Harriman property. It leaves the good woods road it has been following at 0.9 mi., when it turns sharply L. A downward pitch at 1.2 mi. brings the hiker to the crossing of a wide inlet stream of Lake Capra. The way then leads up a pitch, crosses a woods road and pitches up again, turning L onto a second woods road. At 1.4 mi. the trail turns R at some berry bushes, near a meadow.

Re-entering the woods, the trail swings S to complete the loop around Lake Capra. It crosses a stream on a footbridge at 1.8 mi. and joins another woods road. A small lake can be seen at 2.2 mi.

Bearing R, the trail parallels the shoreline at a distance before crossing the East Kill outlet of the lake. It then traverses a wet area with spindly hemlocks towering over small pine trees, making a L turn at a meadow's edge at 2.4 mi.

Joining the old East Jewett–Catskill road for a short ways, the route bears R from it at 2.6 mi. to skirt a section flooded by beaver activity. Many iron implements used for past lumbering operations can be seen here. The East Kill, now an inlet of the lake, is crossed again at 2.9 mi. The trail rejoins the old road and turns R to follow it up into Dutcher Notch.

From an extensive meadow, posted "no camping," Blackhead Mt. can be seen looming above. The trail begins to climb on easy grades to a cascading brook R at 3.6 mi. Climbing becomes steeper at 3.8

mi., where a large rock overhang suitable as a shelter can be seen among some large rocks.

The grade then moderates before reaching the 4-way jct. with the Escarpment Trail (see above) at 4.25 mi. The trail continues straight ahead, as the Dutcher Notch Trail (trail 7). There is a good spring a steep 0.35 mi. further along the trail. The Notch jct. has a large clearing, which DEC has posted with signs prohibiting camping within 150 ft. of the trail. Stoppel Point is 2.2 mi. S and Blackhead Mt. is 2.5 mi. N on the Escarpment Trail from this jct.

On return, hikers may enjoy a swim and picnic at Colgate Lake. It is on Co. Rd. 78, on the opposite side of the trailhead, and 0.1 mi. towards East Jewett. A DEC sign marks the parking area.

Distances: *To Lake Capra inlet stream, 1.2 mi.; to footbridge, 1.8 mi.; to meadow at second crossing of East Kill, 2.9 mi.; to Dutcher Notch jct. Escarpment Trail, 4.25 mi. (6.9 km). Elevation 2550 ft (765 m); ascent 430 ft. (129 m).*

(9) Black Dome Mt. Trail

Map 41: O-2
NE Catskills

Rated as third highest in the Catskills, Black Dome Mt. is a frequent destination of hikers from both Big Hollow Rd. and Elmer Barnum Rd. In this guide, the E end of what is generally called the Blackhead Range Trail is described as the Black Dome Mt. Trail, to assist hikers starting from Big Hollow Rd.

Trailhead: *The trailhead is near the parking area at the E end of Big Hollow Rd. (see above). Walk the gravel road to a jct. 0.05 mi. E of the parking area. A DEC signpost is found at the trailhead (0.0 mi.).*

Red DEC trailmarkers lead SE, 150 ft. to a trail register. The trail crosses a bridge at 0.1 mi. and continues E. The Batavia Kill is recrossed at 0.3 mi. The Batavia Kill Trail jct. is at 0.5 mi. (The yellow-marked Batavia Kill Trail leads 0.75 mi. to a lean-to and another 0.25 mi. to the Escarpment Trail; see above.)

The red-marked trail climbs a gradual grade and then crosses a small brook and at 0.8 mi. a stream (often dry). The slope becomes moderate. At 1.1 mi., a sign indicates a spring L of the trail. The grade now becomes moderately steep.

The Blackhead Mt. Spur Trail jct. is at 1.4 mi. in this col. (This yellow trail leads steeply 0.6 mi. to the Blackhead Mt. summit; see below.) Turn R at this jct. and continue W on the red trail. It climbs steeply up Black Dome Mt. At 1.7 mi., it swings L under a ledge, then circles R to the top of the ledge. A spur trail leads R to a magnificent viewing point from which the Helderbergs, the Hudson Valley, Blackhead Mt., High Peak, and the Devil's Path can be seen in a wide sweep.

The trail is moderately steep from there, becoming a gradual grade near the summit, which is reached at 2.0 mi. Balsams prevent a view N, but an extensive vista to the S is outstanding. Beyond the Devil's Path of Indian Head, Twin, Sugarloaf, Plateau, Hunter, and Westkill mts., Rusk, Cornell, Wittenberg, Slide, and Table mts. are visible. It is particularly impressive in winter.

Distances: *To Batavia Kill jct., 0.5 mi.; to spring, 1.1 mi.; to Blackhead Mt. Trail jct., 1.4 mi.; to ledge lookout, 1.7 mi.; to Black Dome summit, 2.0 mi. (3.2 km). Ascent, 1780 ft. Summit elevation, 3980 ft. (1217 m).*

(10) Blackhead Mt. Spur Trail

Trailhead: The Blackhead Mt. Spur Trail originates at the 1.4-mi. point of the Black Dome Mt. Trail at Lockwood Gap (see below). It ascends to the summit of Blackhead Mt.

The trail climbs E from the Black Dome Mt. jct. (0.0 mi.), marked with yellow DEC trail markers. The moderate upgrade soon reaches the DEC 3500 ft. elevation sign.

At 0.2 mi., the trail opens. Steps are cut into the slope at the base of a short, loose rock slide. The grade continues to steepen. Excellent views are had to the S and W.

The route nearly levels, close to the summit, at 0.4 mi. It continues through conifers to the summit. Blueberries abound in open places. The trail meets with the blue-marked Escarpment Trail (see above) at 0.6 mi.

Distances: To steps at slide, 0.2 mi.; to leveling point of the trail, 0.4 mi.; to summit jct., 0.6 mi. (1.0 km). Ascent from col, 500 ft. Summit elevation, 3940 ft. (1205 m).

(11) Blackhead Range Trail (Thomas Cole Mt., Black Dome Mt.)

The Blackhead Range of Caudal, Camel's Hump, Thomas Cole Mt., Black Dome Mt., and Blackhead Mt. offers the hiker one of the finest sequences of open-ridge hiking to be found in the Catskills. The trail as described here terminates at the summit of Black Dome Mt., but the hiker can refer to the Black Dome Mt. Trail (trail 9) and the Blackhead Mt. Spur Trail (trail 10) for through trips (see above). Carry plenty of water.

Trailhead: *The trailhead is at the end of Barnum Rd., 0.9 mi. E of Maplecrest Rd. There is room for parking several vehicles at the road end turnout.*

Red DEC trailmarkers lead SE up the gradual grade of a woods road to a trail register at 0.4 mi. The route turns sharply NE from the register, leaving the old road. A few moderate pitches precede the state Forest Preserve boundary at 0.4 mi. From this point, the way is moderately steep to steep, climbing over rock slabs to the top of a knob, called Caudal, at 1.2 mi. Elevation is 3300 ft. (In anatomy, a caudal part is found near the tail. It has been suggested that this knob represents the tail of the camel.) Views S at 1.0 mi. include most of the Devil's Path.

The trail ascends on varying grades to 1.3 mi., levels for 0.1 mi., then descends a short pitch and is level to 1.8 mi. From there, moderate grades upward bring the hiker to a passage between two boulders and then to the top of Camel's Hump at 2.0 mi. Elevation is 3500 ft. Indian Head Mt., Stoppel Point, and Kaaterskill High Peak can be seen to the SE on a clear day. Windham High Peak is N.

After a slight descent, the trail again becomes level. At 2.0 mi., the trail is open and, in places, almost a meadow. Thomas Cole Mt. is in full view as the route swings broadly SE. The trail gains nearly 500 ft. in elevation from this point at moderate grade before the trail is again level.

The flat ridge trail actually passes just below the true summit and there are no views N. Summit elevation is 3940 ft. A yellow-marked spur trail R leads to a lookout at 2.9 mi.

Thomas Cole Mt. is named for the painter who is credited with establishing the Hudson River School of Painting in the 19th century. Onteora Mt. and Parker Mt. are across the valley below you.

The mountains of the Devil's Path are in the distance.

The trail soon descends at a moderate rate, with occasional very steep pitches. The col (3550 ft.) between Thomas Cole and Black Dome is quickly reached at 2.8 mi. The short section to the summit of Black Dome Mt. at 3.25 mi. is moderately steep. Summit elevation is 3980 ft.

Though only 40 ft. higher than Thomas Cole, the summit of Black Dome Mt. offers far more open viewing from a large flat rock shelf. It is a perfect lunch spot. Views can be seen from 150 degrees to 260 degrees, including the Hudson Valley, Kaaterskill High Peak, Indian Head, Twin, Sugarloaf, Plateau, Stony Clove Notch, Cornell, Wittenberg, Slide, Table, Westkill, and Rusk.

The trail beyond leads to Big Hollow Rd. or to the summit of Blackhead Mt.; see above.

Distances: *To state land, 0.2 mi.; to Caudal, 1.2 mi.; to Camel's Hump, 2.0 mi.; to Thomas Cole Mt. summit, 2.5 mi.; to Black Dome Mt., 3.25 mi. (5.3 km). Ascent from parking area, 2080 ft. Summit elevation, 3980 ft. (1217 m).*

View from Long Path on shoulder of Kaaterskill High Peak, Palenville side

Palenville–
North Lake Section

Millions of years ago, it is believed, the outlet of North and South lakes drained SW to Gooseberry Creek, Lake Rip Van Winkle, and the Schoharie Creek basin. A classic case of stream piracy occurred when the Kaaterskill Falls eroded back into Lake Creek, stealing the Schoharie-bound waters.

Much later, in 1741, John Bartram, the famous Philadelphia botanist, sought out the Balm of Gilead, today's balsam fir, that was in such demand for the gardens of Europe. He found an abundance of them around North and South lakes. Captivated by the region, he returned in 1753 with his son to study the area.

Still later, in 1823, the view from the escarpment was immortalized by James Fenimore Cooper's Natty Bumpo in *The Pioneers.* When asked what he could see when he got there, he replied, "Creation, all creation, lad."

Perhaps no other place in America had such significant impact in changing the prevailing view of nature held by 18th-century minds than did this little region around the Kaaterskill Clove. Before then, wilderness was evil—something to avoid or conquer. By the end of the 19th century, romanticists saw nature as a place of overpowering beauty, drawing one towards spiritual uplift. The magic of the Land of Falling Waters (Palenville), where Rip Van Winkle escaped Dame Van Winkle's scolding by tramping the hills with his dog, Wolf, did much to change the image of the forests from a place of danger to a retreat. Thomas Cole's Hudson River School of Landscape Painting centered on this region. Steamboats brought the elite and powerful of the world here. Wagons (later railroads) carried them through the Wall of Manitou to the Mountain Top, with its Mountain House, Hotel Kaaterskill, Laurel House, and other hotels. Here, one became renewed and enjoyed nature.

It is the same today. The glades are as enchanting and the vistas as awe-inspiring as ever they were in the past. But let the hiker be cautioned. The cliffs and crags are rugged and can be extremely dangerous.

General access from the east is from Exit 21 (Catskill) of I-87, the New York State Thruway. One can get to NY 23A and Palenville via NY 23 and NY 32. One can also exit I-87 at Exit 20, but it is advisable to take NY 32 N to Palenville rather than to go W to West Saugerties and up Platte Clove Mountain Rd., which is officially closed from November to April each year and is hazardous to drive the rest of the time. From the W, this region can be reached via NY 23 and NY 23A.

Trail in winter: North/South Lake State Campground is excellent for cross-country skiing and snowshoeing. However, extreme care must be taken when you are near the escarpment. A winter walk to the base of Kaaterskill Falls is short, but interesting.

Short Hikes:

Kaaterskill Falls—*0.8 mi. round trip. A short walk with a little scrambling to one of the most impressive waterfalls in New York State.*

Mary's Glen—*1.4 mi. round trip. A pretty walk to a mossy glen, with a quiet waterfall.*

Boulder Rock—*1.4 mi. round trip. Visit the site of the former Catskill Mt. House and then climb the steep shoulder of South Mt. to one of the best vistas on the escarpment wall.*

Rip Van Winkle Hollow—1.9 mi. round trip. Walk into the land of Rip Van Winkle, along the Sleepy Hollow Trail to the very spot at the bend in Sleepy Hollow where Rip is said to have slept those 20 years.

Moderate Hikes:

Inspiration Point Circuit—4.7 mi. loop. Follow the Escarpment Trail from Schutt Rd. to the second Schutt Rd. jct., visiting Inspiration Point, a favorite spot of President Grant; then return via the Schutt Rd. Trail.

Buttermilk Falls—8.0 mi. round trip. A good day trip, with quite a bit of climbing, to two exquisite waterfalls.

Harder Hikes:

Escarpment Trail–Sleepy Hollow Trail—7.7 mi. through trip. Walk the Escarpment Trail from Schutt Rd. to the Sleepy Hollow Trail and then through to Palenville Lookout, Rip Van Winkle Hollow, and Mountain Turnpike Rd.

North Point Circuit—9.4 mi. loop. Follow the Escarpment Trail from Schutt Rd. to North Point, returning via the Mary's Glen and Rock Shelter trails.

Trail Described	Total Miles (one way)	Page
Sleepy Hollow	4.55	64
Harding Rd.	3.3	67
Buttermilk Falls	4.0	69
Kaaterskill Falls	0.4	71
Kaaterskill Falls from Laurel House Rd.	0.2	72

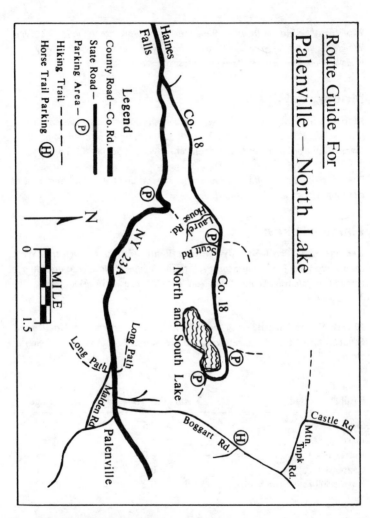

Route Guide For
Palenville – North Lake

Legend

County Road – Co. Rd.
State Road –
Parking Area – ⓟ
Hiking Trail – – –
Horse Trail Parking Ⓗ

N

0   MILE   1.5

Haines
Falls

Co. 18

ⓟ

Laurel House Rd.

ⓟ

Scutt Rd

Co. 18

North and South Lake

ⓟ

NY 23A

Long Path

ⓟ

Long Path

Long Path

Malden Rd.

Palenville

Boggart Rd.

Ⓗ

Castle Rd

Mtn. Tnpk. Rd.

ROUTE GUIDE FROM PALENVILLE TO NORTH LAKE

Mileage E to W	Description	Mileage W to E
0.0	Intersection of NY 23A and NY 32A in Palenville.	8.9
0.15	Boggart Rd. jct. (Sleepy Hollow Trail).	8.75
0.6	Beginning of Section 21, the Long Path. 100 ft. E of Catskill Park sign, three horse-trail markers on telephone pole.	8.3
0.9	Malden Avenue.	8.0
3.4	Bastion Falls, start of Kaaterskill Falls Trail at horseshoe turn.	5.5
3.6	Molly Smith parking area.	5.3
4.9	North Lake Rd. (Co. Rd. 18)–NY 23A jct. Turn E for North–South Lakes Public Campground.	4.0
6.7	Laurel House Rd., S side.	2.2
7.1	Schutt Rd., S side. (200 ft. to parking area; Rock Shelter trailhead, N side of road at same jct.)	1.8
7.2	Toll gate, North–South Lakes Public Campground. (Bear L at fork immediately past gate.)	1.7
8.1	Trailhead, Mary's Glen Trail on L.	0.8
8.2	Day-use parking on L for Mary's Glen Trail.	0.7
8.8	North Mt. Trail trailhead on L.	0.1
8.9	Beach, bath houses, picnic area.	0.0

(12) Sleepy Hollow Trail

The Sleepy Hollow Trail is a little-used but most rewarding hiking route. The vale where some have said Rip Van Winkle bowled ninepins with the ghosts of Henry Hudson's *Half Moon* crew and a continuous vista of the Hudson River are but two of the joys awaiting the walker.

Much of this historic path was part of the Little Delaware Turnpike. Passengers left ship at Catskill for stagecoaches that bounced and jostled their way up this road to North Lake. In time it became part of the second DEC horse trail developed in New York State. However, the upper reaches, beyond Palenville Overlook, are difficult for horses. Much of that section is seldom used by riders.

Trailhead: *Access is off NY 23A at Boggart Rd. in Palenville. (See Route Guide for Palenville-North Lake.) The Sleepy Hollow Horse Trail parking area is on the L side of Boggart Rd. at 2.1 mi., but this is not the hiker's trailhead. Continue past it, bearing L at the Penn. Ave. jct. Note the old stone building foundation on the L at 2.3 mi. This is the remains of a turnpike station, where two or more were added to make six-horse teams before stagecoaches started up the mountain.*

Turn L onto Mountain Turnpike Rd. at 2.4 mi. The trailhead begins at the end of pavement, 0.8 mi. up this road. Do not use the private home parking area at the road end. Use the wide shoulder of the road, at least 100 yds. back along the lane.

From the trailhead (0.0 mi.) the old turnpike trail heads into Rip Van Winkle Hollow (Sleepy Hollow). It soon swings W, following the N bank of Rip Van Winkle Brook (Stony Brook). Sounds of falling water play in your mind as you watch the flow spill over the brinks of endless small cataracts amongst the deepening walls of the hollow.

Sometimes called the Mt. House Rd., this trail gradually ascends, being drawn into an ever-narrowing vale where hemlocks darken the way and eerie thoughts of times long past come to mind. At 0.5 mi. the trail crosses tiny Black Snake Bridge. A trail register is within sight of a sharp horseshoe bend at 0.95 mi., where the roadway swings SE. Take time here to look at the stone foundation of the Rip Van Winkle House, once a small inn. Seek out Rip's Boulder, a large flat rock behind the inn site, where Rip allegedly slept away those 20 long years. If you have time, bushwhack up some 600 vertical ft. to Rip's Rock.

From here, the route ascends Dead Ox Hill. Initially, the way is gradual, though more rocky. Forbidding cliffs are on the R; a broadening valley floor is to the L. The grade becomes moderate; it is evident why two more horses were needed for a stage's climb and why passengers often had to get out to walk the steeper sections.

A spur road L leads to a lookout at 1.5 mi., where a fireplace and picnic table are found. A yellow barrier gate is 100 ft. farther along the road. A sharp switchback, called Cape Horn, heads N at 1.65 mi. It was possible to see the Catskill Mt. House on the escarpment from this point in the 1800s, but forests block the view today.

The grade soon moderates as you travel through the Short Level. Another switchback S, at 1.95 mi., sends you up Featherbed Hill at moderate grades. At 2.35 mi., just before it levels off again, the trail becomes more rocky and curves L. Where several large boulders stand out on the L, an unmarked side trail cuts back to the R of the road. It is easy to miss, coming up the hill, if you are not looking for it. (It runs N over two mi., mostly on state land, before entering the private trail network at Winter Clove.)

The nature of the route greatly changes, as an almost flat grassy lane greets you. This is the Long Level. The roadway is nearly level or gradually up until a jct. at 2.6 mi. Here, a DEC signpost blocks the way. (The old Mt. House Rd. continues another 0.6 mi. to North Lake.)

The Sleepy Hollow Trail makes an abrupt turn L and drops 0.1 mi. down a series of switchbacks at moderate grade. Leveling, it continues S through a less appealing short section. A gradual downgrade finally levels as the trail passes under a high electric utility line. The line follows the course of the old stationary engine Otis Railroad line, which carried guests almost to the very door of the Catskill Mt. House. (An informal path follows the rail bed's course, both R and L.)

The trail is now essentially level and straight, making a jog L at 3.4 mi. before resuming its direction S to a jct. at 3.75 mi. (The yellow spur trail L leads 0.3 mi. on the level to an escarpment cliff called Palenville Overlook. There is a picnic table and fireplace, but the best lunch spot is 100 ft. farther, on the open ledge.)

From the jct., a series of switchbacks climbs steeply upward 0.1 mi. to the next rock shelf level, some 150 vertical ft. above. While most of this section is quite suitable for riding, a few short parts are very demanding for horses. As a result, the route is an attractive footpath, essentially level, often shrouded by mountain laurel. The direction of travel is still S. Views of the Hudson eventually open up to the L rear.

At 4.1 mi., a swing NW offers views across Kaaterskill Clove. Gradual and moderate grades alternate as the wide path gains elevation. The trail crosses a creek at 4.3 mi. in a nice stand of hemlocks. A short pitch up ends at a T-jct. at 4.45 mi.: the Harding Rd. Trail (trail 13, also with yellow trail markers) enters from the L. (Palenville is 3.3 mi. down this trail; see below.) Bear R to a second T-jct. at 4.55 mi. The blue-marked trail running each direction from this jct. is the Escarpment Trail (trail 18).

Distances: *To Rip Van Winkle Hollow, 0.95 mi.; to spur lookout, 1.5 mi.; to Winter Clove spur trail, 2.35 mi.; to North Lake spur jct., 2.6 mi.; to Palenville Lookout spur, 3.75 mi.; to Harding Rd. Trail T-jct., 4.45 mi.; to*

Escarpment Trail T-jct., 4.55 mi. (7.4 km). Ascent 1490 ft. (447 m).

(13) Harding Rd. Trail

This trail has very nice walking over a little-used old carriage road. A party with two vehicles can have a through trip by starting at the Schutt Rd. parking area near North Lake and then walking the Schutt Rd. trail and short sections of the Escarpment and Sleepy Hollow trails to connect with the Harding Rd. Trail. The party will travel on nearly level or downhill grades for the whole trip.

When George Harding built the Hotel Kaaterskill near the top of South Mt. in 1880–81, he also built Harding Rd. for access. Considered an engineering marvel in its time, this road snaked its way up South Mt. to the hotel from Palenville. In more recent years it became part of the Sleepy Hollow Horse Trail network and then part of the Long Path trail.

Trailhead: *The trailhead is 100 ft. E of the large wooden "Entering Catskill Park" sign on the R side of NY 23A in Palenville. (See Route Guide for Palenville–North Lake.) You may note three yellow horse-trail markers on a telephone pole near the trailhead, but the location is otherwise unmarked. Parking space is very tight here; do not block the trailhead road. Squeeze off the road in front of the sign or leave your vehicle back in the village somewhere.*

The trail heads NE on the unmarked gravel carriage road. It soon begins a gradual climb, curving W at 0.2 mi. Avoid the side road R at 0.35 mi. (In the future, this side road may lead to a new trailhead on Whites Rd. if the Unit Management Plan proposal drafted in late 1994 is accepted.) The trail enters state land at 0.5 mi. Interesting views open up to the L into Kaaterskill Clove, while the bank sweeps steeply upward on the R side of the road. The roadway levels at 1.0 mi., but not before it becomes clear why hiking down from the mountaintop has some advantages.

The trail passes a trail register and horse tie rail at 1.25 mi. Here, on a very sharp curve R, there is a splendid lookout into Kaaterskill Clove. Just around the curve, on the R side of the road, is a large fireplace cleverly built into the cliff.

The trail continues N, beginning an extensive V-shaped course on contour to where it crosses a major tributary of Kaaterskill Creek. The birches are lovely in this section. Tall hemlocks and stately pines give off entrancing scents as cool breezes waft up from the valley below.

At 1.6 mi. the route crosses the tributary and winds back out of the tributary valley to continue its generally W course. High rock cliffs bare themselves on the R at 2.0 mi.

At 2.4 mi., at a major switchback, the trail sharply turns ENE. The gradual slope becomes moderate and the views are now out of Kaaterskill Clove instead of up it. It must have been a fascinating trip by stagecoach a century ago. Interesting rock slabs can be seen L at 2.6 mi. The trail nearly levels at 2.7 mi. Then, at 2.85 mi., the Harding Rd. Trail joins a section of the Sleepy Hollow Trail that was once part of the old Mountain Turnpike Rd. (The Sleepy Hollow Trail [trail 12] turns R here, descending to Rip Van Winkle Hollow, where Rip bowled ninepins with the ghosts of Henry Hudson's *Half Moon* crew, and then goes on to Boggart Rd.; see above.)

Those walking the trail as part of the Long Path should continue L on the Sleepy Hollow Trail to join the Escarpment Trail (trail 18) at a jct. 0.1 mi. SW.

Distances: *To first lookout, 1.25 mi.; to tributary, 1.6 mi.; to switchback,*

2.4 mi.; to Sleepy Hollow Trail, 2.85 mi. (4.6 km). Ascent, 1300 ft. (390 m). Elevation, 2000 ft. (600 m).

(14) Buttermilk Falls Trail

Map 41: P-4
NE Catskills

Buttermilk Falls sits far up the shoulder of Kaaterskill High Peak. For years, the only short trip to Buttermilk Falls was across Twilight Park Association land, on the old Twilight Park–Palenville Trail. Then, in 1987, the so-called "missing link" of the Long Path between Platte Clove Valley and Palenville was opened. Day trippers can now reach this history-filled section. (For the full Long Path section description, see Platte Clove Section.) It is beautiful in June, when the mountain laurel is in bloom.

Trailhead: *The actual trailhead is 0.35 mi. down Malden Avenue, off NY 23A at Palenville, but the small parking space beside it is a homeowner's private parking spot, not open for public use. The closest large area is at the NY 23A–Malden Avenue jct., where several cars can be left off the shoulder of the road. From this spot, walk E along Malden Avenue. Note the occasional blue paint blazes indicating the Long Path.*

At a curve in the road at 0.35 mi., on a wooded slope on the R between two white houses, three blue blazes on a large tree mark the trailhead (0.0 mi.). Head S up the slope, soon turning R behind private homes. This is the old Red Gravel Hill Rd. It winds a bit before steadily climbing a grade to the SW.

Grade steepness increases and as elevation is gained, views of the Hudson River open up generally S. State land is reached at 0.5 mi. Blue DEC trail markers now guide you.

At 1.1 mi. the route makes a broad horseshoe turn N. The way almost levels. Mountain laurel abounds here in spring. Then, at 1.4 mi., the trail swings W, ascending varying grades.

Height of land provides some views, but the trail soon enters the woods. At 2.0 mi. the trail reaches a jct. with a spur trail N to Poets Ledge (0.5 mi.), which provides outstanding views of Kaaterskill Clove. Gradual downgrades lead SSE into the upper reaches of Hillyer Ravine. The trail crosses a small brook at 2.2 mi., and then at 2.6 mi. a much larger brook of two sections 100 ft. apart from each other. This is the main flow that enters Hillyer Ravine.

The trail is now rather flat and enjoyable, as it follows the edge of the escarpment. The path abruptly turns from NNW to SW at 2.7 mi., near a larger boulder, then passes through a narrow rock outcrop and turns R.

The trail breaks out of the woods at 3.5 mi., by the stream atop Wildcat Falls. This is a spectacular place. The stream drops precipitously from the great rock ledge. The view looks across the distant Hudson River directly at artist Frederick Church's home, Olana. One feels a part of one of his Catskill paintings in this setting.

The trail continues NW on level terrain to Buttermilk Falls at 4.0 mi. Here, one can look almost 2000 ft. below to the Rip Van Winkle Trail (NY 23A), wending its way through Kaaterskill Clove. Directly across the valley are North Mt. and Stoppel Point.

The ambitious can continue along the trail another 0.2 mi. to where it swings sharply S, ascending another 1475 ft. in the next 1.6 mi. to the summit of Kaaterskill High Peak.

Distances: *To state land, 0.5 mi.; to horseshoe turn, 1.1 mi.: to Poets Ledge Trail jct., 2.0 mi.; to Hillyer Ravine double brook, 2.6 mi.; to Wildcat Falls, 3.5 mi.; to Buttermilk Falls, 4.0 mi. (6.5 km) (4.3 mi. from parking). Ascent, 1507 ft. (452m). Elevation, 2180 ft. (654 m).*

(15) Kaaterskill Falls Trail

Kaaterskill Falls is one of the most striking natural features in New York State. It has two great tiers: the upper falls drops 175 ft., the lower falls drops 85 ft. The overhang of the upper falls cap rock is so prominent that a great amphitheater exists behind the waterflow. William Cullen Bryant immortalized it in his poem "Cauterskill Falls"; Currier and Ives prints were made of it; great painters made their reputations trying to duplicate its glory.

Trailhead: Access is from the Molly Smith parking area on 23A. (See Route Guide for Palenville–North Lake.) A DEC signpost marks the trailhead (0.0 mi.) down the hill from the parking area. Care should be taken while walking the section of NY 23A.

Bastion Falls is the cataract at the trailhead. The trail proceeds steeply up the S side of Lake Creek, passing a second, smaller waterfall and then an even smaller falls in the first 0.1 mi. The grade eases and shale cliffs rise sharply across the stream.

Moving away from the water, the grade moderates its climb through picturesque territory, finally climbing over large rocks to reach the base of the falls at 0.4 mi. The first full view of Kaaterskill Falls is breathtaking. It is a photographer's delight. Do *not* attempt to climb the falls from the base. Many deaths and injuries have occurred here.

The original Escarpment Trail used to ascend to the top of the falls by circling to the R in the woods. A spur trail from it led to the base of the upper falls. This original section of the Escarpment Trail is now officially closed and is not maintained. The Escarpment Trail now starts at Schutt Rd., near the entrance gate to North-South Lakes Public Campground (see below).

Distances: *To third waterfall, 0.1 mi.; to base of Kaaterskill Falls, 0.4 mi. (0.6 km).*

(16) Kaaterskill Falls from Laurel House Rd.

Kaaterskill Falls is best seen via the Kaaterskill Falls Trail, starting at Bastion Falls, off NY 23A (see below). However, the hiker who would like to be at the top of the falls can get there via Laurel House Rd. (See *Route Guide* for Palenville to North Lake.)

Trailhead: *Turn R off North Lake Rd. and travel 0.5 to its terminus, where parking is available.*

From the yellow barrier gate, walk S along a gradually descending broad path to a log railing at 0.2 mi., near the top of the falls. From this point, several informal paths lead another 40 ft. to the brink of the falls.

A fine view out into the valley is available, but do not try to see the base of the falls. It is extremely dangerous to go near the edge of this precipice.

When the Laurel House hotel operated in the 1850s, near today's parking area, guests walked W a short distance to Prospect Rock, where a good view of the whole falls could be had. The DEC Kaaterskill Wild Forest unit management plan proposes building a trail W along the old Ulster and Delaware railway course from the parking area to a point near Prospect Rock, where an observation deck would provide a safe vantage point for viewers.

Distance: *To Kaaterskill Falls, 0.2 mi. (0.3 km).*

(17) Rock Shelter Trail

Map 40: P-3
North/South Lakes Area

The Rock Shelter Trail provides hikers on the Escarpment Trail with a means to reach the Schutt Rd. parking area without having to walk the paved roads of the North-South Lakes Public Campground. This makes for a far more pleasant and comfortable day. It is a relatively level trail to the jct. with Mary's Glen Trail.

Trailhead: See Route Guide for Palenville–North Lake for access information.

From the Schutt Rd. jct. trailhead the trail heads N, crossing a wet spot on large flat rocks. There is a trail register at 0.05 mi. The route begins a broad swing E at 0.1 mi. The course is nearly level, with only minor grade changes, as it winds through open deciduous forest.

At 1.4 mi. the trail joins the Mary's Glen Trail (trail 20) and follows it for 200 ft. In this open area, a rock ledge with attractive mosses is found; in wet weather, they are rich, lush green. (The Mary's Glen Trail turns L, providing the shortest route to North Point from here, 0.8 mi.; Mary's Glen is 0.55 mi. R; North Lake Rd. is 0.7 mi. See below.)

The last section of the Rock Shelter Trail has a much longer history than the relatively new part before this jct. It ascends 200 vertical ft. before reaching its terminus. The trail climbs in steps of steep and level sections. A campsite with a fire ring up against a boulder is at L at 1.6 mi. After topping the ridgeline, the path drops down slightly, reaching the Escarpment Trail (trail 18) at 1.75 mi. (From this jct., North Point is L 0.8 mi. and North Lake parking area is R 2.5 mi. See below.)

Distances: To Mary's Glen Trail jct., 1.4 mi.; to Escarpment Trail, 1.75 mi. (2.8 km). Ascent, 380 ft. (114 m). Elevation, 2640 ft. (792 m).

(18) Escarpment Trail (Southern Section)

This section of the Escarpment Trail has some of the nicest and most sustained vistas in the Catskills. It is a tough trail on which to carry a full backpack, but it is delightful for day trips with a light day pack.

Trailhead: The trail now originates on Schutt Rd. near the entrance gate to North-South Lakes Public Campground. (See Route Guide to Palenville– North Lake Section.)

Carry plenty of water and allow yourself much longer time for hiking than the distance suggests you need. You'll stop often to observe the views, and the cliff edges are no place to hurry. The general course of the trail in this section circles South Mt. to North Lake and then ascends North Mt.

Background information for the Escarpment Trail can be found in the chapter "Extended and Challenging Opportunities." Refer to the Black Dome Valley–North Point Section for the description of the northern 15.9 mi. of the trail beyond North Point.

North–South Lakes Public Campground is a splendid place for recreation. Not only is the hiking very special, but one can also round out the trip with a swim and picnic. Boats can be rented at the South Lake beach (first R past the entrance gate). A small day-use charge per vehicle is levied for those entering through the campground gate; there is no charge for hikers parking outside the gate at the Schutt Rd. DEC parking area.

Trailhead parking is at the DEC parking area on the R, 200 ft. down Schutt Rd. (See *Route Guide* to Palenville–North Lake.) The trailhead is directly across the road from the parking area.

Blue DEC trail markers lead through tall hemlocks and small spruces on a very gradual descent, parallel to Schutt Rd. The trail crosses a narrow old railroad bed and then a wider railroad bed at 0.4 mi.; then, dropping down a small slope, the route passes over a bridge at Lake Creek.

Immediately past a second bridge, the trail reaches a jct. at 0.5 mi. Here, an unmarked roadway, immediately L, heads towards the South Lake perimeter road. The red-marked Schutt Rd. Trail (trail 19) bears SW up a gradual grade; see below.

The Escarpment Trail turns R, joining the site of the old parking area at the end of Schutt Rd., 100 ft. down the grade. Beyond, it soon reaches the S side of Lake Creek. The trail pitches sharply upward to the L at 0.65 mi. and then arrives at a trail register at 0.75 mi. (The faint trail R is the original, abandoned part of the Escarpment Trail.)

The route soon reaches a height of land and descends slightly through maple/birch/oak forest. There is a jct., where the trail makes a sharp R turn at 1.1 mi. (The unmarked path L is a cross-over route, staying on contour, rejoining the trail.) Layman Monument is at 1.2 mi.; here the trail makes a sharp turn L at the escarpment edge. (Frank Layman lost his life here, fighting a forest fire on August 10, 1900.) Molly Smith parking area, just above the Kaaterskill Falls Trail, can be seen far below on the Rip Van Winkle Trail (NY 23A).

From this place, the trail steeply regains lost elevation. The unmarked cross-over trail re-enters at 1.25 mi., where an open cliff ledge provides excellent viewing. Many lookouts are afforded as the hiker continues along the escarpment edge.

The trail ascends steeply at 1.5 mi., reaching a jct. at 1.6 mi. (The unnamed yellow trail L joins the Sleepy Hollow Horse Trail (trail 12) in 0.15 mi. and the Schutt trail in 0.5 mi.) Sunset Rock is passed at 1.7 mi. and Inspiration Point at 1.9 mi. From here on, sights from several lookouts stretch to the E, far across the Hudson River. Views S across Kaaterskill Clove, of the ravines coming off the shoulder of Kaaterskill High Peak, keep your attention. The walking is nearly level, but it is not a place to be unwatchful of your step, especially if you have children with you. The trail narrows in places and is close to the brink of the escarpment. This is a fascinating section.

The trail traverses a minor descent, followed by a slight upgrade, before it joins the Sleepy Hollow Horse Trail at 2.55 mi. The Escarpment Trail turns R, coming to a second jct. 200 ft. farther along the route. Here, the trail turns L up a winding grade. (The horse trail continues straight ahead on the Harding Road, now part of the Long Path).

Gradual climbing along the roadway leads to yet another jct. at 3.1 mi. Here, the Escarpment Trail turns sharply R at a DEC signpost. This is near the high point of South Mt. (The red-marked trail straight ahead is the Schutt Rd. Trail, which runs 1.1 mi. to a jct. with the Escarpment Trail. The road to the Hotel Kaaterskill site immediately branches off it to the NW.)

The nearly level roadbed trail is relaxing. The trail passes a large rock outcrop at L at 3.7 mi., just before a jct. at 3.8 mi. The blue Escarpment Trail turns R. (The red cutoff trail straight ahead bypasses the Boulder Rock vista.) It passes Split Rock at 3.9 mi.; huge blocks of a rock massif have split off as gravity slowly pulls them apart. Then, at 4.0 mi., Boulder Rock sits on a large open ledge. Before you lies an immense section of the Hudson River. On a trail having dozens of wonderful vistas, the view from Boulder Rock stands out as truly spectacular.

From here, the trail pitches upward and passes the other end of the red cutoff trail at 4.1 mi., then bears R at the height of land. A short, moderate pitch downward soon levels off. There are more lookouts before the trail steeply descends.

At 4.5 mi. the hiker arrives at the site of the former Catskill Mt. House in the Pine Orchard, where John Bartram came seeking the Balm of Gilead in 1741. Both hotel and pines are gone, but large exhibit boards provide maps and historical information about this famous spot. In its day, four presidents came here to rest. Night boats on the Hudson beamed spotlights on the hotel for their passengers. A railroad climbed the escarpment to deliver the cream of society to its doors. Now there is no trace of this illustrious past, save two stone posts at the entrance of the carriage road.

There is a trail register and bulletin board W of the exhibit area. The trail follows a curving roadway from here to the North Lake beach area. It passes a yellow metal barrier gate just before reaching a DEC signpost at 4.7 mi. The route crosses an open zone, enters a light woods, and then eases by the rear of the picnic area. The beach is on the other side of the picnic area.

A jct. near the beginning of a high wire mesh fence appears at 4.8 mi. (The red-marked snowmobile trail at R joins into the Sleepy Hollow Horse Trail network.) The Escarpment Trail follows the L side of the fence, re-entering woods at 4.9 mi.

Soon, a rock outcrop presents a steep climb to a trail register at 5.05 mi. Then the trail crosses a flat rock zone, covered with pitch pine similar to that which must once have been found in the Pine Orchard. Vistas abound from the escarpment edge. Finally, the trail ends up at a rock ledge, called Artist Rock, at 5.1 mi. Thomas Cole used to bring fellow artists here to point out his home, miles away on the Hudson in the village of Catskill.

A steep pitch up red shale is engaged at 5.3 mi. and then the trail follows the base of a long, thick layer of conglomerate cap rock. The path climbs steeply again before reaching a jct. at the foot of a cliff at 5.7 mi. (Here, a yellow-marked spur trail R cuts back a short distance to Lookout Rock and then, at a total of 0.2 mi., terminates at Sunset Rock. An open rock zone cleaved with deep rock joints requires careful footwork but leads to a place of magnificent views of North and South lakes, far below. Beyond, L to R, are Kaaterskill High Peak, Roundtop, Plateau, Hunter, and Rusk mts. This is an excellent lunch spot.)

The Escarpment Trail continues from the jct., soon climbing a pitch. It then slabs along the escarpment edge to open Newman's Ledge, at 5.8 mi. Here, one can see N beyond Albany. The route climbs again, levels occasionally, and then resumes its ascent. At 6.4 mi., just below Badman Cave, where it is thought 18th-century outlaws lived, there is a jct. with the yellow-marked Rock Shelter Trail (trail 17), which runs straight ahead 1.75 mi. to the Schutt Rd. parking area, near the campground gate. See below.

The Escarpment Trail steeply ascends R of the cave. Beyond the overhang, the slope is more moderate. Eventually, the woods are more open. There is a level campsite 50 ft. L of the trail on a side path at 6.55 mi. Climbing resumes, again leveling at 7.05 mi., 100 ft. before a jct. (The red-marked trail at L is the Mary's Glen Trail, which leads 1.35 mi. to the N/S Lakes Campground; see below).

From the junction, the trail rises steeply, easing in grade just before it turns R and steeply bolts up 50 ft. to a last vertical rock abutment. There are magnificent views from the open shelf.

The trail leads NW a short distance to a DEC signpost at 7.2 mi. This is North Point. Excellent views are found to the S. North and South lakes stand out, as do mountains on the horizon.

The Escarpment Trail continues N another 15.9 mi. Refer to the Escarpment Trail (Northern Section, trail 6) in the Black Dome Valley–North Point Section of this book for the trail description.

Distances: *To Schutt Rd. Trail jct., 0.5 mi.; to Layman Monument, 1.2 mi.; to Sleepy Hollow Horse Trail jct. (Long Path), 2.55 mi.; to second Schutt Rd.*

Trail jct., 3.1 mi.; to Boulder Rock, 4.0 mi.; to Catskill Mt. House site, 4.5 mi.; to North Lake picnic area, 4.7 mi.; to jct. with yellow spur to Sunset Rock, 5.7 mi.; to Newman Ledge, 5.85 mi.; to Rock Shelter Trail jct., 6.4 mi.; to Mary's Glen Trail jct., 7.05 mi.; to North Point, 7.2 mi. (11.7 km).

(19) Schutt Rd. Trail

Map 40: P-3
North/South Lakes Area

The Schutt Rd. Trail is a short trail that climbs South Mt. to the site of the old Hotel Kaaterskill. When Catskill Mt. House owner Charles Beach refused to provide a chicken dinner for George Harding's daughter and told him to build his own hotel if he didn't like it, Harding built the Hotel Kaaterskill. The largest hotel of its time, it could handle 1200 guests. The hiking trail follows one of the routes to this old hotel, providing walking of little challenge but pleasant surroundings.

In 1852, Peter Schutt and his son, Jacob, started the Laurel House Hotel to provide rooms for vacationers who couldn't gain booking into the larger hotels. It is believed that what many trail guides refer to as the Scutt Trail, an extension of Schutt Rd., should properly be called Schutt Rd. Trail, and it appears as such in this book.

Trailhead: Schutt Rd. Trail used to start at the S end of Schutt Rd. at a corral and parking area. Today, a parking area and corral are found at the N end of Schutt Rd. where the Escarpment Trail (trail 18) now begins. Schutt Rd. Trail begins 100 ft. W of its earlier starting point, where the relatively new section of the Escarpment Trail joins it at a jct.

From the jct. (0.0 mi.), the red-marked DEC trail climbs SW up the gradually curving grade of an old carriage road. It passes remnants of two stone gate posts at 0.05 mi. just before reaching a trail register on the R. Great hemlocks and attractive birches interest you until the trail reaches a second trail register at a jct. at 0.25 mi. (The unnamed yellow-marked trail R joins the Escarpment Trail 0.5 mi. SE.)

The trail continues at comfortable grades, sometimes nearly level and sometimes slowly ascending the mountain. Large overhangs are seen L at 0.5 mi., where great rock outcrops stand out. The grassy road swings NE at 0.6 mi., reaching an unmarked jct. at 1.05 mi. Here a trail L leads a short distance to the area where the Hotel Kaaterskill once stood. The unmarked trail straight ahead continues NE, but the Schutt Rd. Trail turns sharply SW to a DEC signpost at a jct. at 1.1 mi. Here, the blue-marked Escarpment Trail enters from the SE and turns abruptly NE (see above).

Distances: *To yellow cross-over trail, 0.25 mi.; to Escarpment Trail, 1.1 mi. (1.8 km).*

(20) Mary's Glen Trail

Map 40: P-3
North/South Lakes Area

Mary's Glen Trail is the shortest route to North Point from North Lake Rd. North Point offers dramatic views both N and S. The northern half of the Escarpment Trail starts at North Point.

The Mary of Mary's Glen was Mary Scribner. Ira and Mary Scribner built the Glen Mary Cottage in 1844, near Lake Creek. Over the years, the little cottage was frequently used to care for the overflow of the large hotels, and it is said that Henry David Thoreau spent a night there.

Trailhead: *Access to the trailhead is via North Lake Rd. (See* Route Guide *for Palenville–North Lake.) A parking area is a short distance past the trailhead.*

The trail runs N from the trailhead (0.0 mi.), following the W side of Ashley Creek. The primary water source of North Lake, it once provided water for the Catskill Mt. House. The red-marked trail is criss-crossed by tree roots, but large stepping stones keep you dry in wet spots. A particularly large hemlock is at L of the level trail at 0.1 mi. A trail register is located at 0.15 mi.

At a jct. at 0.2 mi., the whisper of a falls is heard. A short walk R on the spur trail brings you to the base of Ashley Falls. Several slabs of rock lean at sharp angles. Above, two upper pitches of the falls can be seen.

The Mary's Glen Trail becomes moderately steep for a short distance; a side trip R reveals the top of Ashley Falls. Further ascent is more moderate. The mossy stream edge, pleasant forest, and sounds of water create an enjoyable effect.

The way heads NW away from the stream, and then N before reaching a jct. with the Rock Shelter Trail at 0.7 mi. (The Rock Shelter Trail [trail 17] leads R, 0.35 mi. to the Escarpment Trail (trail 18). The Mary's Glen Trail turns L, parallel to a high ledge with a waterfall on the R, sharing the route with the Rock Shelter Trail. (The latter trail departs L about 100 yds. from the first jct., just after a turn N, and proceeds 1.4 mi. to Schutt Rd.; see above.)

At 0.9 mi. the route becomes moderately steep before leveling off again. It passes below ledges where huge sedimentary rock slabs are tumbled together. Another steep rock zone pitches up to ledges where views of North Point become evident. The rock type changes to red shale and the path steepens; it is muddy in wet weather.

At 1.35 mi., the trail joins the Escarpment Trail at a jct. (The Escarpment Trail heads steeply L 0.15 mi. to North Point, and R 2.35 mi to the parking area at North Lake; see above.)

Distances: To Mary's Glen, 0.26 mi.; to Rock Shelter Trail jct., 0.7 mi.; to Escarpment Trail jct., 1.35 mi. (2.2 km). Ascent from trailhead to North Point, 840 ft. (252 m).

Platte Clove Section

This section offers the hiker some of the most fascinating outings in the Catskills, and its trailheads are among the easiest to reach in these mountains.

The Mohawk Joseph Brant marched his Revolutionary War prisoners along Overlook Rd. in the 1700s, and Mink Hollow Rd. was used for hauling in the early 1800s. Summer visitors of the 19th century visited Plattekill Clove, where they could look down from platforms to the rock formations called Devil's Kitchen.

Several of the trails were started by Twilight Park Association and Elka Park members. The fanciful names of waterfalls, boulders, and lookouts hark back to the 1800s, when summer residents tramped over every inch of these mountains. The Devil's Path begins in this section, running over Indian Head and Twin, Sugarloaf and Plateau mts. before heading over Hunter and West Kill mts.

Plattekill Creek has headwaters on the shoulder of Kaaterskill High Peak, while Schoharie Creek begins on neighboring Indian Head Mt. Plattekill Creek water flows E to Esopus Creek and then to the Hudson, about 10 miles away. The Schoharie flows W and N, first entering the Mohawk, before also reaching the Hudson. Its water has to flow 175 mi. to reach the same point in the Hudson where the Plattekill's water enters, though they started their journeys within 3 mi. of each other.

Trail in winter: *Climbers have to be careful on the steep rock along the Devil's Path in winter. This is particularly true on Sugarloaf Mt. and at the W end of Plateau Mt. The Kaaterskill High Peak (Alternative Trail) is not recommended in winter due to the steep cliff descent in places. However, a descent from the summit to the cliff edge for a good view is rewarding.*

Cross-country skiing on the Kaaterskill High Peak Trail and on the Old Overlook Rd. Trail is excellent.

Short Hikes:

Devil's Kitchen Lean-to—2.7 mi round trip. Walk the first section of the Devil's Path through pleasant forest to a lean-to by the Cold Kill.

Huckleberry Point—4.8 mi. round trip. Plan on arriving at lunchtime, so you can spend lots of time at this magnificent vista.

Moderate Hikes:

Kaaterskill High Peak—8.8 mi. round trip. A long hike through attractive forest to an isolated mountain top.

Indian Head Mt.—7.0 mi. loop trip. A good scramble to introduce you to the Devil's Path.

Harder Hikes:

Devil's Path–Sugarloaf, Twin, Indian Head mts.—8.65 mi. through trip. Be in good shape for these three mountains, but you can bail out at the Jimmy Dolan Notch Trail if it's too much.

Long Path via Kaaterskill Mt. Trail and on to Malden Ave. in Palenville—9.5 mi. This is a great woods walk, but be sure to start at the Platte Clove end.

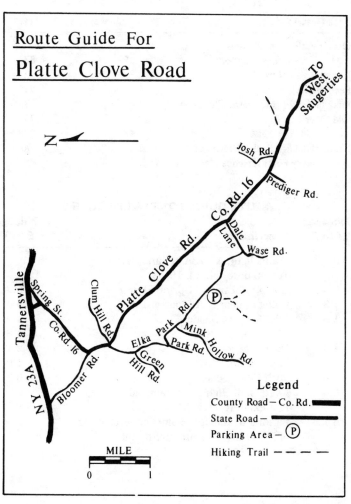

Route Guide For
Platte Clove Road

N

To West Saugerties

Josh Rd.

Prediger Rd.

Co. Rd. 16

Dale Lane

Wase Rd.

Platte Clove Rd.

Clum Hill Rd.

Tannersville

Spring St.

Co. Rd. 16

Bloomer Rd.

Elka Park Rd.

Green Hill Rd.

Park Rd.

Mink Hollow Rd.

NY 23A

P

Legend

County Road – Co. Rd. ▬▬
State Road – ▬▬
Parking Area – (P)
Hiking Trail – – – –

MILE

0   1

Trail Described	Total Miles (one way)	Page
Devil's Path (Plateau–Indian Head Wilderness Section)	13.05	87
Jimmy Dolan Notch	2.3	92
Pecoy Notch	1.15	93
Mink Hollow (from Platte Clove)	1.0	93
Old Overlook Rd.	4.8	95
Kaaterskill High Peak	4.4	97
Kaaterskill High Peak (Alternate)	2.4	100
Huckleberry Point (Friends Nature Trail)	1.3	101

ROUTE GUIDE FOR PLATTE COVE

Mileage W to E	Description	Mileage E to W
0.0	Traffic light, NY 23A in Tannersville. Turn S onto Co. Rd. 16.	6.7
0.3	Going S, bear R at Spring St. jct.	6.4
1.3	Going S, bear L at Bloomer Rd.	5.4
1.8	Elka Rd. jct., S side.	4.9
1.9	Clum Rd. jct., N side.	4.8
4.6	Dale Lane jct., S side.	2.1
5.7	Prediger Rd., S side.	1.0
6.0	Josh Rd., N side.	0.7
6.6	Kaaterskill High Peak trailhead, N side; Plattekill Preserve, N and S.	0.1
6.7	Parking turnabout, S side, on level at top of Platte Clove Mountain Rd. hill.	0.0

(21) Devil's Path Trail (Plateau–Indian Head Wilderness Section)

This 12.05-mi. section of the Devil's Path climbs Indian Head, Twin, Sugarloaf, and Plateau mts. Perhaps even more challenging are the descents into Jimmy Dolan, Pecoy, Mink, and Stony Clove notches. This is an exciting region with many excellent views. However, in wet weather or winter it can be dangerous. The hiker should carry plenty of water and allow extra time for careful climbing.

Trailhead: *Access to the eastern end of the Devil's Path is 0.4 mi. off Platte Clove Rd. on Prediger Rd. (See* Route Guide *for Platte Clove.) The best approach to Prediger Rd. is from Tannersville rather than from West Saugerties because Platte Clove Rd. from West Saugerties climbs a treacherously steep, narrow road past the Devil's Kitchen. (This road is not open in the winter.) The parking area at the end of Prediger Rd. can hold several vehicles, but space is cramped.*

From the end of Prediger Rd. (0.0 mi.), the trail passes through a narrow opening in the log fence, crossing a small tributary brook on a wooden bridge. Red DEC trail markers lead SW on a nearly level woods road. Wide and grassy, it would be good for cross-country skiing. A trail register is found at 0.1 mi. Small intermittent streams cross the trail in several places in wet weather.

Nearing a stream at 0.4 mi. and a trail jct. at 0.5 mi. the trail goes straight following red trail markers. (The Jimmy Dolan Notch Trail [trail 22] goes R with blue trail markers; see below.)

Gradual inclines continue and the woods road narrows to a footpath at 0.7 mi. Gently rolling terrain generally follows contour as the route angles SE around the base of Indian Head Mt.

At 1.8 mi., the trail merges with the Old Overlook Rd. Trail (trail 25) for a short distance. This old road dates back to colonial days. Bear R. (The Old Overlook Rd. to the L runs 0.85 mi. to Platte Clove Rd., passing through the Catskill Center's Platte Cove Preserve.) The woods road swings S, reaching another jct. at 1.9 mi. The Devil's

Kitchen lean-to is 0.2 mi. straight ahead on the blue trail.

The Devil's Path turns R, heading W, up a gradual slope. It soon changes to a moderate grade with occasional short level sections. At 2.7 mi. the trail becomes steep to Sherman's Lookout (the chin of the Indian) at 3.2 mi., where there is an excellent 180-degree view. From here the route climbs very steeply to a second lookout point to S at 3.4 mi. From this point, there is a small loss of elevation before steep climbing resumes. At 3.7 mi. there is an extensive overlook E from the top of a cliff.

The grade lessens at 3.9 mi. and is easy for the rest of the way to the wooded summit at 4.2 mi. Ascent from the parking area is 1573 ft.; summit elevation is 3573 ft.

The trail begins its 475-ft. descent into Jimmy Dolan Notch with gradual grades, but then drops steeply before easing again in the col. The Jimmy Dolan Notch Trail (trail 22) enters from the R at 4.7 mi. (It descends 1.5 mi. to rejoin the Devil's Path, 0.5 mi. from the Prediger Rd. parking area.)

The Devil's Path heads W through the small notch. It climbs steeply up a rock bluff towards the summits of Twin Mt. The sharp profile of Indian Head Mt. can be seen to the E. The trail reaches a rock overhang at 4.9 mi. and then steeply ascends a scramble over tree roots up 10 ft. of nearly vertical rock.

Hiking then becomes easier past the 3500 ft. elevation sign. Switchbacks lead steeply up to 5.0 mi., where the trail levels. A lookout bluff to the L has views to the SE.

Wind-swept spruces and blueberry bushes cloak the trail as it skirts the SW edge of the mountaintop, reaching the lower of the two summits of Twin Mt. at 5.1 mi. Extensive open rock ledges afford 180-degree views far S, E, and to nearby Sugarloaf Mt. Ascending again, the trail reaches the true summit of Twin Mt. at 5.7 mi. Ascent from Jimmy Dolan Notch is 640 ft.; summit elevation is 3640 ft. A flat open rock ledge provides views to the S.

The trail swings L, circling below the bluff and descending gradually to 5.9 mi. Here, one of the steepest parts of the whole Devil's Path drops between narrowly spaced boulders. A large overhang cave R is an excellent emergency shelter, capable of holding several hikers. There is a lookout L, 100 yds. farther along the trail.

A short, gradual grade prefaces a second steep downgrade, followed by more steep descents, with open viewing NE. Eventually, the trail moderates, reaching the col of Pecoy Notch at 6.5 mi. Col elevation is 2810 ft. The Pecoy Notch Trail (trail 23) enters from the R. (It descends 1.97 mi. to Roaring Kill Rd.; see below.)

The red-marked Devil's Path continues straight ahead towards Sugarloaf Mt. Initially level, it soon turns L and ascends the mountain. At 6.9 mi., the climb becomes steep and rocky in places. Occasional lookouts present themselves.

At 7.3 mi., the grade becomes gradual again as the trail passes the 3500-ft. elevation marker. Near the summit the trail almost levels; low evergreens and ferns are abundant. The trail reaches the summit at 7.7 mi. Summit elevation of Sugarloaf Mt., once known as Mink Mt., is 3800 ft. Ascent from Pecoy Notch is 822 ft. A spur trail L, at 7.8 mi., leads to a lookout to the S.

The path remains nearly level for a few minutes of easy walking before descending over large boulders, from which there are good views NW towards Plateau Mt. It passes the 3500-ft. elevation mark at 8.1 mi., just before reaching a spring (which fails in dry weather).

The trail drops with varying grades between boulders that close in on it in places. Several caves are found here. Open viewing is frequent along the often-turning trail.

At 8.4 mi. the route passes under a natural rock arch, turning sharply L. (Pay attention here.) The grade then moderates, finally becoming gradual before reaching a 4-way trail jct. in the Mink Hollow col at 8.65 mi. Elevation is 2600 ft. Descent from Sugarloaf Mt. is 1200 ft. A trail register is located here. To the L, the Mink Hollow Trail follows blue markers 0.1 mi. to the Mink Hollow lean-to and 2.9 mi. S to a parking area. To the R, the Mink Hollow Notch Trail (trail 24) leads 0.8 mi. N to the trailhead on Mink Hollow Rd. (See below.)

The trail heads W from Mink Hollow Notch toward Plateau Mt., ascending in moderate and gradual sections. It swings R at 8.75 mi. and soon after passes a spring. The route then slabs a shoulder, which drops off to the R, becoming steeper.

Grades are uneven as the route climbs a rocky path. A steep rock bluff at 9.05 mi. is followed by switchbacks and a steep climb up through a rock cut at 9.2 mi. Moderate and steep grades continue to a small rock overhang at 9.4 mi., followed by another steep section. Thereafter, a more comfortable grassy section gives the hiker a breather.

Then, at 9.65 mi., stone steps lead up through one last rock cut to a large flat boulder from which splendid views are seen. Sugarloaf Mt. is directly E. Kaaterskill High Peak and Roundtop mts. stand out clearly to the NE.

This spot is sometimes called the E summit, but actual height of land is still 0.2 ahead. Nearly level grades lead through spruce to the actual Plateau Mt. summit (hard to discern) at 9.85 mi. Summit elevation is 3840 ft. Ascent from Mink Hollow Notch is 1240 ft.

The reason for its name is obvious, since the top of Plateau Mt. is nearly flat, with only mildly undulating grades. The hiker walks through thick spruce growth, with few glimpses of distant points, to the W end of the plateau. This is an attractive walk, but one that somehow doesn't make you feel that you are on a mountaintop.

The trail runs NW to the first of several increasingly better look-outs at 11.6 mi. The site where the old Plateau Mt. lean-to once stood is on the L at 11.7 mi. Danny's Lookout, a rock ledge offering clear views of the Blackhead Range and the Escarpment Trail, is at 11.9 mi.

The trail swings sharp L and has a minor loss of elevation before reaching Orchard Point (called Orchid Point in a 1969 Conservation Dept. trail guide) at 12.05 mi. This large, open rock ledge looks out directly to the Hunter Mt. fire tower. The West Kill Mt. summit is barely visible over the L shoulder of Hunter. Extensive views present a panorama of peaks and vales from S to N.

From Orchard Point, the trail drops off a ledge and begins nearly 1500 ft. of vertical descent into Stony Clove Notch. Deciduous trees again dominate as elevation is lost. Once beyond the initial drop off the ledge, the route is a gradual downgrade.

After a spring L at 12.25 mi., the slope becomes moderate and very steady. It slabs the mountainside for a while before crossing the first of two loose rock slides at 12.45 mi. (They are not difficult to cross, but one should be careful.) Open woods permit the hiker to see a long distance down the trail as moderate and steep grades continue. Several switchbacks make descent easier. The trail is not so much difficult as relentless in grade.

The trail passes a second spring R at 12.8 mi. Finally, the grade becomes gradual at 12.9 mi. A trail register precedes log steps to the highway at Devil's Tombstone Public Campgrounds in Stony Clove Notch. Across NY 214, at 13.05 mi., there is a large parking area. The Devil's Path continues from the L rear of the parking area. (See Devil's Path–Hunter Mt. section for continuation of the trail description.)

Distances: To Jimmy Dolan Notch Trail jct., 0.5 mi.; to Old Overlook Rd. jct., 1.8 mi.; to Indian Head Mt. jct., 1.9 mi.; to Indian Head Mt. summit, 4.2 mi.; to second Jimmy Dolan Notch Trail jct., 4.7 mi.; to Twin Mt. summit 5.7 mi.; to Pecoy Notch, 6.5 mi.; to Sugarloaf Mt. summit, 7.7 mi.; to Mink Hollow Notch, 8.65 mi.; to Plateau Mt. summit, 9.85 mi.; to Orchard Point, 12.05 mi.; to Stony Clove Notch, 13.05 mi (20.2 km).

(22) Jimmy Dolan Notch Trail

Map 41: O-4
NE Catskills

Trailhead: The Jimmy Dolan Notch Trail branches R from the Devil's Path (trail 21) at its 0.5 mi. point (see above). It climbs 1.5 mi. SW to rejoin the Devil's Path at that trail's 4.7 mi. point. The trail provides the hiker with several options for varying trip distances.

From the 0.5 mi. point of the Devil's Path (0.0 mi.), the Jimmy Dolan Notch Trail crosses a stream and proceeds along a grassy woods road, following blue DEC trail markers. The trail crosses several intermittent brooks. At 0.5 mi. the trail leaves the old logging road and heads L up a gradual grade into hemlocks on a softer footpath.

The slope increasingly steepens as it climbs into the notch. First moderate and then steep, it finally eases at 1.5 mi., reaching the jct. with the Devil's Path in Jimmy Dolan Notch at 2.3 mi. Elevation here is 3098 ft. (Follow the Devil's Path L 0.45 mi. for the summit of Indian Head Mt., or R 0.95 mi. to the summit of Twin Mt.)

Distances: *To point where trail leaves woods road, 1.2 mi.; to Jimmy Dolan Notch jct. with Devil's Path, 1.5 mi. (3.75 km). Ascent, 1098 ft. (336 m).*

(23) Pecoy Notch Trail

Map 41: N-4
NE Catskills

Trailhead: *Access to the trailhead is off Platte Clove Rd. Turn SE onto Dale Lane at a trailhead parking sign 3.7 mi. from Tannersville. At a jct. at 0.5 mi., bear R, crossing a small stream onto Roaring Kill Rd. Follow this road NW 0.7 mi. to a parking area on the L. Roaring Kill itself is about 200 ft. farther. It is 1.0 mi. to Mink Hollow Rd. over a rough dirt roadway that is not maintained in winter.*

At the parking lot is an information board with a trail register 50 ft. up the trail. From the rear of the parking lot (0.0 mi.), the yellow-marked trail heads SW through a small grassy area before crossing a small drainage and entering the woods. It crosses a second small drainage at 0.2 mi. before reaching a trail jct. at 0.3 mi.

The blue trail leading straight ahead and to the R forms part of a loop network over Sugarloaf Mt. It leads 2.5 mi. to the Devil's Path in Mink Hollow (see below, trail 24). For Pecoy Notch, bear L.

The Pecoy Notch trail continues S from the jct., soon beginning a short, moderate climb along an old quarry road through a steep area. At 0.4 mi. the grade eases as the trail passes a large boulder at 0.5 mi. and an intermittent spring about 70 yds. past it.

The trail traverses Mudd Quarry at 0.6 mi., after a short, steep pitch up through the talus slope below the quarry. The next third of a mile is level through a mature hardwood forest before the trail reaches Dibbles Quarry at 0.9 mi. This quarry offers good views of the upper Schoharie Valley in the foreground, to Round Top and High Peak in the N, around to the Hudson Valley to the E and Twin Mt. looming above to the SE. This is an excellent destination for families with small children or individuals with limited abilities.

After traversing the open talus slope, the trail re-enters the woods at 1.0 mi. and crosses a reliable stream in a hemlock grove at 1.1

mi. It now follows a low ridge E of the stream, reaching a small wet-weather pond at 1.4 mi. Natural ponds are rare in the Catskills; this one is typical, holding water only in the spring and after heavy rains.

Turning more easterly, the trail passes through an old beaver meadow at 1.5 mi. Here one can look S to Pecoy Notch with Twin and Sugarloaf flanking it to the E and W respectively.

The trail re-enters the woods and reaches an old trail at 1.6 mi; turn R ascending. The route continues on a rocky treadway, passes a spring on the L at 1.8 mi. and reaches the Devil's Path in Pecoy Notch at 2.0 mi. The red-marked Devil's Path leads L to Twin and Indian mts. and R to Sugarloaf, Plateau, Hunter and Westkill mts.

Distances: *To Mudd Quarry, 0.6 mi.; to Dibbles Quarry, 0.9 mi.; to beaver meadow, 1.5 mi.; to Devil's Path, 2.0 mi.*

(24) Mink Hollow Leg of Sugarloaf Trail System

Map 41:N-4
NE Catskills

Trailhead: *See above, trail 23.*

From the new parking lot on Roaring Kill Rd., follow yellow markers 0.3 mi. to a jct.; see above, trail 23. L leads 1.7 mi. to Pecoy Notch (trail 23), R 2.5 mi. to the Devil's Path in Mink Hollow (trail 24). The two new trails form a bypass of Sugarloaf Mt. and create an opportunity for a loop hike of just under seven miles over Sugarloaf. The through trail from Pecoy Notch to Mink Hollow is marked with blue markers, the quarter-mile spur to the parking lot with yellow markers.

From the jct. (0.0 mi.), bear R on level ground through open hardwoods, shortly joining an obscure quarry road as a gradual grade begins to the first of two quarries. The trail crosses two small streams (not reliable) and reaches the first quarry in dense woods at 0.3 mi. The trail swings around the E side of the quarry on level terrain before beginning a gradual ascent on a quarry road to the second quarry at 0.5 mi.

This second quarry is more interesting, with old walls built of the tailings. It is also in a dense hemlock woods with rocks covered with moss. It is quite extensive, extending to the W several hundred ft. into private property.

Leaving the quarry, the trail climbs moderately to steeply through hemlock woods, reaching a good woods road at 0.7 mi. From the rocks below this road, limited seasonal views can be had to the N and the Blackhead Range.

The trail turns L and ascends moderately, then bears R, easing onto a flat section before negotiating a short rise to yet another woods road at 1.0 mi. The trail follows this road L to the high point of the trail at 1.1 mi. (approx. elev. 2750 ft.).

The route turns S and heads toward Mink Hollow. The next half mile is mostly level through mixed woods. The hemlocks thin out by 1.3 mi., offering limited seasonal views across the Roaring Kill valley to Spruce Top and Plateau.

At 1.6 mi. there is an open view W to Spruce Top and at 1.7 another open view toward Plateau and Mink Hollow. Here the trail makes a sharp switchback R and descends steeply to a cut-over area recently purchased by the state. At 1.8 mi. the trail enters an overgrown area, joining a skidder road to the L. This route descends for a short distance before re-entering the woods and crossing a small stream in a hemlock-lined ravine at 2.0 mi.

Climbing the creek, the trail soon enters another recently cut weedy area, following another skidder road to the SW. At 2.2 mi. the trail bears L, leaving the wide skidder road and passing through young hardwoods before climbing steeply to a level stretch. Heading S with the notch sometimes in sight through the trees, the trail soon passes through a hemlock grove before emerging onto another wide skidder road at 2.3 mi., continuing on the road with slight ups and downs to the jct. with the Devil's Path at 2.5 mi. Sugarloaf Mt. is L, Plateau to the R. To continue S on the Mink Hollow Trail, turn R for 175 yds. to a second jct.; turn L for Lake Hill and Mink Hollow Lean-to, straight ahead for Plateau. The wide woods road to the R is the abandoned N portion of the Mink Hollow Trail.

Distances: *To jct. on trail 23 to second quarry, 0.5 mi.; to height of land,*

1.1 mi.; to ravine, 2.0 mi.; to Devil's Path, 2.5 mi. Total distance from parking lot, 2.8 mi.

(25) Old Overlook Rd. Trail

The Old Overlook Rd. Trail runs from Platte Clove Rd. to the jct. of the Overlook Mt. Trail (see Woodstock–Shandaken Section). Until the middle 1980s, the trail began at the Indian Head Mt. jct. of the Devil's Path Trail. When the Catskill Center for Conservation and Development created the Platte Clove Preserve, their trail system included a section of this old road, which is included here as part of the trail description. The trail makes a delightfully easy and attractive day hike to Echo Lake or up Overlook Mt. (If the skier starts on the Devil's Path at Prediger Rd. trailhead [see above] and picks up the trail at the 1.1 mi. point, this is also a very nice intermediate cross-country trail all the way to the summit of Overlook Mt.)

Perhaps no other Catskill trail can conjure up so much history for such a short distance. The road (then a trail) was used by Indians to force march their Revolutionary War prisoners to their stronghold at Echo Lake. In the Gilded Age of grand hotels, hikers would tramp from the Catskill Mt. House on the edge of the escarpment to the Overlook House on Overlook Mt. for lunch and then return to the Catskill Mt. House for dinner. Today, the old road is narrowing, providing a comfortable path along the edge of Plattekill Clove through a forest that is returning to wilderness.

Trailhead: *Trail access is off the S side of Platte Clove Rd. (See Route Guide for Platte Clove Rd.) This is 0.6 mi. E of Prediger Rd. There is a large new parking area about 0.7 mi. E of Prediger Rd., L up the old woods road marked by a D.E.C. sign.*

The trailhead location (0.0 mi.) is not identified by signs but has Platte Clove Preserve signs posted on trees. Follow the green arrow trail markers; avoid blue trail markers. At an opening in a wire fence, the route of the Old Overlook Rd. Trail drops down a bank 30 ft. to Plattekill Creek. The creek is small here and can be easily rock-hopped in summer.

Across the creek, the trail joins the Old Overlook Rd. and heads SE up a gradual grade. The route follows this woods road all the way to the Overlook Mt. Trail.

At 0.3 mi., the route is over hardscrabble rock, though hemlocks crowd on both sides. The gradual uphill grade is steady and easy. There is a small abandoned stone quarry with interesting small caves on the L at 1.05 mi.

The Devil's Path (trail 21) enters at 1.1 mi. (see above). The route follows red DEC trail markers to a jct. where the Devil's Path bears R up Indian Head Mt. at 1.2 mi. Continue straight ahead, following the blue trail markers of the Old Overlook Rd. Trail.

Another quarry, R at 1.3 mi., is just before the Devil's Kitchen lean-to at 1.35 mi. The lean-to sits 40 ft. above the Cold Kill in a most picturesque location. This is a high use lean-to. Hikers are strongly urged to CARRY OUT anything they carried in, *plus a bit more.* If the lean-to is occupied, overflow campsites are located up the hill about 200 ft. behind the lean-to. Do not use the campsites that are marked NO CAMPING. Camping is permitted across the creek in front of the lean-to.

The trail passes to the rear of the lean-to, crossing the Cold Kill on a log bridge 150 ft. farther along the way. Gradual upgrades continue to a jct. at 1.9 mi., where a yellow-marked spur path L leads to the remains of a very large stone quarry.

At 2.0 mi. the route swings from SE to SW around the shoulder of Plattekill Mt. The trail contours the slope for the next 1.2 mi. As the terrain drops off sharply on the L, views of the Hudson Valley are possible through the trees.

At 2.4 mi. the trail reaches an uncared-for spring pool on the R, and at 2.5 mi. a masonry basin and pipe R is at the base of a tree.

This is Skunk Spring, which has good water flow in all but the driest weather.

The trail goes up and down long, gentle grades before reaching a large boulder marking the jct. of the Echo Lake Trail (trail 49) at 3.4 mi. (The Echo Lake Trail descends R 0.6 mi. to Echo Lake lean-to.)

The Old Overlook Rd. Trail continues straight ahead over rising terrain. There is a moderate rise at 3.7 mi. and then more level ground. Passing a spring at the base of a small cliff on the L at 4.4 mi., the trail ascends slightly. Avoid the woods road that slants back to the L, 100 ft. before the jct. of the Overlook Mt. Trail at 4.8 mi. (Here the red-marked Overlook Mt. Trail ascends L 0.5 mi. to the summit; to the R that trail descends straight ahead 2.0 mi. to Mead's Mt. Rd. See description in Woodstock–Shandaken Section.)

Distances: To Plattekill Creek, 50 ft.; to Old Overlook Rd., 0.1 mi.; to Devil's Path, 1.1 mi.; to Indian Head Mt. jct., 1.2 mi.; to Devil's Kitchen lean-to, 1.35 mi.; to Skunk Spring, 2.5 mi.; to Echo Lake Trail jct., 3.4 mi.; to Overlook Mt. Trail jct., 4.8 mi. (7.8 km). Ascent, 1100 ft. (336 m).

(26) Kaaterskill High Peak Trail   Map 41: O-4

Kaaterskill High Peak stands apart from other Catskill mountains, making it appear higher than it really is, and gives climbers superb views. Originally called Roundtop (Roundtop was called High Peak then), it was renamed Liberty Cap by the French Revolutionist Pierre DeLabigarre in 1793. By the 1820s, it was referred to by many as Mrs. Montgomery's Cap, after the widow's cap worn by Janet Montgomery, widow of General Richard Montgomery, who died leading the attack on the City of Quebec in 1775. An attempt to call it Mt. Lincoln (and neighboring Roundtop Mt., Mt. Stanton) in the 1880s never really took hold. Today, the local people call it Cauterskill High Peak.

This trail to the base of the mountain and the snowmobile loop around Roundtop would be excellent for skiing. The first 3.5 mi. of this trail is part of the Long Path.

Trailhead: *Access to the mountain is via a snowmobile trail off the N side of Platte Clove Rd. (See Route Guide for Platte Clove.) This is 0.9 mi. E of Prediger Rd. A new parking area is a few feet up the snowmobile trail, an old woods road.*

The trail follows orange snowmobile markers N from Platte Clove Rd. The gradual grade of the woods road climbs through hemlock forest. Nearly leveling at 0.5 mi., the rocky road then climbs more gradually, reaching a fork at 0.7 mi. Bear R. Steenburg Rd. jct. is at 1.0, where the marked snowmobile trail again bears R.

Then, at 1.1 mi., there is a jct. where the yellow-marked trail leads 1.3 mi. SE to Huckleberry Point. See Huckleberry Point Trail, below.)

The High Peak Trail continues N, crossing a wet area and then two branches of Upper Plattekill Creek at 1.4 mi. The route begins to climb easy grades. As elevation is gained, the slopes are drier. Flora changes to maple and white and gray birches.

The route almost levels, becoming a grassy lane, still heading N. By 2.3 mi., the route approaches 3000 ft. elevation. Blueberries, spruce and a few balsam fir now dominate. The trail follows a small brook at L before passing over the almost flat height of land, and starts to descend. Brooks now flow N.

At 3.5 mi. at a jct. the marked snowmobile trail veers sharply L. (Straight ahead, through the jct., this section of the Long Path continues on the level 0.2 mi., merging there with the old Twilight Park Trail. From there, it descends a steep series of switchbacks, leveling and turning sharply R before reaching Buttermilk Falls at 5.0 mi. See Buttermilk Falls Trail (trail 14), Palenville–North Lake

Section, for continuation to Malden Avenue in Palenville.)

The marked snowmobile trail heads S from the jct., soon climbing a moderate grade, before swinging sharply N again. At another jct., at 3.7 mi., a DEC sign marks the beginning of the 7.64-mi. snowmobile loop around Roundtop Mt. Bear R and follow the wide, grassy loop trail 0.1 mi. to where it dips to cross a small brook. A small rock cairn may be seen here in summer. The informally marked Twilight Park Trail crosses the loop trail here and ascends the mountain to the L. Look carefully just before the small brook, because blue markings are now scant; the informal trail's beginning crosses a rocky wet area and is nearly indiscernible. Turn L (S) and follow the informal blue trail markers of the Twilight Park Trail.

The route quickly passes a wet zone and follows blue paint blazes. The rough trail steepens, climbing through a rock cut at 4.0 mi. At its top, views N begin to open up. The route passes between large boulders at 4.1 mi., jogging E and then back S before ascending steeply up another rock cut in a cliff wall. At its top, the footpath circles L, where at 4.2 mi. a boulder top provides a clear lookout N to Stoppel Point and the Blackhead Range.

The grade is now almost level. Blowdown increases near the top. After a few minor bumps, the trail reaches the almost flat, viewless summit at 4.4 mi. in a small clearing. The careful searcher can find a USGS benchmark embedded in a rock some 10 ft. SE. There are excellent views S from grassy, open ledges another 0.3 mi. along the footpath; the hiker is encouraged to walk the extra distance. (See the Kaaterskill High Peak Alternate Trail [trail 27]).

Distances: *To first jct., 0.7 mi.; to Steenburg Rd. jct., 1.0 mi.; to Huckleberry Trail jct., 1.1 mi.; to height of land, 2.3 mi.; to Long Path separation jct., 3.5 mi.; to Roundtop Mt. loop jct., 3.7 mi.; to Twilight Park Trail jct. (cairn), 3.8 mi.; to summit, 4.4 mi. (7.1 km). Elevation, 3655 ft. (1118 m). Ascent from Platte Clove Rd., 1705 ft. (521 m).*

(27) Kaaterskill High Peak Alternate Trail

This trail offers a loop option to the hiker on Kaaterskill High Peak. It provides splendid views S from the peak, but it does add 1.7 mi. to the trip. It is a challenging summer descent from the summit, and the hiker is advised to wear long pants because of the presence of nettles along the way. Because of its steepness in places, this trail is not recommended for the winter climber.

Trailhead: The trail begins at the 3.7 mi. point jct. of the Kaaterskill High Peak Trail (see above). From the DEC signpost (0.0 mi.), follow the orange marked snowmobile trail L (SSE). The route circles the base of Kaaterskill High Peak. The almost level loop trail has wet spots at 0.3 mi. At 0.5 mi. a brooklet of a spring flows from the R. The woods become open as the trail continues to circle the mountain. Keep a sharp eye for trail markers.

Gradually losing some elevation, the trail swings from W to SW before reaching a 4-way jct. at 1.65 mi. Here a rock cairn marks the R turn up the mountain. (The L turn heads S towards Josh Rd., soon entering private land. This jct. might be difficult to find in winter if snow covers the cairn.)

The trail climbs gradually N, becoming a moderate grade at 1.7 mi. Then, alternately moderate and steep grades wind up switchbacks. At 1.9 mi., a large overhang forms a cave-like area of significant size. The route swings R, resuming moderate grade to 2.0 mi., where very steep climbing leads up a section ending in a short vertical scramble up a narrow shoot. On top of this is a marvelous grassy meadow slope from which splendid views of Overlook, Plattekill, Indian Head, Twin, Sugarloaf, Plateau and Hunter mts. are afforded to the S.

The trail continues upward, leveling at a broad clearing outlook at 2.1 mi. Beyond this point, blue paint blazes must be followed carefully to the summit. A summit clearing is reached at 2.4 mi. The Kaaterskill High Peak Trail (trail 26) continues N with blue paint blazes (see above).

Distances: *To spring, 0.5 mi.; to 4-way jct., 1.65 mi.; to cave overhang, 1.9 mi.; to lookout meadow, 2.1 mi.; to summit clearing, 2.4 mi. (3.9 km). Summit elevation, 3655 ft. (1118 m). Ascent, 605 ft. (185 m). Ascent from Platte Clove Rd., 1705 ft. (521 m).*

Huckleberry Point Trail (Friends Nature Trail)

Map 41: O-4

Huckleberry Point has one of the truly magnificent vistas in the Catskills. From its precipice one looks directly S to Overlook Mt.; to the SE and E are the Hudson River and New England; to the W is the awesome steepness of the Plattekill Clove walls abutting the shoulder of Indian Head Mt. Straight down, over 1000 ft., is the narrow ribbon of Plattekill Creek, cutting through its narrow canyon, spilling over waterfalls, shimmering in the sunlight.

Trailhead: *Trail access is via the Kaaterskill High Peak Trail (trail 26) at its 1.1 mi. point (see above). Informal yellow trail markers lead R to the SE. The nearly level trail slowly loses elevation, passing several rock piles at 0.1 mi. Plattekill Creek must be rock-hopped at 0.4 mi.*

There is a short, moderate upgrade at 0.5 mi., followed by a general increase in elevation to 0.6 mi., where leveling occurs. After a slight dip, the trail climbs again, and then descends a steep slope at 0.8 mi. The next several minutes are spent walking amongst mountain laurel, which makes a mid-June trip especially nice.

Avoid a side trail R, marked by a cairn. The birch forest is interrupted by a grove of pine. At a T-jct. at 1.2 mi. a cairn blocks the way S, and the well-marked trail turns R. This level section soon reaches Huckleberry Point and descends a short distance to the precipice edge, at 1.3 mi.

A sheer drop of over 1000 ft. into Plattekill Clove immediately draws your attention; then you are captivated by the view SE across the Hudson towards New England. Later you see Overlook Mt. across the clove, and to the R, Plattekill Mt. and Indian Head Mt. Another ledge to the L permits a more directly E view. This is a wonderful place to have lunch while watching hawks glide on air currents.

Distances: *To creek crossing, 0.4 mi.; to height of land, 0.8 mi.; to T-jct., 1.2 mi.; to Huckleberry Point, 1.3 mi. (2.1 km) (2.4 mi. from Platte Clove Rd.).*

Stony Clove Section

Hunter Mt., the principal feature in this section, was not named after the colonial governor, Robert Hunter, but rather for a landlord, John Hunter—a rascal who endlessly sought backrents from his tenants in the mid-1800s. For a while, there was a movement to change its name to Mount Guyot in honor of Arnold Guyot, the great map maker of the Catskills. His August, 1871 ascent proved Kaaterskill High Peak was not the highest in the Catskills, though he was yet to find that Slide Mt. was even higher than Hunter.

Raging forest fires swept the mountain in 1893, only eight years after the Forest Preserve was created. The first fire tower was built in 1909 at the 4010 ft. level, where the Becker Hollow Trail joins the Hunter Mt. Trail. The foundation bolts are still visible. The present tower is at the 4040-ft. summit and is open to the public.

The four major trails on Hunter Mt. are Spruceton Trail, Becker Hollow Trail, Devil's Path, and the Colonel's Chair (Shanty Hollow Trail). All but the Spruceton Trail are described in this section. The old Taylor Hollow trail, which ties in with the Spruceton Trail, is closed to hikers now.

Stony Clove more clearly demonstrates the concept of a notch than any other rock cut in the Catskills. It was so narrow before the building of a road and then a railroad widened it that in the 1840s the painter Charles Lanman said, "It is the loneliest and most awful corner of the world that I have ever seen—none other, I fancy, could make a man feel more utterly desolate. It is the type of valley of the shadow of death; in single file did we pass through it and in single file must we pass to the grave." Take your time and explore it, for you will see, from NY 214, high on a cliff of Hunter (best viewed from the south), the stone face of the Devil himself. The Devil's Tombstone is at Devil's Tombstone Campground. Notch Lake was formerly called Stygian Lake (mythical source of the River Styx, across which the souls of the dead are ferried in Hades).

Trail in winter: This is nice snowshoe terrain. Diamond Notch also has good cross-country skiing, but the upper elevations of the notch often have hard crust. Good skills are needed here. The summit of Hunter Mt. is quite flat and permits skiing also, but the ascent to the top is easier on showshoes. Perhaps a ski-shoe trip, where one snowshoes the steeper sections and skis the rest, makes the most sense if skiing on Hunter is desired.

Short Hikes:

Becker Hollow to Concrete Dam—*1 mi. round trip. A very pleasant walk on mostly level terrain by a brook to a 50-ft. concrete dam.*

Moderate Hikes:

Becker Hollow Trail/Connector Trail to Hunter Mt.—*4.4 mi. round trip. Steady grades up a beautiful deciduous forest vale to a summit with a fire tower and excellent views.*

Colonel's Chair Trail—*Take a ski chair lift to a ski lodge, then go on a 4.2 mi. round trip to the summit of Hunter Mt. Return by chairlift.*

Diamond Notch Trail to lean-to—*3.6 mi. round trip along a brook and up a pleasant valley.*

Harder Hikes:

Plateau Summit—*6.4 mi. round trip. Climb steeply to Orchard Point for a good view and then take an easy walk to the summit and back.*

Hunter Mt. Loop—*5.95 mi. This trip reaches the summit of Hunter Mt. from Becker Hollow, swings over to the Devil's Acre lean-to, and then returns* *to Devil's Tombstone Campground via a steep Devil's Path. A second vehicle is needed for return to Becker Hollow trailhead.*

Trail Described	Total Miles (one way)	Page
Colonel's Chair	1.1	107
Becker Hollow	2.05	108
Becker Hollow Connector	0.3	109
Devil's Path (Hunter Mt. Section)	4.15	110
Hunter Mt. Spur	1.35	112
Plateau Mt. from Stony Clove	3.2	113
Diamond Notch (Hollow Tree Brook)	3.2	115

ROUTE GUIDE FOR STONY CLOVE

Mileage N to S	Description	Mileage S to N
0.0	Jct. of NY 23A and NY 214, E of village of Hunter.	13.5
0.7	Ski Bowl Rd. to Hunter Mt. (to Shanty Trail trailhead).	12.8
1.3	Parking, Becker Hollow Trail.	12.2
2.6	The Devil's face in stone, W side of rd., on cliff of Hunter Mt.	10.9
2.8	Notch Lake.	10.7
2.9	Parking, Devil's Path to Hunter and Plateau mts.	10.6
3.1	Office of Devil's Tombstone Campground, W side of rd.	10.4
3.3	Devil's Tombstone with DEC Forest Preserve Centennial Plaque on it, E side of rd.	10.2

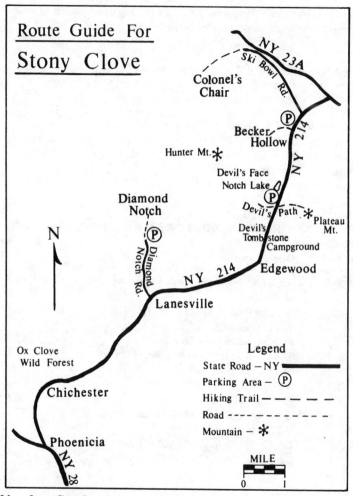

Route Guide For
Stony Clove

NY 23A

Ski Bowl Rd.

Colonel's Chair

Becker Hollow

Ⓟ

NY 214

Hunter Mt. ✳

Devil's Face

Notch Lake

Ⓟ

Diamond Notch

Devil's Path ✳ Plateau Mt.

Devil's Tombstone Campground

N

Diamond Notch Rd.

Ⓟ

NY 214

Edgewood

Lanesville

Ox Clove Wild Forest

Legend

State Road — NY ▬▬▬

Parking Area — Ⓟ

Hiking Trail — — — —

Road ---- — — —

Mountain — ✳

Chichester

Phoenicia

NY 28

MILE

0   1

Mileage N to S	Description	Mileage S to N
7.5	Diamond Notch Rd., Lanesville; Diamond Notch Trail.	6.0
10.5	Ox Clove (Westkill Mt. Wilderness Area)	3.0
11.5	Chichester	2.0
13.5	Phoenicia, NY 214-NY 28 jct.	0.0

(28) Colonel's Chair Trail

**Map 41: M-3
NE Catskills**

The Colonel's Chair Trail is somewhat unique in that one must take a chairlift at the Hunter Mountain ski slope up to the lodge atop Colonel's Chair in order to reach the trailhead. This spot on the shoulder of Hunter Mt. was named for Col. William Edwards, a major leather tanner in this region in the early 1800s. From the valley floor, this bump on Hunter's shoulder resembles a chair.

Summer tourists, as well as winter skiers, can ride the chairlift and then continue to the summit of Hunter Mt. The chairlift normally operates until 4:30 P.M each day, though the hiker had better verify this before starting out—especially if there is inclement weather.

Trailhead: *The trail leaves the upper-level exit of the lodge (0.0 mi.) and heads generally S, following yellow DEC trail markers. It passes a group of picnic tables, charcoal burners, and the starting points of several ski runs. At 0.1 mi. a monument commemorates John Clair, for his contributions to skiing, and Jean Wald, who lost his life while serving as a member of the ski patrol.*

The route then follows a grassy path L of the service road a short distance before rejoining it. Avoid the windmills and other apparatus on the R side of the trail at 0.2 mi. Continue along the flat trail to a jct. at 0.5 mi. Bear L and begin gradual climbing past the 3500 ft. elevation level at 1.0 mi. The moderate grade levels just before the trail reaches the Spruceton Trail (trail 92) jct. at 1.1 mi. (see Spruceton Trail, Prattsville–Shandaken section).

(By turning L and walking another 1.0 mi., the hiker can reach the fire tower summit of 4040-ft. Hunter Mt., second highest peak in the Catskills.)

Distances: *To monument, 0.1 mi.; to jct., 0.5 mi.; to Spruceton Trail jct., 1.1 mi. (1.8 km). Ascent to Spruceton Trail jct., 530 ft. (162 m); ascent to Hunter Mt. summit, 940 ft. (287 m).*

(29) Becker Hollow Trail

Map 41: M-4
NE Catskills

This is the shortest trail to the summit of Hunter Mt. It ascends 2200 ft. and, while at steady grade, is a rather tough little climb.

Trailhead: *Trail access is off NY 214 (see Route Guide for Stony Clove) at the DEC trail sign and parking area 1.3 mi. S of NY 23A. A trail register is at the trailhead (0.0 mi.).*

The trail heads W on a gravel roadway, past a vehicle barrier, following blue DEC trail markers. At 0.1 mi. the route enters hardwood forest. Shortly after, the gravel trail branches L, while the hiking trail continues straight ahead. It soon parallels a brook, which it crosses on a footbridge at 0.3 mi. (Avoid the unmarked path R.)

At 0.4 mi., the trail passes a three-tiered cascade of the brook and then a 50-ft. concrete dam. Once across a creek at 0.5 mi., a pitch up pulls away from the water. The way is still wide as the old woods road ascends the mountain. The grade eases briefly at 0.9 mi. before resuming its moderate slope. A sign indicating an elevation of 3500 ft. is reached at 1.8 mi. A fieldstone path guides hikers through an open area to a jct. at 1.9 mi. (A spring is 250 ft. R along the yellow-marked Becker Hollow Connector Trail [trail 30], which leads 0.3 mi. to the fire tower on the Hunter Mt. summit; see below).

The blue Becker Hollow Trail continues straight ahead up several steep pitches to the jct. with the Hunter Mt. Spur Trail (trail 32) at 2.05 mi. Steel rods of the former fire tower protrude from the bedrock here.

Distances: *To concrete dam, 0.4 mi.; to 3500-ft elevation, 1.8 mi.; to Becker Hollow Connector Trail, 1.9 mi.; to Hunter Mt. Spur Trail jct., 2.05 mi. (3.3 km).*

(30) Becker Hollow Connector Trail

Map 41: M-4
NE Catskills

This short trail saves the hiker on the way to the Hunter Mt. summit on the Becker Hollow Trail a few minutes and provides a source of water for hikers who need to refill their water bottles. The condition of the trail is less stable than that of other trails on the mountain, but it is pleasant to walk.

Trailhead: *The trail begins at the 1.9 mi. point of the Becker Hollow Trail (trail 29) (see above) and climbs to the 3.4 mi. point of the Spruceton Trail (trail 93) (see Prattsville–Shandaken section).*

From the jct. (0.0 mi.) at the 1.9 mi. point of the Becker Hollow

Trail, the yellow-marked trail very gradually descends NW 250 ft. through a wet area to good spring water delivered from a metal pipe. The trail then travels on contour to 0.2 mi., where it swings L and pitches upward through conifers. One has to be careful to follow trail markers here. It enters the clearing at the summit of Hunter Mt. at 0.3 mi.

Distances: To spring, 250 ft.; to pitch up, 0.2 mi.; to Hunter Mt. summit clearing, 0.3 mi. (0.5 km).

(31) Devil's Path (Hunter Mt. Section)

Map 41: M-4 to L-4
NE Catskills

For the complete sequencing of the Devil's Path, refer to the Devil's Path description in the Extended and Challenging Opportunities chapter.

This is the heart of the Devil's territory in the Catskills and has some extremely steep climbing. It is not a place in which to rush, for you may have a devil of a time.

Trailhead: The trailhead is off NY 214, 2.9 mi. S of Hunter (see Stony Clove Route Guide), where the Devil's Path drops off Plateau Mt. and then climbs Hunter Mt. The route passes through the parking area on the W side of the road. Leaving the L rear of the parking area (0.0 mi.), it bears R, following red DEC trail markers.

After 100 ft. the trail drops down a bank and crosses the outlet of Notch Lake on a wide log bridge below a small cement dam. It then heads SW, reaching a trail register at 0.1 mi. From there, the trail continues to the base of a rock bluff at 0.3 mi., where large boulders seem to surround you. Continue straight ahead up the sloping rock.

The grade steepens, with some excellent stone trailwork, to a second rock bluff at 0.35 mi. After following the base of the cliff, the trail climbs very steeply up a 50-ft. vertical zone known as the Devil's Portal, passing a small stone overhang before reaching the top of this wall.

(Years ago, another trail left the main trail at the top of the Devil's Portal and led to the Devil's Pulpit, above the stone face of the Devil, at the cliffs to the N. It is nearly impossible to locate this path today.)

The trail continues to climb at varying steep, moderate, and gradual grades to 1.8 mi., where it levels and contours a side slope, having ascended 1500 ft. from Stony Clove Notch.

The trail reaches the Hunter Mt. Trail jct. at 2.15 mi. at 3500 ft. elevation. (The Hunter Mt. summit can be reached another 1.6 mi. from this jct. via the yellow Hunter Mt. Spur Trail [trail 32] and a short section of the blue Spruceton Trail [see Prattsville–Shandaken section]. There is an increase of 540 ft. elevation.)

Continue straight ahead on the red-marked Devil's Path. A gradual descent to Diamond Notch Falls begins from this jct. Devil's Acre lean-to is 300 ft. farther along this trail at 2.2 mi. There is a good spring here.

Several informal camping spots can be found on a knoll clearing just past a brook at 2.4 mi. Here one can see remnants of the stationary engine railroad equipment used by the Fenwick Lumber Co. in the late 1800s to transport logs to its sawmill near Diamond Notch.

The route bears R from the clearing (avoid the unmarked trail straight ahead). At Geiger Point at 2.65 mi., a spur trail L leads 30 yds. to a fine lookout W from an overhang.

The trail swings sharply N and continues on the level to the 2.7 mi. point, where a steady downgrade to Diamond Notch, 1200 vertical ft. below, begins. Rushing water in the ravine at L can be heard at 3.3 mi. The trail climbs briefly, passing a large rock overhang.

A distinct spur trail leads L at 3.4 mi., through an informal campsite to a large flat boulder overlooking the valley of the West Kill. Excellent views invite a rest here.

At a stream crossing at 3.7 mi., the grade becomes more gradual. Several more small brooks and a large brook at 4.0 mi. make this a wet section during inclement weather.

One last drop brings the hiker into a large clearing beside Diamond Notch Falls at 4.15 mi. Here a trail register, bulletin board, and several informal campsites mark the Diamond Notch Trail jct. (The Spruceton Trail [trail 93] is 1.0 mi. NW on the Diamond Notch Trail [trail 34]; NY 214 is 4.0 S on the Diamond Notch Trail.)

The Devil's Path crosses the bridge above the falls and immediately turns R towards West Kill Mt. (See Devil's Path–West Kill Mt. in the Prattsville–Shandaken section.)

Distances: To trail register, 0.1 mi.; to Devil's Portal, 0.35 mi.; to leveling of trail, 1.8 mi.; to Hunter Mt. Trail jct., 2.15 mi.; to Devil's Acre lean-to, 2.2 mi.; to Geiger Point, 2.65 mi.; to second lookout, 3.4 mi.; to Diamond Notch Falls, 4.15 mi. (6.7 km) (16.2 mi. from trail origin; 16.6 mi. from Platte Clove Rd.).

(32) Hunter Mt. Spur Trail

Map 41: M-4
NE Catskills

The original fire tower on Hunter Mt. was where the Becker Hollow Trail (trail 29) now ends, near the summit of Hunter Mt. Both the Hunter Mt. Spur Trail (trail 32) and the Spruceton Trail (trail 93) (see Prattsville–Shandaken section) ended at this tower. When the present tower was constructed at the actual summit, the trails were never adjusted to end at the new tower. Consequently, the trail markers are the same as originally set out, and the Hunter Mt. Spur and Spruceton trails still both end at the original tower site. This is why hikers sometimes become confused when the trail markers they have been following suddenly change color at the top of Hunter Mt.

Trailhead: *The Hunter Mt. Spur Trail connects the Devil's Path (see above) to the Becker Hollow Trail. The trail (0.0 mi.) leaves its jct. with the Devil's Path and very gradually ascends Hunter Mt. to the NE. It begins a counter-clockwise swing to the NW at 0.3 mi., following a wide old woods road. At 1.0 mi. the trail steepens briefly as it climbs two switchbacks. It then resumes its nearly flat grade to the jct. with the Becker Hollow Trail at 1.35 mi. At this point a short level walk of 0.1 mi. W brings you to a ledge with a good view of the Westkill Valley.*

Distances: *To beginning of swing to NW, 0.3 mi.; to switchbacks, 1.0 mi.; to Becker Hollow jct., 1.35 mi. (2.2 km).*

(33) Plateau Mt. from Stony Clove

Map 41: M-4

NE Catskills

Plateau Mt. offers exceptional viewing from three sides. From the top of this huge block, the trail enters a spruce forest more typical of the Adirondacks than of the Catskills. Once in the center of this flat table, one almost forgets it is a summit, until reaching the opposite end of the plateau.

Trailhead: *The trailhead is on the E side of NY 214 at the Notch Lake parking area of Devil's Tombstone Campground. (See Route Guide to Stony Clove.) A day-use parking permit must be obtained from the campground office, 0.2 mi. S of the parking area.*

The trail climbs a set of log steps (0.0 mi.) and swings R past restroom facilities and then L to a trail register. Red DEC trail markers guide you toward a rushing brook. The trail turns L and begins a series of steep switchbacks.

A spring is to the L at 0.25 mi. Moderate to steep grades slab the mountainside. The trail crosses the first of two closely spaced, open rock slides at 0.5 mi.

Passing large flat boulders, be alert for a sharp turn L at 1.0 mi. where the trail ends slabbing the mountainside and climbs rocky terrain, now well-maintained by needed trailwork. Swinging L the trail traverses wet rocks by a spring and crosses a very wet, flat meadow-like area. The 3500-ft. sign is passed, and soon the trail winds below interesting ledges at 1.1 mi. The rocky route ascends to 1.25 mi., where it reaches the base of Orchard Point. It is necessary to scramble up. (A 1969 Conservation Dept. Hiking Guide calls it Orchid Point.) From this broad ledge there are magnificent views from S to N. Directly across Stony Clove Notch stands huge Hunter Mt. with its fire tower. West Kill Mt. can barely be seen over Hunter's L shoulder.

The elevation is near 3600 ft. The casual day hiker might well stop here but will miss much by not walking the next 2.2 mi. to the true summit, even though it is only 240 ft. higher. The trail continues at gradual grade to 1.4 mi., where Danny's Lookout is located by an enormous erratic boulder. The Blackhead Range and Escarpment Trail to North Mt. can be seen from this point.

The trail makes a sharp R turn and continues on a nearly level route. Occasional lookouts appear to the NE; and the site where the Plateau lean-to once stood is passed at 1.35 mi. From this point to the summit, the spruce woods close in and very few distant vistas are to be had. The undulating trail climbs so gradually that it doesn't seem like the top of a mountain. However, the quality of the forest makes for a very pleasant walk.

The true summit is at 3.2 mi., but most hikers will be past it without realizing it. There is no view from this place, but if the hiker continues to the 3.4 mi. point, a large flat boulder top provides a lookout E to Sugarloaf Mt. and NE to Kaaterskill High Peak and Round Top Mt.

Distances: *To first spring, 0.25 mi.; to rock slides, 0.5 mi.; to second spring, 0.8 mi.; to Orchard Point, 1.25 mi.; to Danny's Lookout, 1.15 mi.; to summit, 3.2 mi. (5.2 km); to E Lookout, 3.4 mi. Summit elevation 3840 ft. (1174 m). Ascent, 1840 ft. (563 m).*

(34) Diamond Notch Trail (Hollow Tree Brook Trail)

Map 41: L-4
NE Catskills

The Diamond Notch Trail follows the route of an old wagon trail, connecting Lanesville to Spruceton. Sometimes called the Hollow Tree Brook Trail, the state made it into a ski trail in 1937. (The upper reaches of the Lanesville side of the notch require considerable skill, but intermediate skiers can handle the rest of the trail.) In summer, it is a delightful hiking route.

Trailhead: *Access to the Lanesville trailhead is at the end of Diamond Notch Rd., off NY 214. (See Route Guide for Stony Clove.) Drive 1.3 mi. on Diamond Notch Rd. to a parking area. The last part of this road is unpaved.*

The blue-marked DEC trail leaves the parking area (0.0 mi.) and heads N. It crosses a footbridge at 0.1 mi., 50 yds. before reaching a trail register. The woods road follows the course of Hollow Tree Brook into Diamond Notch.

The trail begins to climb moderately, leaving the brook far below in the ravine bottom. It crosses a brook from a good spring at 1.1 mi.

At 1.2 mi. the route becomes fully open and offers good views down the valley. A sharp drop L and then a scramble R up a steep embankment of loose rock require some caution. (In winter, this can be a windswept snow-crust zone.)

A col (2650 ft. elevation) at 1.3 mi. is tree-covered, but views continue back through the valley just ascended. The trail passes a second spring at 1.5 mi. and reaches the Diamond Notch lean-to at 1.8 mi. (A spur trail R leads a short distance to the lean-to, the open front of which faces away from the trail.) There is a stream for water 0.1 mi. N, down the trail.

Long, winding stretches gradually sweep downward from here. The trail reaches the West Kill Mt. jct. of the Devil's Path (see Prattsville–Shandaken section), heading S to West Kill Mt. at 2.5 mi. This is immediately before the bridge over Diamond Notch Falls. From the bridge the hiker looks down over a 12-ft. plunge of water into a deep pool of water. Beyond the stream is a large clearing, where a trail register and bulletin board mark the 4-way trail jct. with the Devil's Path. (The red-marked Devil's Path [trail 44] turns R and ascends Hunter Mt.)

The Diamond Notch Trail turns L and continues to follow blue markers along an old woods road by the brook.

Gradual downgrades continue NW towards Spruceton. A barrier cable at 3.2 mi. marks the end of the Diamond Notch Trail.

A large parking area is 0.1 mi. farther along the road at L. The Spruceton Trail (trail 93) parking area is another 0.2 mi. beyond the first parking area. (See *Route Guide* to Spruceton Rd., Prattsville–Shandaken section).

Distances: To spring, 1.1 mi.; to height of land, 1.3 mi.; to Diamond Notch, 1.5 mi.; to Diamond Notch lean-to, 1.8 mi.; to Diamond Notch Falls and 4-way jct., 2.5 mi.; to barrier cable, 3.2 mi. (5.2 km).

Big Indian–Upper Neversink Section

This section of the Catskills was long overshadowed by the Great Wall of Manitou rim hotels in and around Haines Falls and Tannersville. After Prof. Guyot of Princeton University showed that Slide Mt. was the highest peak in the Catskills, however, people began to take notice of points farther inland from the Hudson. When the naturalist John Burroughs started writing about the region, the whole nation took interest. It was T. Morris Longstreth who said, "God made the Catskills; Irving put them on the map; but it is John Burroughs who brought them home." It is fitting that the United States Geological Survey now officially recognizes Slide, Cornell, and Wittenberg mts. as the Burroughs Range.

The southern part of this section is in the watershed of the Neversink River, sometimes called the Minisink. Both its east and west branches rise on the shoulders of Slide Mt.

It was in the Neversink Valley that Gross Hardenbergh was shot in 1808, ending the Hardenbergh War. At one time, wild pigeons came here in thousands to eat beechnuts each fall, but commercial interests wiped them out by 1870. The low gradients of the stream channels resulted in many sandbars and other obstacles that made it difficult to get saw logs to market in the old days. These same factors created pools where great trout lurked.

Just as it was difficult to reach these branches in the 1800s, it is still a test of one's will to get to many of the trailheads today. For those who accept the challenge, some of the best wilderness in the Catskills awaits. The mountains in this section are generally hard to climb, but the views from the peaks are commensurate with the efforts expended.

Map aficionados cannot help but notice the dendritic (branch-like) pattern of river systems in the Catskills. An exception to this is Esopus Creek. As it flows near Panther Mt. it begins a long, almost perfectly circular, course around the mountain. Geophoto studies, supplemented by magnetic and gravitation field data, suggest that at sometime millions of years ago a huge meteorite hit this spot. Later, ocean sediments filled in the region, and still later Panther Mt. formed. This caused the flow pattern of the Esopus and the "rosette" pattern of streams that run into it from Giant Ledge-Panther Mt. Ridge.

Travelers in this region should be sure they have full gas tanks. In earlier days county election results were often held up a week or more because poor roads kept recorders from getting out the results.

Trail in winter: *Slide Mt. summit in winter is magnificent. The climb to the summit from the Co. Rd. 47 trailhead, SW of Winnisook Lake, is not difficult. However, the descent beyond the summit, via ladders in places, to the col on the way to Cornell Mt. is very steep and should not be taken lightly. To do the whole Burroughs Range in one winter day is challenging and should be attempted only by experienced winter climbers.*

Lone and Rocky peaks seem to be done more in winter than summer because it is possible to snowshoe right over much of the blowdown found on those climbs.

The Belleayre Trail from Pine Hill and then along the Belleayre Ridge to the ski area is good for experienced skiers. Skiing the Cathedral Glen Trail is definitely for experts only. Rochester Hollow is excellent for intermediate and novice skiers.

Short Hikes:

Rochester Hollow—*Up to 6.0 mi. round trip. Just a stroll in the woods along a woods road. Turn around whenever you're ready.*

Moderate Hikes:

Giant Ledges and Panther Mt.—*6.6 mi. round trip. Some stiff climbing takes you to fabulous vistas.*

Slide Mt.–Curtis-Ormsbee Loop—*5.75 mi. Climb the highest mountain in the Catskills and return to the trailhead by a different route.*

Harder Hikes:

Slide–Cornell–Wittenberg Mts.—*9.75 mi. through trip. Probably the hardest day trip in the Catskills, but a superb outing for those in good shape. Need cars at each end.*

Table–Peekamoose Mts.—*7.4 mi. round trip. A lovely trail, but don't underestimate the time it takes to travel.*

Biscuit Brook–Pine Hill Trail Backpack—*14.9 mi. through trip. One of the nicest backpacking trails in the Catskills.*

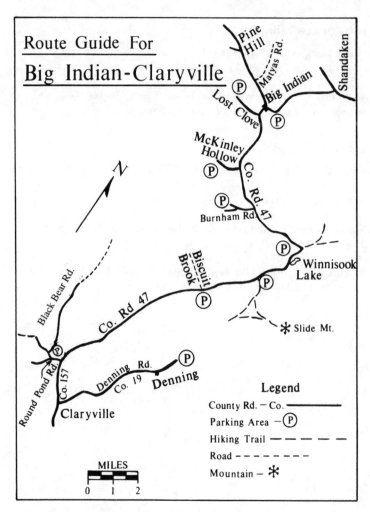

Route Guide For
Big Indian-Claryville

Legend

County Rd. – Co.	——
Parking Area – Ⓟ	
Hiking Trail	— — —
Road	- - - - -
Mountain – ✳	

MILES
0   1   2

ROUTE GUIDE FOR BIG INDIAN TO CLARYVILLE

This route guide begins in the hamlet of Big Indian at the jct. of NY 28 and Co. Rd. 47. It follows Co. Rd. 47S. This becomes Co. Rd. 157 near Claryville, where it crosses from Ulster Co. to Sullivan Co. Local names for the road vary as you travel along it. Initially it is Big Indian Hollow Rd.; then it becomes Slide Mt. Rd.; finally, it is either

West Branch Rd. or Frost Valley Rd., depending on your preference.

Mileage N to S	Description	Mileage S to N
0.0	NY 28 and Co. Rd. 47 jct. at hamlet of Big Indian; there is a general store here.	20.9
0.5	Lost Clove Rd.	20.4
2.9	Oliveria	18.0
3.0	McKenley Hollow Rd.	17.9
3.7	Burnham Hollow Rd./Association Rd. (Forest Preserve Access parking at end).	17.2
7.4	Hairpin turn; trail to Giant Ledges and Panther Mt. and Woodland Valley; parking area.	13.5
8.5	Winnisook Lake	12.4
9.4	Slide Mt. parking area; Woodland Valley–Denning Trail passes through parking area.	11.5
12.8	Biscuit Brook parking area. Big Indian Mt. Trail is 100 ft. W on road from parking area, opposite side.	8.1
14.0	Frost Valley YMCA Camp—some trails open to public.	6.9
19.6	Jct. Co. 47 and Co. Rd. 157 (Willowemoc Rd.)	1.3
20.0	Town line	0.9
20.9	Claryville	0.0

Rochester Hollow

Map 42: I-5
Central Catskills

Rochester Hollow is part of the Shandaken–Pine Hill Wild Forest. It is undeveloped, except for a woods road that wanders 3.0 mi. through Rochester Hollow.

Trailhead: *Access is at the end of Matyas Rd., which leaves NY 28, 1.05 mi. W of the intersection of NY 28 and Co. Rd. 47 at Big Indian. Drive 0.1 mi. N on Matyas Rd. to a pair of stone entry columns, where state land begins. There is a small parking zone for a few cars 100 yds. beyond the stone columns.*

The road continues on state land as a woods road, paralleling a stream for a little over two miles. It then curves W at a plaque, leaving state land at 3.0 mi. The road continues over private land another 0.2 mi. and is not open to the public.

This woods road provides a place for relaxed walking through a deciduous forest.

Distances: *To end of stream, 2.0 mi.; to end of state land, 3.0 mi. (4.9 km).*

(35) Cathedral Glen Trail

**Map 42: I-4
Central Catskills**

The Cathedral Glen Trail is unique. The first half of the trail descends quite steeply down Belleayre Mt.'s easternmost ski slope, providing unusually good views of the distant landscape to the N. The second, lower, half of the trail passes through a delightful stand of old-growth hemlock.

Access: *As of this writing, trail access to the Cathedral Glen Trail is available only from the south (the Belleayre Ridge Trail); legal access from the railroad bed in Pine Hill is not available.*

From the jct. with the Belleayre Ridge Trail 0.2 mi. E of the E summit of Belleayre Mt., or 0.8 mi. E of the true summit at

Chairlift #1, turn L on the blue-marked Cathedral Glen Trail and begin the descent through a moderate and then gradual grade before joining the fern-covered ski slope at 0.2 mi. Turning R and continuing downward quite steeply, the trail levels off twice prior to the base of the ski slope at 0.7 mi. An old woods road continues downward, following the course of a brook, through a magnificent stand of old growth hemlock. Circling R of Belleayre Mt.'s snowmaking reservoir, the trail descends and terminates at the railroad bed.

Distances: *To top of ski slope, 0.2 mi.; to base of ski slope, 0.7 mi.; to railroad bed, 1.7 mi. Ascent 1590 ft.*

(36) Belleayre Mt. Trail

In the heyday of hotels in the Catskills, Pine Hill was a railroad stop and had many small hotels. Guests climbed to the fire tower on Belleayre's E summit for a marvelous view of the region. Today, the fire tower is gone and so is the summit view. However, the climb is still a most pleasant one and a short extension of the trip along Belleayre Ridge to the true summit at the Belleayre Ski Area provides excellent views. The Belleayre Mt. Trail is the first part of the Biscuit Brook–Pine Hill Trail (trail 43) from the N.

Trailhead: From NY 28 in Pine Hill, turn S on Elm St. Turn R from Elm St. onto Main St., L on Bonnie View Ave., L on Station Rd., crossing the open area to Woodchuck Hill Rd. above the RR. Travel 0.55 mi. up Woodchuck Hill Rd. to a parking clearing on the R. The trail begins beyond the gate.

The road turns sharply E soon and becomes a nearly flat route. It continues through quiet deciduous forest to 0.4 mi., where arrow signs at a clearing indicate an abrupt R turn into forest on a woods road that leads up a moderate grade. The grade becomes gradual at 0.5 mi. Soon after, the trail enters state land. The old grass-covered jeep road to the summit provides a very enjoyable woods walk.

The Lost Clove Trail (trail 38) jct. enters from the L at 1.4 mi. (It leads 1.3 mi. down moderate to steep grades to a parking area on Lost Clove Rd.; see below).

The enjoyable trail reaches Belleayre Mt. lean-to at 1.6 mi. Beyond the lean-to, the grade becomes moderate to steep, curving past a pipe spring on the L at 1.75 mi.

At 1.85 mi. the grade becomes gradual again until the grassy clearing of Belleayre Mt. E summit is reached at 2.1 mi. The trail leads L another 2.2 mi. to the summit of Balsam Mt., continuing S (as the Biscuit Brook–Pine Hill Trail [trail 43]; see above). The Belleayre Ridge Trail (see below) heads W from the clearing toward the Belleayre Mt. Ski Area, to the true summit of Belleayre Mt. It is well worth walking the nearly level trail to there for the views. (The W summit is 45 ft. higher than the E summit.) A picnic table and fireplace are found at the N edge of the clearing under trees.

Distances: *To clearing, 0.4 mi.; to Lost Clove Trail jct., 11.4 mi.; to Belleayre lean-to, 11.6 mi.; to Belleayre Mt. summit, 2.1 mi. (3.4 km). Summit elevation, 3375 (1032 m). Ascent from Pine Hill village, 1475 ft.*

(37) Belleayre Ridge Trail

Map 42: H-5
Central Catskills

The Belleayre Ridge Trail is a short connector trail between the Biscuit Brook–Pine Hill Trail (trail 42) (Belleayre Mt. Trail [trail 36]) and the Belleayre Ski Area. The use of it today is quite different from its original purpose. Years ago, when there was a fire tower on Belleayre's E summit, the tower was the focal point for area trails. Hikers from Arkville and Fleischmanns used a trail from Hanley Corners up the Belleayre Ridge to the E summit. Today, the Belleayre and Highmount ski areas block this trail. Principal use of the trail is for hikers heading from Belleayre's viewless E summit to the ski area, where excellent views N and fair views S are found on the true summit. The route is an almost level grass-covered jeep trail. Views gained at the ski area are well worth the short time it takes to travel the ridge.

Trailhead: *The trail leaves Belleayre's E summit (0.0 mi.), following red DEC trail markers W. A slight decrease in elevation occurs before the Cathedral Glen Trail (trail 35) intersects the trail from the R at 0.25 mi. (see above). The grade becomes gradually uphill, reaching the Hirschland lean-to at 0.45 mi. (A spur trail R leads a few ft. to the lean-to, which sits at the top of a ski slope. From here a narrow view N is available.)*

Rolling grades again lose elevation at 0.3 mi. A jct. at 0.9 mi. has a few picnic tables at the top of another ski slope. A level dirt roadway leads straight ahead to an open field at Chairlift #1 and a summit ski lodge at 1.0 mi. This is as far as most people wish to travel, although it is possible to walk along the ridge through the ski area another mile before reaching the end of state land, where the old trail enters Highmount Ski Area.

The best views from the lodge area are N. Immediately below in the valley is small Monka Hill, with Halcott Mt. behind it in the distance. Rose Mt. is R of Monka Hill, with Balsam, Sherrill, and North Dome mts. behind it. Still farther R, West Kill Mt. blocks the fire tower on Hunter Mt. From the deck of the lodge, the fire tower on Balsam Lake Mt. is S, just over the top of Hirams Knob in the valley.

Distances: *To Cathedral Glen Trail jct., 0.25 mi.; to Hirschland lean-to, 0.45 mi.; to Chairlift #1, 1.0 mi. (1.6 km). Elevation, 3420 ft. (1026 m).*

(38) Lost Clove Trail

The Lost Clove Trail provides access to the summit of Belleayre Mt. over private land in Big Indian. The trail is a little-used woods road that presents the climber with some stiff climbing before intersecting the Biscuit Brook-Pine Hill Trail.

Trailhead: *Access is off Co. Rd. 47 in Big Indian Hollow, via Lost Clove Rd. (See* Route Guide *from Big Indian to Claryville.) Drive 1.4 mi. up Lost Clove Rd. to a parking area on the R.*

The trail leaves the rear of the parking area (0.0 mi.), crosses a small brook, and enters an open field at 0.05 mi. Turn L and climb a steep grade on a woods road. Grades are steep or moderate for most of the next mile. Avoid side trails and bear L at the jct. at 0.3 mi. Go straight through the X jct. at 0.55 mi. Bear L at another jct. at 0.85 mi. There are occasional gradual grades in the upper reaches, before the jct. with the Biscuit Brook–Pine Hill Trail (trail 43) at 1.3 mi. (Turn L for Belleayre Mt. summit and R for Pine Hill.)

Distances: *To open field, 0.05 mi.; to X jct., 0.55 mi.; to second jct., 0.85 mi.; to jct. with Biscuit Brook–Pine Hill Trail, 1.3 mi. (2.1 km). Ascent, 780 ft. (234 m).*

(39) McKenley Hollow Trail

The DEC Oliverea–Mapledale Trail is seldom hiked as a through trip. Instead, hikers climb from either end to join the Biscuit Brook–Pine Hill Trail on top of the ridge. In this guide, the E side of the Oliverea–Mapledale Trail is referred to as the McKenley Hollow Trail and the W side is called the Rider Hollow Trail (trail 64).

McKenley Hollow is the usual way up Balsam Mt. from Oliverea, but the hiker should be ready to earn his spurs. This is the type of climb that stays in the memory, especially if done in winter. It is a good way to get off the Biscuit Brook–Pine Hill Trail (trail 43), but not a good way to get on it if toting a heavy backpack.

Trailhead: *Access is via Co. Rd. 47 at Oliverea. (See Route Guide from Big Indian to Claryville.) Drive 1.0 mi. along the McKenley Hollow Rd. to the DEC parking area on the L near Mountain Gate Lodge.*

Walk W 0.1 mi. along McKenley Hollow Rd. to an arrow trail marker which points L, off the road. Follow red DEC trail markers along McKenley Brook. Cross a bridge over the brook and reach a trail register at 0.2 mi. There are a few private camps across the brook.

The trail proceeds along the S bank of the brook, crossing back to the N side just before reaching a large boulder. The nearly level trail continues upstream along a woods road to 0.65 mi., where the McKenley Hollow lean-to is located beside the creek at L.

The trail crosses a tributary of McKenley Hollow Brook at 0.7 mi., heading SW a short distance before beginning a broad swing at gradual grade to the NW. The route returns to the brook and becomes moderate to steep as it sidles up the wall of the hollow. The brook is far below to the R.

The trail reaches a long series of stone steps at 1.2 mi. It climbs steeply upward to 1.4 mi. and continues at a moderate grade. It becomes gradual at 1.7 mi., reaching the jct. of the Biscuit Brook–Pine Hill Trail (trail 43) at 1.85 mi. (Turn R for Balsam Mt. and L for Haynes Mt. Water is located at the base of a rock outcrop, 65 ft. ahead towards Rider Hollow; see below.) (Refer to Rider Hollow Trail,

Arkville–Seager section, for the remainder of the Oliverea–Mapledale route.)

Distances: *To trail register, 0.2 mi.; to McKenley Hollow lean-to, 0.65 mi.; to stone steps, 1.2 mi.; to Biscuit Brook–Pine Hill Trail jct., 1.85 mi. (3.0 km). Ascent from McKenley Hollow lean-to, 1375 ft.*

(40) Giant Ledge–Panther Mt. Trail (Southern Section)

The Giant Ledge–Panther Mt. Trail runs 7.45 mi. from a jct. on the Denning–Woodland Valley Trail (trail 46) N to Fox Hollow. Since hikers from the S rarely continue N past the Panther Mt. summit, this trail description covers only the southern portion of the trail, reached from Big Indian Hollow or Woodland Valley. (Through hikers can refer to the Panther Mt. Trail description, Woodstock–Shandaken section, for the northern part of this trail.)

Trailhead: *Trail access is from a large DEC parking area on the S side of Co. Rd. 47, 7.4 mi. S of Big Indian at a hairpin turn. (Refer to Route Guide from Big Indian to Claryville.) Follow the yellow markers of the Denning–Woodland Valley Trail (trail 46) E towards Woodland Valley. The trailhead jct. of the Giant Ledge–Panther Mt. Trail is 0.75 mi. from the parking area, after an ascent of 580 ft.*

From the trailhead jct. (0.0 mi.) the route leads N, following blue DEC trail markers. The route is almost level for 0.5 mi. and then ascends gradually. A spring 50 yds. L of the trail at 0.55 mi., on a yellow-marked spur trail, immediately precedes the site of the former Giant Ledge lean-to.

The slope increases to a moderate-to-steep grade as it

switchbacks up through rock outcrops. The trail levels at 0.75 mi. near 3200 ft. elevation. Several outlooks in the next 0.3 mi. provide excellent views of Woodland Valley, Wittenberg Mt. and Cornell Mt. An informal spur trail L at 0.95 mi. leads to a lookout with views SW to Fir, Spruce, and Hemlock mts.

The trail then descends gradual to moderate grades into the col between Giant Ledge and Panther Mt. at 1.5 mi. The col is fairly flat. (Hikers returning to the parking area from Panther Mt. may wish to drop down the E side of the col and do a bushwhack through open forest along the base of Giant Ledge rather than reclimb the ridge. The trail can be intersected near the former lean-to site at the S end of the base of Giant Ledge. This alternative is especially attractive on snowshoes or skis in winter.)

A vertical ascent of 725 ft. must be made from the col to the Panther Mt. summit. Moderate grades steepen as the trail switchbacks up to a fine lookout at 1.8 mi., 100 ft. R of the trail. There is an undependable spring R at 2.0 mi. The 3500-ft. sign is passed at 2.1 mi.

The relatively flat top of Panther Mt. eases the strain of climbing but makes it difficult to be sure of the true summit. It is at 2.55 mi. Thick conifers open briefly at a cliff's edge for a magnificent vista of the Burroughs Range of Wittenberg, Cornell and Slide mts. A classic cirque formation gives proof of local mountain glaciers in the recent geological past.

The trail continues another 4.9 mi. over a bumpy ridge to the trailhead at Fox Hollow. Refer to the Panther Mt. Trail description (trail 56), Woodstock–Shandaken section.

Distances: *To spring, 0.6 mi.; to leveling on Giant Ledge, 0.75 mi.; to col between Giant Ledge and Panther Mt., 1.5 mi.; to lookout on Panther Mt., 1.8 mi.; to Panther Mt. summit, 2.55 mi. (4.1 km) (3.3 mi. from parking area). Summit elevation, 3720 ft. (1138 m). Ascent from parking area, 1545 ft.*

(41) Slide–Cornell–Wittenberg Trail

This trail has a little bit of everything. The walk up Slide Mt., almost all of it at gradual grade, is one of the most enjoyable outings in the Catskills. Its upper reaches are almost a stroll in a park-like atmosphere. The vistas are magnificent. Then, in the next 0.9 mi. beyond the summit, the trail drops 930 vertical feet down cliffs and ladders. The ensuing route to Wittenberg from Slide Mt. is challenging.

Trailhead: *Access to the trail is from the upper reaches of the West Branch of the Neversink, via the Denning–Woodland Valley Trail (trail 46). A parking area is on the S side of Co. Rd. 47 (Slide Mt. Road). (See* Route Guide *for Big Indian–Claryville.)*

Follow the yellow DEC trail markers of the Denning–Woodland Valley Trail past the trail register at the rear of the parking area. Cross the cobblestone bed of the West Branch of the Neversink River and head E on a flat trail. The route climbs gradual grades from 0.1 mi. to 0.2 mi., where it changes to a moderate grade over slab rock. The trail climbs stone steps at 0.4 mi. to a woods road. Turn R. After a spring L at 0.6 mi., the road reaches the Slide–Cornell–Wittenberg Trail jct. at 0.7 mi. (The Denning–Woodland Valley Trail continues straight ahead; see below.)

Turn L at the jct. trailhead (0.0 mi.) and follow red DEC trail markers E up a remarkably gradual old cobblestone woods road. In time the grade slowly, but progressively, becomes moderate. Soon after passing the 3500 ft. elevation sign at 1.1 mi., the trail turns N and then E again. Views N open up before the Curtis-Ormsbee Trail jct. on the R at 1.35 mi. (This trail runs SW to intersect the Denning–Woodland Valley Trail. See below.)

This section of trail is most enjoyable, with a fine view S towards Table Mt. off a spur trail R at 1.41 mi. and an excellent trailside lookout N past Cornell and Wittenberg on the L at 1.9 mi. The trail reaches the Slide Mt. summit (4180 ft. elevation and highest in the Catskills) at 2.0 mi. Only the base support of the fire tower remains.

Continue to 2.05 mi. (2.75 mi. from the parking area), where a broad open rock shelf rewards the climber with a marvelous view over Friday and Balsam Cap to the Ashokan Reservoir and beyond. On a clear day, Mt. Everett in Massachusetts can be seen. The profile of mountains on the NE horizon resembling a reclining figure is called the Old Man of the Mountain. Don't neglect to walk around to the base of the rock shelf lookout to read the John Burroughs Memorial Plaque.

The trail to Cornell leaves the John Burroughs Memorial and rapidly descends, losing 930 ft. in the next 0.9 mi. The route drops at grades varying from moderate to very steep, often at the edge of a cliff. A series of four ladders is found at 2.25 mi. At the base of the last ladder, the blue markers lead L, 25 ft. to a marvelous spring that bursts out of the rock wall. The red trail markers head R from the ladder into the col below. (The view over Woodland Valley and generally NW is spectacular from this location.) Descent continues at a less precipitous rate from here, but there is a 15-ft. vertical drop down a rock outcrop at 2.5 mi., followed by a 35-ft. drop at another outcrop bluff.

Dropping below 3500 ft. the trail passes three designated campsites before reaching the col between Slide Mt. and Cornell at 2.9 mi.

Gradual and moderate grades lead up to Cornell's summit. After three more designated campsites, water crosses the trail at 3.75 mi., indicating a spring 400 ft. R of the trail. Just before a lookout at 4.25 mi., there is a "lemon squeezer," a very narrow curving passage between rock ledges. The lookout provides a good view back towards the slide on Slide Mt. A second viewing spot atop a rock ledge provides a sweeping 180-degree view from Table Mt. in the SW to the Devil's Path.

A blue-marked spur trail at 4.35 mi. leads R 0.05 mi. to the flat
Cornell Mt. summit. Summit elevation is 3860 ft. (1180 m). The view
features a good profile of Wittenberg Mt. The trail descends easily to
4.45 mi., where a deep V-cut at the top of a vertical drop down a
rock bluff requires great care. (Winter climbers may find a rope
handy here.)

Descent into the col continues. Gradual grades continue to the
Wittenberg Mt. summit at 5.15 mi., where the trail breaks out onto a
broad rock shelf. Perhaps the finest view on the whole trail—over
Samuels Point across Ashokan Reservoir to Massachusetts—is from
this location.

The trail continues another 2.2 mi. to Terrace Mt. lean-to and 3.9
mi. to Woodland Valley Public Campground (see p. 146).

*Distances: To Curtis-Ormsbee Trail, 1.35 mi.; to Slide Mt. summit, 2.0 mi.;
to spring, 2.25 mi.; to Slide–Cornell col, 2.9 mi.; to Cornell summit spur trail,
4.35 mi.; to Wittenberg Mt. summit, 5.15 mi. (8.3 km). Summit elevation,
3780 ft. (1156 m). To Terrace Mt. lean-to, 7.35 mi.; to Woodland Valley
Public Campgrounds, 9.05 mi. (9.75 mi. from Slide Mt. parking area).*

(42) Curtis-Ormsbee Trail

**Map 43: J-7
Southern Catskills**

This trail provides a very attractive and enjoyable route up Slide
Mt. From a jct. at the 2.95 mi. point of the Denning–Woodland
Valley Trail (see below), it climbs NE to a jct. with the Slide–Cornell–
Wittenberg Trail (trail 41). Both William Curtis and Allen Ormsbee,
builders of the trail, died in a snowstorm on Mt. Washington in
June, 1900. A monument commemorating Curtis is at the
trailhead jct.

Trailhead: The trail heads E from the Denning–Woodland Trail (trail 46) jct., following blue DEC trail markers. After 0.15 mi. of gradual climbing, the trail swings R around the base of a great rock cut and pitches steeply upward. The trail follows the edge of the cliff at the top, for spectacular views downward into the rock formations.

Soon, gradual and moderate grades alternate, briefly becoming steep, before the trail reaches the 3500 ft. elevation marker at 0.5 mi. Gradual grades continue from there to 0.6 mi., where the trail again pitches steeply up rock ledges. At 0.65 mi., an unmarked spur trail R leads 75 ft. to Paul's Lookout. Table, Lone and Rocky Mts. can be seen from this rock shelf.

The trail soon levels, crossing 125 ft. of wet area on log walkways. Then, moderate and gradual grades again alternate as the route passes over interesting terrain. Wooden steps ascend a steep spot at 1.5 mi. Gradual and then nearly level grades end at the jct. of the Slide–Cornell–Wittenberg Trail (trail 41) at 1.6 mi. The Slide Mt. summit is 0.65 mi. E.

Distances: To rock cut, 0.15 mi.; to Paul's Lookout, 0.65 mi.; to log walk, 0.7 mi.; to log steps, 1.5 mi.; to jct. 1.6 mi. (2.6 km). Ascent from trailhead, 830 ft.

(43) Biscuit Brook-Pine Hill Trail   Map 43: I-7
(Pine Hill-West Branch Trail) Southern Catskills

The Biscuit Brook–Pine Hill Trail offers some of the best backpacking and general hiking in the Catskills. While few long views present themselves, the quality of the trail is excellent. It is said the route as far as Belleayre Mt. is through virgin timber. The recreationist who simply wants to relax in beautiful surroundings will find this region most enjoyable. The long gentle upgrades to summits followed by steeper downgrades, make hiking from S to N the easier direction of travel with heavy backpacks.

Trailhead: Access to the trail is off West Branch Rd. (Co. Rd. 47) at the large Biscuit Brook parking area. (See Route Guide from Big Indian to Claryville.) The trailhead is 100 ft. E of the parking area on Co. Rd. 47.

The trail follows blue DEC trail markers generally N over a gradual upgrade, as it hugs the Forest Preserve boundary. After several small brooks, the trail becomes moderate at 0.5 mi. and climbs a ridge. It swings L near the ridgeline, levels, and then turns sharply R through a small col. From this point, a long gradual grade descends to Biscuit Brook.

At 1.9 mi., a yellow-marked spur trail leads L, 250 ft. to the Biscuit Brook lean-to. This lean-to sits above a steep bank on Biscuit Brook. It is advisable to obtain water from a tributary 0.05 mi. farther along the main trail rather than to seek it by descending this bank. It makes a good base camp for ascending Big Indian and Eagle mts. by trail or for bushwhacking up Fir Mt.

The blue-marked trail swings R and upstream, soon crossing a tributary and then crossing Biscuit Brook at 2.3 mi. It follows the W bank of the creek to 2.5 mi., where a 730-ft. trail relocation was made in 1992. The gradual grade becomes moderate at 2.7 mi. and presents a stiff climb for 0.2 mi. before easing. The route is well above the brook, but within sight of it for much of the way. The trail pulls away from the water and steeply climbs a pitch at 3.9 mi., leveling again just before reaching the old Seager Trail jct. at 4.0 mi. (It is barely discernible as a trail jct. but is readily identified as the place where the trail makes a sharp turn from W to NE.)

The route continues at gradual grade towards Big Indian Mt. Red paint blazes mark boundary lines at two points before the trail reaches a small open area and lookout towards the W at the 3500-ft. elevation marker. (This is the place to bushwhack E, 0.25 mi. to the canister, if peak bagging the true summit of Big Indian Mt.)

The trail climbs easily to a high point at 4.5 mi. and then

descends gradual grades, with occasional moderate pitches. It passes the 3500-ft. elevation marker again at 5.0 mi. The trail levels in a col and, soon after beginning to climb again, reaches the Seager–Big Indian trail (trail 66) jct. at 5.85 mi.; see Arkville–Seager section. (The Shandaken lean-to is located 0.9 mi. down this trail and a trailhead parking area is 3.0 mi.)

The trail climbs R around a rock wall at 6.2 mi. and then ascends easily to a pair of short pitches that bracket the 3500-ft. elevation marker on Eagle Mt. It reaches the flat summit at 6.95 mi. (Summit elevation is 3600 ft.) There is no view. The true summit is off the trail to the west a short distance.

After some flat trail, the grade again gradually descends. A pretty little mossy opening dominates the minor col between Eagle and Haynes mts. Again, gradual slopes predominate until a short steep pitch at 8.3 mi. alerts you that you are nearly to the top of Haynes Mt., whose crest is at 8.35 mi. (Summit elevation is 3420 ft.)

Gradual slopes continue the descent through interesting forest to a final, moderately steep pitch to the 4-way jct. with the Oliverea–Mapledale Trail (see trail 39) at 9.1 mi. (Water can be found 100 ft. NW at the base of a rock wall, where the trail makes an abrupt turn R. Rider Hollow lean-to is 1.25 mi. towards Mapledale down moderate and then gradual grades. The McKenley Hollow lean-to is 1.2 mi. towards Oliverea. The descent to the McKenley Hollow lean-to is very steep.)

The trail up Balsam Mt. from the jct. is generally gradual. A small pitch up at 9.4 mi., a moderate grade at 9.6 mi., and a few minor steep spots lead to the balsam-covered summit at 9.85 mi. (Summit elev. is 3600 ft.) The summit is at the S end of the ridge on a small bump. Posted property signs may help winter climbers identify it.

The trail passes beyond the tree-shrouded summit, continuing N. A slight decrease in elevation occurs before the trail reaches a small boulder at 9.95 mi. This is a very good lookout. One can look directly E down to the hamlet of Big Indian.

The trail progresses over essentially flat terrain, running through an open area at 10.1 mi. A short distance past this point, the trail drops through a steep rock cut. From here to the col, the descent is moderate or steep. A shallow col at 11.0 mi. is followed by a gradual climb to the Mine Hollow (trail 65) Trail jct. at 11.15 mi. (The Mine Hollow Trail drops steeply 1.0 mi. to a lean-to in Rider Hollow; see Arkville–Seager Section.)

The trail continues N to Belleayre Mt. Climbing from the jct. to the E summit is excellent. Except for three short pitches near the top, the route is very gradual and the forest is most attractive. A 3-way trail jct. is reached at 12.05 mi. (Though USGS topographic maps still use Belle Ayr, New Yorkers generally call this peak Belleayre Mt.) Its 3375-ft. E summit no longer has a fire tower, but the hiker can obtain excellent views by walking 1.0 mi. NW from the jct. along the Belleayre Ridge Trail (trail 37) to the true summit (3420-ft.) at the ski lodge at Chairlift #1 of the Belleayre Ski Area.

The Biscuit Brook–Pine Hill Trail leaves the open clearing and continues E. The route is now on an old fire road, transformed by age to a grassy lane. Gradual grades change to moderate slopes at 12.25 mi., swinging S. A pipe spring is on the R at 12.35 mi. and Belleayre lean-to is on the L at 12.5 mi.

Descent from the lean-to to Pine Hill village is almost leisurely in difficulty. The fire road reaches Lost Clove Trail (trail 38) jct. at 12.7 mi. (It descends moderate to steep grades on a woods road to a parking area 1.4 mi. from Co. Rd. 47 in Big Indian Hollow.)

The descent continues with enjoyable grades to private lands at 13.4 mi. A pitch down at 13.6 mi. ends at a shale bed roadway. Turn L, following DEC arrow signs, and walk W on this road. The route through pleasant forest brings you to a sharp turn NE at 14.05 mi. The grade steepens somewhat before reaching a gate at 14.1 mi. (The route becomes a public road here, and vehicles can be driven up the steep hill to this point from the village.

Distances: *To Biscuit Brook lean-to, 1.9 mi.; to old abandoned Seager trail, 4.0 mi.; to Big Indian Mt., 4.45 mi.; to Seager Trail jct., 5.85 mi.; to Eagle Mt., 6.95 mi.; to Haynes Mt., 8.35 mi., to Oliverea–Mapledale Trail jct., 9.1 mi.; to Balsam Mt., 9.85 mi.; to Mine Hollow Trail jct., 11.15 mi.; to Belleayre Mt., 12.05 mi.; to Belleayre Mt. lean-to, 12.5 mi.; to Lost Clove Trail jct., 12.7 mi.; to railroad bridge, 14.65 mi.; to NY 28, 14.9 mi. (24.1 km).*

Doubletop Mt. (Bushwhack)

Map 43: H-6
Southern Catskills

Doubletop Mt., once called Roundtop Mt., is a bushwhack peak. For many years, the usual way up Doubletop was from the Frost Valley YMCA. Use of this property by the general hiking public is no longer permitted (1993).

A good way up the mountain is from the Biscuit Brook–Pine Hill Trail (see above). One can walk to the top of the first ridge, at 0.7 mi., and then follow the Forest Preserve boundary line NW to Pigeon Brook. A tributary of Pigeon Brook, just upstream from the state boundary line, runs NW up to the ridgeline of Doubletop. Here an informal trail can be followed to the N end of the ridge. There is one good lookout near the flat summit, but the canister is past it in the conifers. You may have to search a bit to find it.

A second approach is from the Seager Trail (see Arkville–Seager section). This route gives the hiker a chance to climb Big Indian Mt. on the same trip. The Biscuit Brook–Pine Hill Trail is followed S of its jct. with the Seager Trail, to the very sharp turn where the original Seager Trail intersection was located. (If you go too far S, a steep descent soon begins.) From this turn, follow the ridge directly W into the col leading to Doubletop Mt. The easiest route is to hike S up the ridge from the Seager Trail, just after crossing Flatiron Brook, though much private land must be crossed.

Summit elevation of Doubletop is 3860 ft. (1158 m).

Big Indian Mt. (Bushwhack)

Big Indian Mt. is a bushwhack peak, but just barely. Legend says Winnisook was the "Big Indian"—seven feet tall. All sorts of stories, ranging from his being killed by wolves to tales of romance and vengeance, were popular when the hotel business was crisp in the late 1800s.

The usual approach to the summit is from Biscuit Brook via the Biscuit Brook–Pine Hill Trail (see above). The canister is at the S end of the ridge, about 0.25 mi. E of the 3500-ft. elevation sign.

Another approach is via the Seager Trail (see Arkville–Seager section).

Summit elevation is 3700 ft. (1131 m).

Fir Mt. (Bushwhack)

Fir Mt. is NE of Biscuit Brook lean-to. There is some evidence that Arnold Guyot got mixed up when labeling Spruce and Fir mts. on his early Catskill map. It is likely that Spruce Mt. was the original name for this peak.

The usual approach is to take a compass bearing from Biscuit Brook lean-to for a straight bushwhack to the summit. Shorter approaches from Big Indian Hollow or Maben Hollow require gaining permission from landowners before crossing private land.

Summit elevation is 3620 ft. (1107 m).

(44) Neversink– Hardenburgh Trail

Map 43: G-7 to G-6
Southern Catskills

This trail follows a dirt road N from the West Branch of the Neversink, over the Beaver Kill Range, and then into the valley of the Beaver Kill. It progresses from a rough drivable road to a road often too rough for the normal car, to a very pleasant woods road. How far one drives along it depends on the vehicle, the weather, and the wisdom of the driver. Trail descriptions are given from the DEC parking area on Black Bear Rd., since that is the farthest point to which one can legally drive a vehicle. While most of the road is drivable to this point, ruts, mud holes, and loose hardscrabble rock in places may, at any point, require the driver to park on the road shoulder and walk a few more miles than originally intended.

Trailhead: Trail access is via Round Pond Rd., on the W side of Co. Rd. 47/157. (See Route Guide for Big Indian–Claryville.) It is easy to miss this road if you are not alert. Round Pond Rd. climbs a grade. Bear R onto Black Bear Rd. at a fork at 0.6 mi. (Round Pond is L; Round Pond Rd. forks L and becomes Pole Rd. when it crosses into Sullivan Co.).

Continue along Black Bear Rd. to the Basily Rd. jct. at 0.8 mi. where there is a 15-vehicle parking area. Black Bear Rd. bears R from this fork.

There is an unmarked pulloff on state land on the R at 3.2 mi., and another at 3.8 mi.

From the N most pulloff, 3.0 mi. N of Black Bear Trailhead parking area (0.0 mi.), continue walking N along Black Bear Rd., following yellow DEC trail markers. The route re-enters private land, passing the edge of a clearing that has a large camp L. The road returns to the forest at the far side of the clearing, at an elevation near 2575 ft. You are soon back on state land; from this point onward, the absence of vehicles results in a very nice woods road for hiking.

The trail makes a sharp horseshoe turn, crossing an attractive tributary of Fall Brook at 0.65 mi. The way is enjoyable, with gradual grades. It crosses another small brook at 1.4 mi., and then reaches Fall Brook lean-to L, at 1.55 mi. This lean-to is in excellent condition. A good spring at 1.7 mi. provides water. Here, 40 ft. L of the trail, a pipe emerges from the ground and gives a steady flow across the trail.

The trail is nearly level as it leaves the Neversink watershed and drops into the Beaver Kill valley at 2.0 mi. A benchmark indicates that the elevation is 2653 ft.

The reason for this valley's name is made evident by a beaver pond at 2.25 mi. At 2.35 mi. a second large pond shows off a nice beaver house. Across the water are Doubletop Mt. NE and Graham Mt. N.

The trail becomes a footpath, skirting the W side of the pond on a wet slope. Once at the end of the pond, the path continues through a narrow valley.

The upper Beaver Kill is a rippling brook that grows in size as the trail descends to the lowlands. At 2.55 mi. there is a small island.

The stream begins a great bend from W to SW and the hiker must rock-hop across to the N bank at 2.65 mi. This section is most picturesque, with small riplets of water singing to you and green mossy boulders providing a feast for your eyes.

At 2.75 mi. the woods road resumes again, running NW parallel to the creek. The route continues straight ahead to a jct. at 2.8 mi. (A bridge L crosses the creek and a narrow woods road leads to private land.) The trail passes a small clearing and fire ring. At 2.95 mi. an open clearing extends some 200 ft. off to the R, with a brook at its back edge. This is an ideal location for camping away from the trail.

The woods road is now wider, but still pleasant to walk. Tunis Pond outlet bridge is reached and soon thereafter, at 3.65 mi., **the relocated section** of trail turns N from the woods road. It crosses a brook and then winds NW, where Vly Pond Outlet is negotiated on stepping stones, just S of Vly Pond. The route crosses a woods road and then passes over the Gulf of Mexico Brook bridge at 4.3 mi.

Swinging SW, the S end of a low ridge is topped before the trail turns NW again, descends and then at 5.2 mi. reaches Black Brook. Once across the bridge, the route follows a woods road, reaching the Balsam Lake Mt. trailhead parking area at 5.8 mi. This is located at the end of Beaver Kill Rd. Continue 2.0 mi. SE along the Beaver Kill Rd. to the Hardenberg Trailhead parking area on the N side of the road.

Distances: To horseshoe curve, 0.65 mi.; to Fall Brook lean-to, 1.55 mi.; to divide, 2.0 mi.; to trail crossing Beaver Kill, 2.65 mi.; to where trail leaves road, 3.65 mi.; to Gulf of Mexico Brook bridge, 4.3 mi.; to Black Brook bridge, 5.2 mi.; to Balsam Lake Mt. parking area, 5.8 mi. (9.4 km); Hardenberg Trailhead parking area, 7.8 mi.

(45) Long Pond–Beaver Kill Ridge Trail (Black Bear Rd.–Flugertown Rd.)

Map 43: G-7 to F-7
Southern Catskills

The Long Pond–Beaver Kill Ridge Trail runs 7.45 mi. from the jct. of Black Bear Rd. and Basily Rd. to a jct. with the Mongaup–Hardenburgh Trail up on Beaver Kill Ridge. The description given here is the first part of the Long Pond–Beaver Kill Ridge Trail as far as Flugertown Rd. Used as a snowmobile trail in winter, it has potential as a ski trail.

Trailhead: *Trail access is from Round Pond Rd. (See Route Guide for Big Indian–Claryville.) Climb the grade off the paved road. Pass Round Pond and bear R at a jct. onto Black Bear Rd., at 0.6 mi. Basily Rd. is the L branch of a second fork at 0.8 mi. This jct. (0.0 mi.) is the beginning of the Long Pond-Beaver Kill Ridge Trail. Park in the 15-vehicle parking area at the jct.*

The road climbs a long gradual grade and then descends. At 2.0 mi. the woods road hiking trail makes a sharp L to the S at a road jct. (Basily Rd. continues R.) From here it is essentially flat for the remaining 1.55 mi. to the Long Pond lean-to.

At 2.4 mi. there is another fork. The trail bears R and follows red DEC trail markers. Avoid a side trail L at 3.2 mi. After a grassy area, the trail reaches a spur trail L, leading to the Long Pond lean-to at 3.55 mi. There is a trail register at this jct.

(The spur snowmobile trail heads W but soon swings to the S. Long Pond lean-to clearing is at 0.2 mi., 150 yds. W of Long Pond. A recently constructed snowmobile trail continues S from the lean-to 1.4 mi. to the Long Pond Trailhead parking area on Flugertown Rd.)

The level trail continues generally N, soon crossing a stream on rocks. At 3.8 mi. a gradual descent begins, becoming a sharp descent at 3.9 mi. Drawing close to a brook at 4.0 mi., the route makes a sharp R turn to the E. A bridge over the stream can be seen, but the trail continues upstream, reaching height of land at 4.1 mi.

An unmarked trail continues straight ahead from a jct. at 4.3 mi., where the red-marked trail makes a L turn, descends, and crosses a tributary bridge before crossing the bridge over Willowemoc Creek. Flugertown Rd. is just beyond the bridge at 4.4 mi. (Note: a new Long Pond Trailhead parking area has been constructed 1.0 mi. S on Flugertown Rd.)

Turning R, the Long Pond–Beaver Kill Ridge Trail follows Flugertown Rd., 0.05 mi. to a DEC signpost. Here it turns L and heads N towards Beaver Kill Ridge. (See Long Pond–Beaver Kill Ridge Trail [Flugertown Rd. to Beaver Kill Ridge (trail 81)], Delaware–Beaver Kill Section, for description of the rest of this trail.) Willowemoc Rd. is 2.5 mi. W and then S along Flugertown Rd.

Distances: To first road jct., 2.0 mi.; to parking jct., 2.4 mi.; to lean-to spur trail, 3.55 mi.; to Flugertown Rd., 4.4 mi.; to DEC signpost for N half of trail, 4.45 mi. (7.2 km).

(46) Denning–Woodland Valley Trail (Phoenicia–East Branch Trail)

Map 43: I-7 to K-6
Southern Catskills

This trail provides the backpacker with a number of options. It crosses the divide from the East Branch to the West Branch of the Neversink River and then crosses another divide into the Esopus Creek watershed. The Giant Ledge–Panther Mt. Trail (trail 40), the Burroughs Range (Slide, Cornell and Wittenberg mts.), Table and Peekamoose mts. can all be reached from this trail, as well as bushwhack peaks such as Lone and Rocky mts.

The original route (still marked) began closer to Denning than it does today and ended only a mile from Phoenicia. Hence, it is sometimes called the Phoenicia–East Branch Trail. Now, because of improved roads, most hikers begin at the Denning parking area and end at the Woodland Valley Public Campground. This shortened trail is not necessarily easier. Much elevation must be lost and regained because of rerouting around the private Winnisook Club, which forces the hiker onto paved highway.

Trailhead: The trail begins at the Denning parking area trailhead (see

Route Guide *for Big Indian–Claryville) at the end of the road, 8.0 mi. E along Co. Rd. 19 from its Co. Rd. 157 intersection in Claryville. There are few facilities to help the stranded driver. The road bears slightly R and becomes unpaved at 6.7 mi., some 0.2 mi. past Strauss Center. Pass by the large estate of the Tison Trust, 0.1 mi. before reaching the trailhead. A trail register and accompanying information board are located at the N end of the parking area, just before the gate.*

From the large parking area (0.0 mi.), the yellow-marked trail follows a woods road NE up gradual grades. The route through hemlock forest is both comfortable and pleasant. A gradual down-grade at 1.0 mi. leads to a bridge over a small stream. Lost elevation is then slowly regained to a jct. at 1.2 mi. (The blue trail R, the Table–Peekamoose Trail [trail 47], leads to the summits of Table and Peekamoose mts.; see below.)

Gradual climbing continues along the woods road. The road passes a spring L at 1.75 mi. and crosses a brook at 2.05 mi. Level trail runs from 2.2 mi. to 2.7 mi., where gradual climbing resumes. Height of land occurs at 2.95 mi. at 3050 ft. elevation, some 1000 ft. above the trailhead. At this point the Curtis-Ormsbee Trail enters from the R. A monument to William Curtis is found at this jct. (The Curtis-Ormsbee trail [trail 42] ascends 1.6 mi. up the shoulder of Slide Mt., joining the Slide–Cornell–Wittenberg Trail 0.65 mi. from the summit of Slide Mt.; see above.)

The trail descends slightly, passing a spring R at 3.25 mi. Footing is less rocky and more comfortable before 3.55 mi., where the route crosses a bridge over a large tributary of the West Branch. The route again levels before reaching the jct. of the Slide–Cornell–Wittenberg Trail (trail 41) at 3.75 mi. (This red-marked trail ascends 2.0 mi. to the summit of Slide Mt. and then continues across the Burroughs Range; see above.)

The yellow-marked Denning–Woodland Valley Trail continues

straight ahead, passing a pipe spring on the R at 3.85 mi. It leaves the road at 4.05 mi., abruptly turning L at a trail sign arrow. Descending a stone stairway, the trail continues at moderate grades over rocky terrain before easing at 4.25 mi. The path crosses the rocky West Branch of the Neversink at 4.4 mi., reaching the trail register at the rear of the Slide Mt. parking area at 4.45 mi. Here the trail turns R onto Co. Rd. 47 and wends its way gradually uphill.

The trail passes the Winnisook Club at 5.35 mi. just as it reaches the height of land between the West Branch and Esopus Creek watersheds. From here, at the end of Winnisook Lake, follow the old Denning Trail into the woods. (The Winnisook Club has provided an easement to hike this trail, and asks hikers to stay on the trail until State land is reached.)

For hikers climbing Giant Ledge and Panther Mt., the Denning-Woodland Valley Trail leaves the road at a hairpin turn at 6.4 mi. The trail turns abruptly R and crosses a bridge beyond the road guards at a DEC signpost. It then heads E with yellow trail markers to a trail register at 6.45 mi. Beyond some rock walkways, the route drops to a tributary stream, which it crosses on a wide bridge.

The trail swings L up a moderate grade and then jags R before steeply climbing a short pitch at 6.6 mi. Gradual grades with moderate pitches sidle up the ridge to rock steps at 7.0 mi., as the trail curves R up a steep bit of rock cobble to a trail jct. Here, an old woods road at R (DEC alternate route) heads S. (This is the original trail, now unmaintained.)

Turning L and walking another 65 ft. brings the hiker to a DEC signpost at another jct. at 7.05 mi. The blue-marked trail straight ahead (N) is the Giant Ledge–Panther Mt. Trail (trail 40); see above. The yellow-marked Denning–Woodland Valley Trail turns R and continues E.

An almost flat trail crosses the height of land at 7.15 mi. (Avoid a R turn here at a woods road jct.) A long, gradual descent to Woodland Valley commences at this point. The route, along a pleasant woods road through beech-birch forest, is most enjoyable. Following an undependable water flow L at 7.4 mi., the trail bends N. It narrows at 7.8 mi. as the slope drops off steeply to the R and rises on the L.

At a steady flow spring L at 8.05 mi., a large rock slide creates an interesting section. Here a general swing ESE begins and the rate of descent somewhat increases.

Soon, the loose rock of a talus slope draws attention; it occupies the hiker's curiosity for a quarter mile. When the talus slope ends, the grade becomes gradual in a forest of mostly beech.

A modest log barrier at 8.6 mi. blocks further travel on the woods road. The trail forks L into the woods as a foot path, requiring the hiker to keep a sharper lookout for trail markers. Moderate grades descend into a ravine as the route switchbacks several times before bridging a stream on the valley floor.

Turning R from the bridge, the trail immediately swings L through a rocky area. At 8.85 mi. it very steeply climbs more than 100 stone steps and then continues steeply upward over large rocks.

The route turns R at 8.9 mi., when it reaches a broad shelf in the side of Fork Ridge. Nearly level terrain gives a much needed respite. The shelf narrows at 9.1 mi., and a long, gradual downgrade to Woodland Valley begins. A trail register at 9.75 mi. precedes a short steep pitch, followed by wooden steps, to the rear of the parking area of the Woodland Valley Public campground at 9.8 mi. (The campground office is 500 yds. R along the paved road; Phoenicia is 5.6 mi. L along the road.)

Distances: *To Table–Peekamoose Trail jct., 1.2 mi.; to Curtis-Ormsbee Trail jct., 2.95 mi.; to Slide Mt. Trail jct., 3.75 mi.; to Slide Mt. parking area, 4.45* *mi.; to Giant Ledge parking area, 6.4 mi.; to Giant Ledge–Panther Mt. Trail jct., 7.05 mi.; to stone steps, 8.85 mi.; to Woodland Valley Public Campground, 9.8 mi. (15.9 km).*

(47) Table–Peekamoose Trail (from Denning–Woodland Valley Trail)

Map 43: J-7 to J-8
Southern Catskills

From the Denning parking area, it is 3.95 mi. to the summit of Table Mt. After some preliminary ups and downs from the parking area, the hiker leaves the Neversink Valley and ascends 1617 ft. before reaching the summit. It is a tiring trip, but not nearly as tough as the 2600-ft. ascent on the 3.35-mi. climb via the trail to the summit from Peekamoose Rd. The mountain, one of the less often climbed peaks, offers a truly wilderness experience. This is unlike the woodland road ascents so common in the Catskills; the hiker must scamper up a narrow, rocky foot trail to the summit.

Trailhead: *Access to the Table–Peekamoose Trail is at the jct. of the Denning–Woodland Valley Trail (trail 46), 1.2 mi. from the Denning parking area (see above).*

From the jct. (0.0 mi.), the blue-marked trail heads E, 100 ft., descending a slope. The trail turns N and gradually descends to the flood plain of the Deer Shanty Brook–Neversink River area. At the toe of the slope the trail turns sharply SW, crossing Deer Shanty Brook. It then crosses another small brook on a second log bridge.

The trail passes the site of the former Denning lean-to (removed in 1999) at 0.3 mi., where Deer Shanty Brook and the East Branch of the Neversink River come together. Camping is prohibited at the old lean-to site. The broad flood plain and shallow braided Neversink make this a wet, dangerous area in times of winter meltwater or heavy rain. In summer, it is mostly sandy soil and bare rock stream bottom.

The trail leads N of the lean-to, immediately crossing the Neversink. Climbing the far bank on a rock staircase, it swings L and crosses a brook at 0.4 mi. An informal path enters from the L at a jct. at the top of the brook's bank. (This path is unofficial, but is used enough by hikers to be easily traveled. The route crosses the Neversink just beyond Donovan Brook, 1.0 mi. from the jct. Many more crossings are made along this very gradual trail before the Slide/Cornell col is reached at 4.5 mi. There is a good ascent route up Lone and Rocky mts. between the tributaries at 2.7 mi. and 2.75 mi. from the jct. It is a beautiful river valley.)

Rolling terrain becomes a moderate grade at 0.7 mi. The trail eventually forms a series of pitches before leveling at 1.0 mi. Here, at 2800-ft. elevation, a spur trail R leads to a lookout S towards Van Wyck Mt. A gradual upgrade soon reaches height of land, descends some pitches to a col at 1.2 mi., and ascends again via a series of moderate pitches and gradual grades.

The trail levels briefly at 1.4 mi. at a fair lookout R. A steep pitch cuts through a large rock outcrop at 1.5 mi.; followed by a second steep pitch. The first of three close spur trails R branches at 1.6 mi. It leads to a cliff edge with excellent views S to Van Wyck Mt. and WNW to the Tison Trust estate near the Denning clearing parking area.

The trail dips slightly at 1.9 mi., levels, and then begins a long, steady gradual upgrade for the next half mile. There is a spring (not dependable) to the L of the trail at 2.4 mi. Just above the spring a path leads R (S) 200 ft. to the Bouton Memorial Lean-to. The route reaches a moderate grade just before passing the 3500-ft. elevation marker at 2.5 mi.

The short, steep ascent at 2.6 mi. provides a good view N to Slide and Lone mts. The grade then eases before reaching the Table Mt. flat summit at 2.75 mi. There are no views from this conifer-shrouded peak, but a prominent herd path heads S just below the true summit. Follow it through evergreens a few yards and look for a ledge to the R, where there is room for two people. The view is magnificent. Summit elevation is 3847 ft.

How Table Mt. gained its name is apparent as the trail continues another 0.3 mi. on the very flat mountain top. Gradual downgrades begin at 3.05 mi. A view of Peekamoose Mt. at 3.1 mi. precedes a descent on a moderate slope into the col between Peekamoose and Table mts.

A herd path to Lone Mt. branches L at 3.25 mi. The col bottom is at 3.3 mi. Here the trail squeezes through tightly spaced conifers that nearly form a tunnel for a short distance.

A gradual grade then climbs to a less obvious unmarked herd path L at 3.55 mi. (Bear R for the summit.) At the summit clearing at 3.7 mi., a 30-ft. diameter opening is completely surrounded by balsam fir and spruce. However, by climbing the immense boulder found at the edge of the clearing, one can gain quite interesting views of the Burroughs Range (Slide, Cornell, and Wittenberg mts.), Lone, Rocky, and Table mts. Summit elevation is 3843 ft. The Peekamoose–Table Trail (trail 58) continues another 3.35 mi. to Peekamoose Rd. near Bull Run.

Distances: *To East Branch of Neversink path, 0.4 mi.; to first lookout, 1.0 mi.; to series of three lookouts, 1.6 mi.; to spring and Bouton Memorial Lean-to, 2.4 mi.; to Table Mt. summit, 2.75 mi. (summit elevation 3847 ft. [1176 m]); to col, 3.3 mi.; to Peekamoose Mt. summit, 3.7 mi. (6.0 km) (4.9 mi. from Denning parking area). Summit elevation, 3843 ft. (1175 m).*

Lone Mt. (Bushwhack)

Map 43: J-7
Southern Catskills

Lone Mt.'s summit canister is on a paper birch- and fern-covered mountain top, indicative of a past forest fire. Time is gradually replacing this flora with balsam. The peak is pesky and its ascent is often combined with ascents of Rocky Mt. or Table Mt. There is a good lunch spot on a ledge with a view, a little E of the canister.

The drop into the col between Lone Mt. and Rocky Mt. has some minor cliffs that are readily negotiable in summer, but they can be a problem in winter. The col itself has a dense thicket of balsam with some blowdown. The whole trek between Lone Mt. and Rocky Mt. is much easier if the hiker swings down the N slope of Lone Mt. and then stays well below the balsam-covered col on the way to Rocky Mt. Summit elevation, 3721 ft. (1138 m).

Rocky Mt. (Bushwhack)

Map 43: K-7
Southern Catskills

Rocky Mt. has gradual to moderate slopes but considerable blowdown and new growth near the summit. This makes a mostly easy climb somewhat hard in its last 200 vertical ft. As with Lone Mt., its long approach, from whatever direction the hiker chooses, necessitates an early start and careful planning by day trippers.

Many hikers climb this peak in winter, when deep snow covers much of the blowdown. However, winter ascents pose their own problems and should not be attempted by poorly equipped or inexperienced people. Summit elevation, 3508 ft. (1073 m).

View from the Cathedral Glen Trail

Typical Catskill hollows

Woodstock–Shandaken Section

The trails of the Woodstock–Shandaken section date back to 1783, when the Schoharie Rd. was built up through Mink Hollow on its way to Prattsville. At that time, it was believed the region's hollows were filled with witches and wizards. People sought out the "witch doctor," Jacob Brinks, to deal with them. It was a region where, much later, a favorite pastime for Overlook Mt. House guests was to push huge boulders off the escarpment's cliffs, just so they could be watched as they crashed through the forest below. One would ride the Ulster & Delaware Railroad in pampered luxury almost to the doorstep of the Tremper House in Phoenicia—and then climb Mt. Tremper for exercise. In a time when Woodland Valley was still called Snyder's Hollow, today's Denning–Woodland Valley Trail was being used by pioneers. It was in this section, almost the center of the Catskill Park, that today's leaders have chosen to build the Catskill Park Interpretive Center.

Trail in winter: Overlook Mt. is not only a short snowshoe climb, but the trail ascends a dirt roadway that is suitable for intermediate skiing. Mink Hollow is also excellent for skiing.

The Burroughs Range is a definite challenge for the experienced snowshoer. Panther Mt., from Fox Hollow, is a great day trip, but takes longer than it would seem from the maps. Get an early start.

Short Hikes:

Mink Hollow—*6.1 mi. round trip. Walk up a beautiful wooded hollow to a lean-to. Turn around whenever you feel like it.*

Moderate Hikes:

Overlook Mt.—*5.0 mi. round trip. One of the best views from a fire tower in the mountains. Easy old carriage road trail.*

Wittenberg Mt.—*7.8 mi. round trip. A stiff climb to the summit, magnificent views of Ashokan Reservoir.*

Harder Hikes:

Panther Mt. from Fox Hollow—*9.8 mi. round trip. A tough trip, but a chance to get away from the crowd. Long but very nice winter trip on snowshoes.*

Wittenberg, Cornell, and Slide mts.—*14.1 mi. round trip. Probably the toughest day trip in the Catskills. Great views. Can be shortened to a through trip if you have two vehicles.*

Trail Described	Total Miles (one way)	Page
Overlook Mt.	2.5	158
Echo Lake	0.6	160
Mink Hollow (S of Devil's Path)	3.05	161
Willow Trail to Mt. Tremper	3.2	162
Phoenicia Trail to Mt. Tremper	3.1	164
Wittenberg–Cornell–Slide mts.	7.05	165
Terrace Mt.	0.9	168
Woodland Valley	2.75	169
Panther Mt. (Fox Hollow)	4.9	170

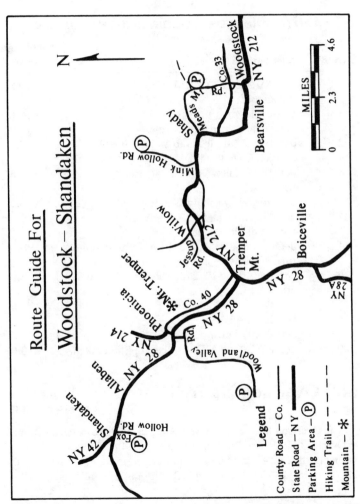

Route Guide For

Woodstock – Shandaken

Mileage E to W	Description	Mileage W to E
0.0	Jct. NY 212 and Co. Rd. 33; village of Woodstock.	20.5
1.9	Bearsville; road turns N-S.	18.6
3.2	Jct. Glasco Turnpike, E side.	17.3
3.7	Jct. Hutch Rd.; leads to Meads Mt. Rd. and Keefe Hollow Rd.	16.8
5.0	Jct. Mink Hollow Rd., N side; village of Lake Hill.	15.5
7.4	Jct. Van Wagner Rd., W side; hamlet of Willow.	13.1
11.4	Jct. Co. Rd. 40 (Old NY 28), W side; hamlet of Mt. Tremper.	9.1
11.6	Jct. NY 28 and NY 212; turn NW if driving W; turn E if driving E.	8.9
15.5	Jct. NY 28 and NY 214; Phoenicia 0.1 mi. N on NY 214.	5.0
16.0	Jct. Woodland Valley Rd., S side.	4.5
19.5	Hamlet of Allaben	1.0
19.9	Jct. Fox Hollow Rd., S side.	0.6
20.5	Jct. NY 28 and NY 42, village of Shandaken.	0.0

(48) Overlook Mt. Trail

Map 41: O-5
NE Catskills

The Overlook Mt. Trail follows the old carriage road to the summit of Overlook Mt. Pierre DeLabigarre, a French Revolutionist, was probably the first to write about the views from this mountain, after his climb in 1793. In 1833 James Booth built a "temporary" hotel there. It took until 1871 to establish a permanent hotel. It burned to the ground on April Fool's Day in 1874, when no one would believe a small child who tried to convince staff that the smoke in the chimney was darker than usual. Rebuilt in 1878, it burned down again in 1924. The struggle to keep it open ended, in the midst of rebuilding yet again, with the stock market crash of 1929. Remnants of the half-finished foundations are still visible. The fire tower is now open.

Trailhead: *Access to the Overlook Mt. trailhead is from Woodstock. Travel 0.6 mi. N on Co. Rd. 33 from Woodstock to the intersection of Glasco Turnpike. Continue 2.1 mi. straight ahead up steep Meads Mt. Rd. to the DEC trailhead signpost and very large parking area on the R side of the road. The large building across the road from the trailhead was once Mead's Mt. House, an early hotel.*

The trail runs E from the trail register (0.0 mi.) on a wide gravel road. Red DEC trail markers guide you but are not needed. The upgrade is steady, ascending 1200 ft. to the jct. with the Old Overlook Rd. Trail. (Both trails are good for skiing or snowshoeing in winter.)

There is a pipe with gushing water on the L side of the road at 0.35 mi. A less obvious spring is on the side of the road at 0.5 mi. Large boulders along the way show signs of frequent use as resting spots, but the way is so easy that a side trip to Echo Lake (trail 49) (see below) is almost necessary to make a full day's outing.

At 1.1 mi. there is a fork; bear L. The ruins of the Overlook Mt. House are on the R at 1.8 mi. The trail circles around to its rear, passing a large antenna, several smaller buildings, and an old stone foundation. It reaches the Old Overlook Rd. Trail jct. at 2.0 mi. (The Old Overlook Rd. Trail [trail 25] runs 2.0 mi. to Echo Lake and 4.8 mi. to Platte Clove Rd.; see Platte Clove Section.)

The Overlook Mt. Trail is now almost level. There is a yellow barrier gate at 2.1 mi. The trail heads E where a path leads to a viewing point R at 2.2 mi. The trail gradually climbs, circling below the summit, to the fire observer's cabin at 2.5 mi. A fireplace and picnic table are across the road. Views are best from the fire tower, which provides magnificent vistas in all directions. The Hudson stands out in the E; Ashokan Reservoir is S; Slide, Cornell, and Wittenberg mts. are W; Indian Head, Twin, Sugarloaf, Plateau, and Hunter mts. are N. On a clear day, seven states can be seen from this summit. Rattlesnakes are seen in the rocky terrain here.

Distances: *To first spring, 0.35 mi.; to second spring, 0.5 mi.; to road fork, 1.1 mi.; to Overlook Mt. House ruins, 1.8 mi.; to Old Overlook Rd. Trail jct., 2.0 mi.; to summit fire tower, 2.5 mi. (4.0 km). Summit elevation, 3140 ft. (960 m). Ascent, 1400 ft. (428 m).*

(49) Echo Lake Trail

Map 41: O-5
NE Catskills

The Echo Lake Trail is a short spur trail to Echo Lake off the Old Overlook Trail (trail 25). Echo Lake is the headwaters of the Saw Kill. Formerly Shue's Pond, it is the only natural lake in a designated wilderness area in the Catskills. It was here that the last Indian encampment in the Catskills was located. Many legends were generated about the lake in the heyday of the Overlook Mt. House.

Trailhead: *From the 1.4-mi. point of the Old Overlook Rd. Trail (0.0 mi.), the Echo Lake Trail gradually descends NW to Echo Lake following yellow DEC trail markers. The route has a constant grade on a cobblestone base.*

At the bottom of the slope, the trail curves SE. It reaches the rear of Echo Lake lean-to at 0.6 mi. The lean-to sits 50 ft. back from the shoreline. Tall trees around the lean-to are widely spaced, allowing excellent views across the lake.

An interesting trip is available to those who follow the lake outlet (Saw Kill) to the SW. A bushwhack of approximately 1.5 mi., it ends at a woods road leading another mile to Keefe Hollow Rd.

Distance: To lean-to, 0.6 mi. Descent, 455 ft. (139 m).

(50) Mink Hollow Trail (South of Devil's Path)

Map 41: N-4
NE Catskills

The Mink Hollow Trail runs N from Lake Hill, crosses the Devil's Path at a height of land, and then descends towards Tannersville. It follows an old hauling road dating back to the 1790s. When Col. Edwards was running the leather-tanning industry in Tannersville, the primary route for transporting hides from the Saugerties port on the Hudson was along this route. The same slope is a good cross-country ski route today.

Trailhead: Access from the S is on Mink Hollow Rd., off NY 212 in Lake Hill. Drive N 2.85 mi. on Mink Hollow Rd. to the snowplow turnabout which is as far as you can legally drive. There is space for several vehicles.

The route follows blue DEC trail markers along a woods road from the turnabout (0.0 mi.). It forks to the R at 0.1 mi., near a trail register. The route narrows at 0.2 mi. and crosses Mink Hollow Brook at 0.3 mi.

From this point, the old road follows the E side of the brook up a lush green hollow that rises sharply to the R. The deciduous vegetation and easy grades make very pleasant surroundings.

At 1.1 mi. the trail jogs R a short distance, avoiding the remains of an old bridge as it again crosses Mink Hollow Brook. (This spot could be a problem for late spring skiers if spring melt has started.)

The valley broadens and the grade steepens a bit before easing again at 2.0 mi. A steady grade finally reaches height of land at 2.8 mi. At 2.95 mi. a spur trail L leads 30 ft. to the Mink Hollow lean-to. Trees are growing more dense around this structure, so good views are decreasing each year. However, there is still a good view of Sugarloaf Mt. to the E from the deacon seat of the lean-to.

A second path leads back to the trail, which reaches the Devil's Path jct. at 3.05 mi. A trail register is at this jct. There is a good spring 150 ft. NW of the jct. on a yellow-marked spur trail. It is 0.95 mi. E on Devil's Path [trail 21] to the Sugarloaf Mt. summit; it's 1.2 mi. W on Devil's Path to Plateau Mt. summit [see Platte Clove Section].

Distances: *To first brook crossing, 0.3 mi.; to second brook crossing, 1.1 mi.; to easing of grade, 2.0 mi.; to lean-to, 2.95 mi.; to Devil's Path, 3.05 mi. (4.9 km). Col elevation, 2600 ft. (780 m). Ascent, 1090 ft. (327 m).*

(51) Willow Trail to Mt. Tremper

Map 41: M-5 to L-5
NE Catskills

The Willow Trail is the longer of the two trails to the Mt. Tremper summit. While the Phoenicia Trail (trail 52) is a short, tough climb, the Willow Trail ascends Hoyt Hollow through forest that becomes increasingly more attractive as you climb. If two vehicles are available, a through trip ascending the Phoenicia Trail and descending the Willow Trail makes a very nice day's outing.

Trailhead: *Access is off NY 212 in the hamlet of Willow. Turn W onto Van Wagner Rd. and drive 0.4 mi. to Jessup Rd. Turn L and drive 1.0 mi. on Jessup Rd. to the point where it begins to climb. This is the trailhead. There is no parking area, and hikers will have to ask landowners for permission to park on their property.*

Where Jessup Rd. begins to climb (0.0 mi.), the trail becomes a rough woods road. Blue DEC trail markers guide you. Avoid all side roads on the lower slopes.

From 0.2 mi. to 0.5 mi., there are enormous numbers of mountain laurel. In late spring, their white and pink blooms literally cover the ground on each side of the trail.

Yellow paint blazes mark the beginning of state land at 0.6 mi. The change in forest quality is very noticeable. At 0.9 mi. the trail becomes a moderate grade. The wall of the hollow drops sharply off on the R; the character of the forest becomes more primitive. The route turns L at 1.4 mi., steeply climbing to a ridgeline, which it reaches at 1.5 mi. It heads SW.

The route is now a well-marked wilderness path. It gains elevation gradually and then levels. Views to the E occasionally present themselves through the trees. The pathway gradually gains elevation again at 2.6 mi. and continues to do so all the way to the summit. The fire tower stands in a clearing at 3.2 mi. providing magnificent views to Slide, Cornell, and Wittenberg Mts., the Devil's Path peaks, and the Ashokan Reservoir. The red-marked Phoenicia Trail (trail 52) continues S, with the Mt. Tremper lean-to another 0.05 mi. along the way.

Distances: *To state land, 0.6 mi.; to ridgeline, 1.5 mi.; to steeper section, 2.6 mi.; to summit, 3.2 mi. (5.2 km). Summit elevation, 2740 ft (838 m). Ascent, 1430 ft. (437 m).*

(52) Phoenicia Trail to Mt. Tremper

The Phoenicia Trail is the shorter of the two trails to the Mt. Tremper summit. Originally named Timothy Berg, the mountain is now named after Major Jacob H. Tremper of Kingston, who, with Captain William C. Romer, owned the Tremper House. This large hotel was one of the first to offer visitors to the Catskills an opportunity to arrive at its door by railroad, with no bumpy stagecoaches needed for transport.

Trailhead: The trailhead is on the N side of Co. Rd. 40 (old NY 28), 1.7 mi. E of Phoenicia.

From the trailhead (0.0 mi.), the red-marked trail slants upward NE, crosses a short foot bridge, then turns R up rock steps and over a knoll to a jct. with the old jeep road route at 0.4 mi. There is a trail register. Turn R and follow the old road uphill at moderate grades. The road grade becomes gradual at 0.8 mi., swinging SE and then S. The route levels at 1.2 mi., where there is a spring L. The trail begins a series of switchbacks, passing a small waterfall on the R at 2.1 mi. Just after a sharp switchback, a spur trail R at 2.2 mi. leads 75 ft. to the Baldwin Memorial Lean-to.

The trail heads uphill to 2.3 mi., where a side trail L runs 30 ft. to a large boulder where water from a spring rushes out from a long metal pipe. At 2.8 mi. the route levels, swinging NE on a grassy lane.

The Mt. Tremper Lean-to is on the L side of the trail at 3.0 mi. The summit is at 3.1 mi. Views from the renovated fire tower are magnificent (see Hike 51).

Rattlesnakes are occasionally seen on this mountain, especially at the old quarry, where they sun themselves on the broad rock faces.

Distances: *To first spring, 1.2 mi.; to Baldwin Memorial Lean-to, 2.2 mi.; to second spring, 2.3 mi.; to Mt. Tremper Lean-to, 3.0 mi.; to summit, 3.1 mi. (5.0 km). Summit elevation, 2740 ft. (838 m). Ascent, 2030 ft. (621 m).*

(53) Wittenberg–Cornell–Slide Trail

Map 43: K-6 to J-6
Southern Catskills

The Wittenberg Mt. Trail is one of the hardest but most rewarding of Catskill trails. The hiker needs good boots and plenty of water. Springs along the trail are not dependable.

Trailhead: *Trail access is from Woodland Valley. (See Route Guide from Woodstock to Shandaken.) Turn L from NY 28 for Woodland Valley and travel 0.3 mi. before crossing the Esopus Creek bridge and reaching a road jct. Turn R and follow Woodland Valley Rd. 4.7 mi. to the Woodland Valley Public Campground. The trailhead is on the L, where a log barrier cable prevents vehicle entry to a service road. A large parking area is on the R, a short distance beyond the trailhead. (Parking permits can be purchased during the summer and fall camping season at an office 500 ft. farther along the road.)*

The trail leaves the trailhead (0.0 mi.) on a macadam service road. It immediately turns L and follows red DEC trail markers between campsites 45 and 46 to where it crosses Woodland Creek on a large wooden bridge. Turning L, it climbs at moderate grade to a trail register at 0.15 mi. The rocky trail becomes a gradual grade at 0.6 mi. and at a trail direction indicator turns sharply L at 0.9 mi. (Avoid traveling straight ahead here.)

Varying grades lead to a bluff at 1.15 mi. The trail difficulty eases. There is a spring 300 ft. R of the trail at 1.45 mi. The route moves away from and then back to the edge of the valley rim two more times before reaching a small down-grade at 2.0 mi. The T-jct. with the Terrace Mt. Trail (trail 54) is reached at 2.6 mi. (The Terrace Mt. Trail leads 0.9 L at gradual downgrade to a lean-to; see below.)

Turn R at the jct. The gradual upgrade soon steepens and is moderate to very steep all the way to the summit.

The trail passes through a sharp rock cut at 3.1 mi. and then ascends a very steep rock bluff at 3.2 mi. Steep pitches of varying size lead past the 3500 ft. sign at 3.4 mi. A spring is 250 ft. R of the trail at 3.6 mi. Rough spur trails lead both L and R near the summit of Wittenberg at 3.9 mi. Summit elevation is 3780 ft. Ascent from Woodland Valley is 2430 ft.

The sweeping view is nearly 180 degrees, from Plateau Mt. in the N to Balsam Cap in the S. Ashokan Reservoir stands out in full glory from the large open rock bluff. Views include dozens of mountains. The isolated peak between Wittenberg and Ashokan Reservoir is Samuels Point. Cornell and Slide cannot clearly be seen.

The trail heads W from the lookout, descending gradually to a col. Climbing out of the col, the trail crosses some log walkways before reaching a large rock bluff at 4.6 mi. Here, a short vertical climb is followed by an ascent through a deep V-cut in the cliff top. (Winter climbers should use a rope here for a safeguard.)

Gradual grades lead this "Bruin's Causeway" to a blue-marked spur trail L at 4.7 mi. This leads 0.05 mi. to the flat-topped "Crown of Cornell" summit of Cornell Mt. Summit elevation is 3860 ft.

From the jct., the red trail descends easily to a good lookout towards Slide Mt. at 4.8 mi. This is followed by a second good lookout in the same direction. This is followed by a narrow "lemon squeezer," a narrow, curved passage between rock ledges. A spring is located to the R of the trail at 5.0 mi., and there may be water across the trail at 5.3 mi. to indicate a spring 400 ft. L of the trail. After passing a spur trail that leads to a designated campsite N, and two more spur trails to designated campsites S, the trail reaches a low point in the col between Cornell and Slide Mts. at 6.15 mi. This is a common place to leave the Burroughs Range trail and bushwhack south to the headwaters of the East Branch of the Neversink River. Eventually herd paths following the East Branch are discernable. (They lead 4.5 mi. to the former Denning Lean-to site; see above.) A spring is located 400 ft. L of the trail.

Leaving the col, the trail passes three more designated campsites before climbing above 3500 ft. Gradual and moderate grades, with occasional pitches, lead upward toward the summit of Slide Mt. A 35-ft. vertical rock outcrop at 6.5 mi. followed by a 15-ft. vertical bluff requires care.

A 25-ft. blue-marked spur trail R at 6.8 mi. leads to the most appreciated spring in these mountains. Water gushes out of the rock in an ice-cold jet. Excellent views of Woodland Valley make this a "must" rest stop.

A series of four large ladders helps the climber past some difficult rock, but the steep scramble to the summit from here requires caution. Finally, the ascent moderates as the trail bursts out of the conifers at the base of the lookout rock shelf at 7.0 mi. Be sure to read the John Burroughs memorial plaque. It was placed here by the Winnisook Club in 1923 to honor Burroughs. Views extend out over Ashokan Reservoir in a wide sweep to the S and E.

The true summit is at 7.05 mi., where a fire tower once stood. Only one base support remains today. The trail continues another 0.65 mi. to the jct. of the Curtis-Ormsbee Trail (trail 42); 2.0 mi. to a jct. with the Denning–Woodland Valley Trail (trail 47); and 2.7 mi. to the Slide Mt. parking area on Slide Mt. Rd. (Refer to Slide–Cornell–Wittenberg Trail [trail 41], Big Indian–Upper Neversink section.)

Distances: To spring, 1.45 mi.; to Terrace Mt. Trail jct., 2.6 mi.; to summit of Wittenberg Mt., 3.9 mi.; to Cornell Mt. summit, 4.7 mi.; to East Branch Neversink path jct., 6.15 mi.; to Slide Mt. summit, 7.05 mi. (11.4 km).

Summit elevation, 4180 ft. (1278 m). Ascent from col, 930 ft.

(54) Terrace Mt. Trail

A trail up Wittenberg Mt. used to start from Woodland Valley Rd., 1.4 mi. closer to Phoenicia than today's trail. (The suspension bridge across Woodland Creek can still be seen.) It ascended the NE slope of Terrace Mt. to the flat tree-covered terrace summit at the 1.45 mi. point. Here, a nice lean-to made a good overnight spot for backpackers. Today, this portion of the trail is no longer used. However, the portion from the lean-to, which leads 0.9 mi. to a jct. at the 2.6-mi. point of the Wittenberg–Cornell–Slide Trail (trail 53), is still maintained so Wittenberg Mt. hikers have access to the lean-to.

Trailhead: *From the jct. at the 2.6 mi. point of the Wittenberg–Cornell–Slide Trail (trail 53), a very gradual grade leads downward to the lean-to. There is a large bare rock clearing at 0.3 mi. A benchmark (2556 ft.) is in a rock 100 yds. R of the trail. There are good views N to Mt. Tremper. Blueberries abound.*

The trail continues to descend, swinging R at a small clearing at 0.5 mi. It levels just before reaching a large clearing at 0.9 mi., where a sign points R to the lean-to, some 40 yds. away.

The lean-to (1987) is very old, but in fair condition, considering its age. How long it will remain is not known, or if the trail will be maintained once the lean-to is gone. Water is not available. The large clearing is attractive and the hike in is very pleasant.

Distances: *To clearing, 0.3 mi.; to second clearing, 0.5 mi.; to lean-to, 0.9 mi. (3.2 mi. from Woodland Valley). Descent to lean-to, 310 ft. (98.4 m).*

(55) Woodland Valley Trail (to Giant Ledges– Panther Mt. Trail)

**Map 43: K-6 to J-6
Southern Catskills**

This trail is the N end of the Denning–Woodland Valley Trail (trail 46) (see Big Indian–Upper Neversink Section); it connects to the Giant Ledges–Panther Mt. Trail (trail 40), offering access to Panther Mt. from Woodland Valley. It is a challenging but rewarding trail.

Trail access is from Phoenicia. (See *Route Guide* for Woodstock–Shandaken.) Turn S off NY 28, 0.5 mi. W of Phoenicia, onto the Woodland Valley Rd. Travel 0.3 mi. before crossing a bridge over Esopus Creek and reaching a road jct. Turn R and follow the Woodland Valley Rd. 4.7 mi. to a large parking area on the R at Woodland Valley Public Campground. (Parking permits can be obtained at an office 500 ft. farther along the road during the camping season.)

Trailhead: The trailhead (0.0 mi.) leaves the rear of the parking area, climbing wooden steps up a short pitch. Yellow DEC trail markers lead 50 yds. to a trail register. From there a very pleasant footpath climbs W through deciduous forest. Occasionally moderate in grade, the incline is generally gradual.

Leveling at 0.7 mi., the footpath joins the beginning of a flat rock shelf. The shelf widens greatly as the trail progresses. Several yards to the R a cliff juts up, while only a few yards to the L the shelf ends and your gaze plummets into the valley below.

At 0.9 mi. the trail turns sharply L and descends very steeply. First, it clambers over large rocks and boulders; then, most enjoyably, over 100 stone steps lead to the valley floor. The path winds a bit before crossing Woodland Creek, and then steeply ascends some switchbacks. The trail soon levels, but the hiker needs to keep trail markers in sight in this little section.

Breaking out of the woods at 1.2 mi., the trail reaches a jct. with an old woods road, which it follows to the height of land. (The original trail was on this road from Woodland Valley, but the present first 1.2 mi. of the trail was added so that the route could be entirely on state land.)

Turning R, the trail follows the old woods road W, climbing at moderate grade, with occasional easier stretches. It climbs a ridge with a large talus slope at R and the valley wall dropping off sharply to the L. At a rocky section and spring on the R at 1.75 mi., the trail makes a swing S and crosses another branch of Woodland Creek.

The route continues to climb, but at more gradual rates. Birch and beech abound here. Beyond an undependable water flow at 2.4 mi., the trail curves W again, reaching height of land at 2.6 mi. (Avoid a side road L.) The now flat route joins the Giant Ledges–Panther Mt. Trail (trail 40) at 2.75 mi. Here, the trail up Giant Ledges follows blue DEC trail markers N. (It is another 0.75 mi. to Giant Ledges and 2.55 mi. to the Panther Mt. summit.) The Denning–Woodland Valley Trail (trail 46) bears L. (See Big Indian–Upper Neversink section for further trail description.)

Distances: *To Woodland Creek bridge, 0.95 mi.; to Woodland woods road jct., 1.2 mi.; to spring, 1.75 mi.; to height of land, 2.4 mi.; to jct. of Giant Ledge–Panther Mt. Trail, 2.75 mi. (4.5 km). Elevation at jct., 3300 ft. (990 m). Ascent, 1850 ft. (555 m).*

(56) Panther Mt. Trail (Fox Hollow Trail)

Map 42: J-5 to J-6
Central Catskills

The climb up Panther Mt. from Fox Hollow may take longer than the distance might suggest. False peaks may discourage the novice;

the unclearly defined summit is not an obvious goal. The shorter trip to the summit, from the S over Giant Ledges, provides more open viewing for less effort. However, the Fox Hollow route gives the climber a longer day of hiking, with less contact with other hikers likely. It is a particularly good winter snowshoe trip, when much more open viewing is possible than in summer.

Trailhead: *Access to the trailhead is via Fox Hollow Rd. off the S side of NY 28 in Allaben. (See Route Guide for Woodstock to Shandaken.) A trailhead parking area is on the R, 1.6 mi. along Fox Hollow Rd. A path to the rear of the parking area leads to a privy.*

From the trailhead (0.0 mi.), the trail leaves a barrier boulder at Fox Hollow Rd. and follows blue DEC trail markers NW, up a woods road. Moderate to steep climbing begins immediately. The trail passes a trail register at 0.1 mi. and crosses a stream over a rickety bridge at 0.3 mi. Still climbing, it reaches the junction of a spur trail and a spring at 0.4 mi. The spur trail R leads 150 ft. to the Fox Hollow Lean-to; the spring is just beyond the lean-to.

The woods road winds back and forth, continuously ascending. Grades ease at 1.0 mi. and the route turns S. Alternating easy and steep grades occur before the route becomes a footpath at 1.4 mi. The moderate slope climbs over some boulders at 2.6 mi. Soon, a view E opens up, but there is no open view at 3.1 mi. on the first false peak, although two more flat bumps can be seen ahead. About 100 ft. of elevation is lost and regained before reaching the second false peak at 3.7 mi.

The trail bottoms out again at 4.2 mi., then ascends and passes the 3500-ft. elevation sign at 4.7 mi. Conifers close in on the trail; care must be taken to watch trail markers in winter. Finally, at 4.9 mi., the trail bursts out on top of an open rock outcrop, with outstanding views E. Looking across to the Burroughs Range, a giant glacial cirque stands out before you; Wittenberg, Cornell, and Slide mts. all are impressive. The Giant Ledges–Panther Mt. Trail (trail 40) continues another 2.55 mi. to the jct. with the Woodland–Denning Trail. (See Giant Ledges–Panther Mt. Trail, Big Indian–Upper Neversink section.)

Distances: *To lean-to, 0.4 mi.; to turn S, 1.0 mi.; to boulders, 2.6 mi.; to first false peak, 3.1 mi.; to second false peak, 3.7 mi.; to summit, 4.9 mi. (7.9 km). Summit elevation, 3720 ft. (1116 m). Ascent, 2420 ft. (726 m).*

Peekamoose Section

The southern border of the Catskills is somewhat isolated from the rest of the Catskill region. It has an older look about it and one gets a glimpse of what it was like in yesteryear.

In the eastern part, Ashokan Reservoir dominates the views from most peaks. Few people realize that seven villages had to be moved so an old glacial lake bottom could be transformed into the reservoir. It takes 92 mi. of tunnels to transport its water to New York City.

The ascents from the S side of the ridges in this section are about 1000 ft. greater than ascents from the N sides, so some challenging climbs can be done here. For example, the ascent of Peekamoose Mt. from Denning is about 1700 ft. over a distance of 4.9 mi. The ascent of the same mountain from Peekamoose Rd. is 2623 ft. over a distance of 3.35 mi.

Buttermilk Falls is a beautiful waterfall along the N side of Peekamoose Rd. (See *Route Guide* for West Shokan–Claryville.) It is unusual in that it has a subterranean source that spouts out of a hole in a cliff. It is a good rest and lunch spot during the long slow trip across Peekamoose Rd.

In a region with names like Bull Run, Sundown, Bangle Hill, Mombaccus, Pataukunk, and Peekamoose, there has to be much history to interest the hiker.

Trail in winter: Balsam Cap and Friday mts. are often climbed in winter. Careful map navigation routes should be planned. Peekamoose and Table are long but not difficult. Recent bridging makes crossing the East Branch of the Neversink easier than it was at one time. The rest of the trips described in this book section are little climbed in winter. This is an isolated area, so have plenty of gas and be sure your vehicle is in good condition.

Short Hikes:

Kanape Brook—*3.0 mi. round trip. Walk along a gurgling brook with occasional cascades. Go to the point where a stone bridge crosses the stream and return.*

Vernooy Falls—*3.6 mi. round trip. Follow woods roads to a 30-ft. waterfall and enjoy the forest before returning.*

Moderate Hikes:

Ashokan High Point—*7.4 mi. round trip. A little bit of everything. First a bubbling brook, then a stiff climb to a mountain peak, and then views of the most beautiful body of water in the Catskills.*

Long Path (Upper Cherrytown Rd. to Peekamoose Rd.)—*8.7 mi. through trip. A long hike along old roads and trails.*

Harder Hikes:

Peekamoose and Table Mts.—*8.6 mi. round trip. One of the highest vertical ascents in the Catskills in very attractive woods.*

Balsam Cap and Friday Mts.—*Approximately 6.0 mi. loop. A longer trip than it looks, but one you'll remember.*

Trail Described	Total Miles (one way)	Page
Samuels Point	trailless	177
Balsam Cap	trailless	178
Friday	trailless	179
Ashokan High Point	3.7	179

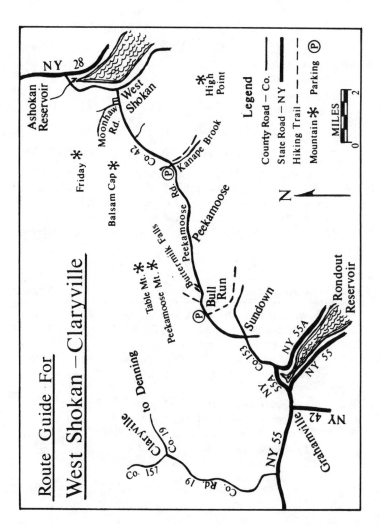

Route Guide For
West Shokan — Claryville

Legend

County Road — Co.
State Road — NY
Hiking Trail
Parking Ⓟ
Mountain ✳

MILES
0   2

N

Ashokan Reservoir

NY 28

West Shokan

Moonhaw Rd.

Friday ✳

Balsam Cap ✳

High Point ✳

Kanape Brook

Co. 42

Peekamoose Rd.

Peekamoose

Table Mt. ✳   ✳ Peekamoose Mt.

Buttermilk Falls

Ⓟ Bull Run

Sundown

Rondout Reservoir

NY 55A

NY 55A   Co. 153

NY 55A

NY 55

Claryville

to Denning

Co. 19

Co. 157

Co. Rd. 19

NY 55

NY 42

Grahamville

Peekamoose Section   175

Trail Described	Total Miles (one way)	Page
Peekamoose-Table (from Peekamoose Rd.)	4.3	181
Long Path (Upper Cherrytown Rd.– Peekamoose Rd.)	8.7	183

ROUTE GUIDE FOR WEST SHOKAN–CLARYVILLE

This route guide runs from West Shokan to Claryville along what is collectively known as the Peekamoose Rd. Actually, under today's road number designations, the route involves several different roads. At times the pavement runs out for short stretches. This is not a rapid-transit road. Plan to take your time, and have a full tank of gas.

Mileage E to W	Description	Mileage W to E
0.0	West Shokan. Jct. of NY 28A and Co. Rd. 42 (Peekamoose Rd.); follow Co. Rd. 42.	26.2
0.9	Moon Haw Rd., N side of road.	25.3
3.9	Kanape Brook, Co. Rd. 42. Trailhead for Ashokan High Point; DEC parking area R side of road.	22.3
8.3	DEC parking, N side of road, for old Peekamoose Mt. Trail, not maintained.	17.9
8.5	Parking, N side of road; Buttermilk Falls.	17.7
10.1	DEC parking, N side of road. Current Peekamoose Mt. maintained trail, 100 ft. W of parking area along road.	16.1

Mileage E to W	Description	Mileage W to E
10.3	DEC open campsite, N side of road; permit needed.	15.9
10.6	Long Path trailhead, S side of road.	15.6
10.7	Open campsite, N side of road.	15.5
11.6	Parking area, N side of road.	14.6
13.2	Sundown. Co. Rd. 153 goes SW; Co. Rd. 42 goes N.	13.0
16.4	Sugar Loaf Rd., N side of road.	9.8
16.6	Lowes Corners. NY 55A goes SW; Co. Rd. 42 goes NE.	9.6
16.8	N end of Rondout Reservoir	9.4
18.6	Jct. NY 55 goes W; NY 55A goes NW.	7.6
19.2	Grahamville. NY 42 jct. to S; continue on NY 55.	7.0
21.6	Jct. Co. Rd. 19 goes N; NY 55 goes E.	4.6
26.2	Claryville. Jct. Co. Rd.19 continues E to Denning; Co. Rd. 157 goes N to Big Indian; Co. Rd. 19 goes S towards Peekamoose.	0.0

Samuels Point (Bushwhack)

Map 43: L-7
Southern Catskills

Samuels Point is a moderately high peak at the end of a ridge extending generally E from Wittenberg Mt. It offers a view of Ashokan Reservoir. For those interested in more strenuous exercise, it is possible to follow the ridge of Cross Mt. and then climb Mt. Pleasant. The whole area may one day become much more utilized, if future development of the Catskill Interpretive Center reaches fruition and recommended changes in the route of the Long Path occur.

Trailhead: Leave NY 28 at Boiceville and follow NY 28A, W and S, 0.9 mi. to Traver Hollow Rd. Turn W and drive 0.7 mi. on Traver Hollow Rd. to Bradken Rd. Follow Bradken Rd. 1.0 mi. to where a stream crosses the road. This can provide a starting point up the state land on the W side of the road. You will need a map.

Samuels Point has a summit elevation of 2885 ft. Vertical ascent from Bradken Rd. is 2785 ft.

Balsam Cap (Bushwhack)

Map 43: K-7
Southern Catskills

Balsam Cap, once called Balsam Top, is in that group of trailless mountains which includes Friday, Rocky, and Lone mts. These are the hardest of the 3500-ft. peaks to reach.

Trailhead: Access from the E is off the N side of Peekamoose Rd., on Moon Haw Rd. (See Route Guide for West Shokan–Claryville.) Travel 1.8 mi. along Moon Haw Rd. to the jct. of private Shultis Rd., on the L. There is a small private parking area at this jct., whose owner has previously let hikers park there. Ask permission for this privilege. Do not proceed along Shultis Rd. with your vehicle.

Shultis Rd. soon branches into a series of woods roads; hikers should study their maps well before starting on this trip. There are some cliffs to negotiate in the upper reaches of the mountain.

Grades are more gradual on the W side of the ridge, but the overall trip in from Denning is much longer. On the W side of the ridge, Balsam Cap can be approached from the upper section of the East Branch of the Neversink via a herd path. The stream running E at 2.75 mi. makes a reasonable ascent route. There is a good view two minutes N of the canister via a herd path.

Summit elevation is 3623 ft. (1087 m).

Friday Mt. (Bushwhack)

Map 43: K-7
Southern Catskills

Friday is a bushwhack peak just N of Balsam Cap Mt. It is generally done along with Balsam Cap Mt. because climbing in this area is so rugged that hikers generally find one long trip preferable to two shorter ones. For unsurpassed primeval grandeur, however, each mountain should be approached separately from the E.

Trailhead: Use the same approaches as mentioned for Balsam Cap Mt. Hikers generally follow the ridge (which is the Delaware-Hudson divide) from Balsam Cap over to Friday. The descent off the E side of Friday is very steep, requiring a bit of jockeying from side to side to find a way down. This is not a good winter descent line. There is a good view via a short bushwhack E of the canister. Summit elevation is 3694 ft. (1108 m).

(57) Ashokan High Point

Map 43: K-8 to L-8
Southern Catskills

Ashokan High Point stands alone and thus offers a more grand view of the countryside around it than is generally the case in the heart of the mountains. A bit off the beaten path, it escaped having a hotel plunked on it in the 1800s. Its summit was never cleared for viewing, so it remains natural. Views are excellent.

Trailhead: Access to the trailhead is off the S side of Peekamoose Rd. at Kanape Brook. (See Route Guide for West Shokan–Claryville.) The Kanape Brook trailhead has a DEC signpost and is marked by a yellow metal barrier gate. A parking area is on the N side of the road.

From the yellow metal barrier gate (0.0 mi.) the red-marked but clear woods road drops down to Kanape Brook, which it crosses on a bridge. The first part of the route is a level course above the N bank of the brook. At a pretty waterfall at 0.6 mi. the trail crosses a pair of stonework bridges. A woods road enters from the L, at 0.9 mi. There is a spring L at 1.3 mi.

Another stonework bridge crosses Kanape Brook at 1.5 mi. After following the S side of the waterway for a while, the brook turns N up the mountain and the hiking trail continues SE. An informal campsite is seen in evergreens at 1.6 mi. There is a woods road R at 2.6 mi.

Height of land is at 2.7 mi., where there is a jct. A DEC sign indicates the trail turns L. (The route straight ahead soon reaches the end of state land. This informal trail leading out to Freeman Avery Rd. is currently posted.)

The trail gradually climbs N from the jct., but by the time it reaches the 2.9 mi. point, the grade is steep. After side roads at 3.1 mi., the woods road you have been traveling ends at 3.3 mi. From there a footpath ascends steeply in pitches. Views begin to open up as the sun begins to penetrate the canopy. Mombaccus Mt. is to the SW. The presence of blueberries whets your appetite.

A steep pitch up at 3.6 mi. is followed by a level stretch with a rock overhang L. At the summit at 3.7 mi., views are found W and N. Others can be found in various places by moving around the summit. The ambitious can take a 25-minute bushwhack down to a knob at 120 degrees magnetic, where there are magnificent views of Ashokan Reservoir and N to the Devil's Path.

Distances: *To waterfall, 0.6 mi.; to spring, 1.3 mi.; to bridge across Kanape Brook, 1.5 mi.; to DEC sign jct., 2.7 mi.; to summit, 3.7 mi. (6.0 km). Summit elevation, 3080 ft. (924 m). Ascent from trailhead, 2070 ft., (621 m).*

(58) Peekamoose–Table Mt. Trail (from Peekamoose Rd.)

Southern Catskills

The lower part of the trail up Peekamoose Mt. was routed in the early 1970s by Ranger Peter Fish to replace the steeper trail then in use. It climbs the ridge between Bear Hole Creek and Buttermilk Brook from Gulf Hollow, where Rondout Creek flows close to the road.

Trailhead: *Access to the trailhead is off the N side of Peekamoose Rd. (See Route Guide for West Shokan–Claryville.) There is parking for a few vehicles 100 ft. W of the trailhead.*

The blue-marked trail leaves the cable barrier at the trailhead (0.0 mi.) and begins a moderate grade ENE up an old woods road. By 0.2 mi. it is heading NE, and at 0.4 mi. it levels. The lower slopes up to 2025 ft. were pasture until the 1920s, when the state purchased the land. Black birch, white ash, red oak, and big-toothed aspen predominate, since they typically are pioneer species where pastures are allowed to return naturally to forest.

Very gradual grades continue along the ridge. At 1725 ft. elevation, there is a red pine grove planted in the 1920s.

The woods road forks L at 0.75 mi., where the hiking trail continues ENE as a footpath. More planted red pines are seen, but hop-hornbeam dominate. Beyond this zone only selective logging was done, and there are far older trees here than are found on the lower slopes.

Grades become moderately steep and then ease as a series of varying grades takes hikers up through rock outcrops. After the route passes between two boulders at 0.95 mi., the grade eases again.

A woods road crosses the trail at right angles and the climb soon becomes steep, passing through a gap in a rock ledge at 1.3 mi. You are now above the zone of past lumbering, among virgin maples and beeches. Peekamoose Mt. can be seen to the NE from time to time. Reconnoiter Rock, a large boulder, is at 1.9 mi. After more steep climbing the path pitches up to a wide ledge where excellent views appear at 2.35 mi.

The ascent up the spine of the ridge leads to the jct. with the old Peekamoose Trail at 2.45 mi. (This red-blazed old route is no longer maintained.) The trail heads N. A spring is L of trail at 2.75 mi.

Steep grades continue to the summit (elevation 3843 ft.; ascent from Peekamoose Rd., 2623 ft.) Here, at 3.35 mi., balsam fir and spruce surround the summit clearing, but the top of a large sloping boulder provides a partial view. The Burroughs Range (Slide, Cornell and Wittenberg mts.), and Lone and Rocky mts. stand out to the NE. Table Mt. is nearby to the NW.

Gradual downgrades lead towards Table Mt. Bear L from a herd path that forks R at 3.7 mi. The trail flattens out in the col at 3.75 mi. and sharp spruces press in on you for a short distance. Then, moderate grades take you upward. In a level spot at 3.8 mi., a herd path on the R heads NE to Lone Mt. There is a good view back to Peekamoose Mt. at 3.95 mi.

The path soon levels and crosses the nearly flat top of Table Mt. to the actual summit at 4.3 mi. There is no view from the wooded summit, but hike down a few yards to a very prominent herd path heading S into evergreens. Look for an open ledge down through the trees, where views are magnificent. Summit elevation is 3847 ft. Ascent from the col is 197 ft. (This trail continues 0.3 mi. to the Bouton Memorial Lean-to and 6.4 mi. to Denning parking area. See Table–Peekamoose Trail [trail 47], Big Indian–Upper Neversink section.)

Distances: *To jct. of footpath, 0.75 mi.; to Reconnoiter Rock, 1.9 mi.; to jct. with old Peekamoose Trail, 2.45 mi.; to spring, 2.75 mi.; to summit of Peeka-moose Mt., 3.35 mi.; to col, 3.75 mi.; to summit of Table Mt., 4.3 mi. (7.0 km).*

(59) Long Path Trail (Upper Cherrytown Rd.–Peekamoose Rd.)

This is the southernmost section of the Long Path found within the Catskill Park. (For a complete sequence of the Long Path in the Catskills, refer to the Long Path in the chapter on Extended and Challenging Opportunities.) This section of the trail passes through the Claryville–Sundown–Sholam Wild Forest, generally following snowmobile trails on old woods roads. Best traveled in a S–N direction, a through trip requires extensive driving to place a return vehicle. A shorter day trip to Vernooy Falls is a good choice if only one vehicle is available.

Trailhead: Access is off NY 209 onto Co. Rd. 3 (Pataukunk Rd.), 0.7 mi. E of the stop light in Kerhonkson. Pass through the hamlets of Pataukunk, Fantinekell and Mombaccus before turning L at an intersection 3.4 mi. from NY 209. After 0.2 mi., bear L at the fork with Ridgeview Rd. Drive another 0.6 mi., passing two more side roads. Stay L at each jct. Just after a small bridge crossing, there is a 3-way jct. (A large concrete building marks the spot.) Turn R here onto Upper Cherrytown Rd. and continue N another 3.1 mi. to the DEC trailhead sign at the R side of the road. There is a large parking area on a side road opposite the trailhead sign. This is a total of 7.8 mi. from NY 209.

From the trailhead (0.0 mi.), follow red trail markers into the woods. There are many trail sign changes along the way, but the blue paint blazes of the Long Path are seen at jcts. and sharp turns. Cross a brook at 0.2 mi. on a small bridge and continue along the woods road. Easy but steady climbing takes you over a ridgeline, and then the drop down to the Vernooy Falls jct. begins. Vernooy Falls and a trail register are reached at 1.8 mi. There is a splendid view of Vernooy Falls from the bridge across the stream, but do not continue beyond it unless you wish to take the snowmobile trail to Greenville. This interesting waterfall has four cascades dropping a total of about 30 ft. Downstream along the Vernooy Kill are the remains of an old stone mill.

From the trail register, the trail makes a sharp R turn and heads NNE up a winding woods road, soon reaching the crest of the rise. Thereafter, nearly level trail takes you through very attractive deciduous woods.

Keep a sharp eye for an unmarked jct. at 2.65 mi. Here the route leaves the woods road and easily climbs to the top of Pople Hill, where it levels and turns R at 3.05 mi., continuing N.

The trail reaches another jct. at 4.3 mi., where it turns L on an old woods road. An informal hunters' camp is found here. Ruts from their vehicles can make spring hiking a little muddy for the next couple of miles. (The R turn leads along Sapbush Creek to Riggsville.)

The route heads W on the level, crossing a bridge with metal culverts over the Vernooy Kill at 4.5 mi.

After an attractive camp up a grade to the R, a slight descent takes you to the crossing of a stony creek at 6.5 mi. Watch for a large stone cairn where the woods road makes a curve to the S at 6.7 mi. Here the Long Path makes an abrupt turnoff to the R and heads uphill on a well marked, but definitely primitive, wilderness footpath. The unwary can easily walk right past the turnoff, since the cairn is on the L and the woods trail, which is to the R, is not clearly indicated. (The woods road continues 0.8 mi. to a paved road; Greenville is another 0.6 mi. to the L on the paved road.)

The rough trail climbs steeply N, making a couple of jags to the R as it climbs. Keep a sharp eye for the trail signs as you ascend the lower slopes of Sampson Mt. The trail swings sharply L when it reaches a woods road, but soon turns R and climbs through woods again with more rough trail. The trail eventually eases, makes a very sharp L turn and then maintains a fairly steady course WNW towards Bangle Hill.

The pathway widens somewhat and provides enjoyable, nearly level, walking. Yellow paint blazes indicating private property are crossed at two points.

The Long Path continues along the base of Sampson Mt. and, after some loss of elevation, crosses the headwaters of Sundown Creek at 7.2 mi. Elevation is regained and the trail heads NW, reaching height of land, and crossing Bangle Hill at 2350 ft. A very steep descent N off Bangle Hill loses 1150 ft. elevation before reaching Peekamoose Rd. (Hikers walking this section from N–S have to be careful to watch trail signs. Some side trails make it easy to ascend the wrong route.)

The trail bears R at a large boulder at 8.6 mi. and breaks out of the woods at Peekamoose Rd. at 8.7 mi. The Long Path turns R and follows Peekamoose Rd. E, 0.5 mi., where it ascends the Peekamoose–Table Mt. Trail (trail 58) N. There is a DEC open campsite (permit needed) 0.2 mi. E along the road. A large parking lot is 0.1 mi. W of the trailhead on Peekamoose Rd. Sundown is 2.6 mi. W along Peekamoose Rd.

Distances: To Vernooy Falls, 1.8 mi.; to jct. before Pople Hill, 2.65 mi.; to jct. past Pople Hill, 4.3 mi.; to Vernooy Kill bridge, 4.5 mi.; to unmarked Sampson Mt. trail, 6.7 mi.; to headwaters Sundown Creek, 7.2 mi.; to top of Bangle Hill, 8.5 mi.; to Peekamoose Rd., 8.7 mi. (14.1 km).

Winter on Balsam Lake Mt.

Arkville–Seager Section

Close to several sizeable villages, the trails of this section seem little used by hikers, although hunters and anglers know the area well. No railroads entered these hollows, nor were there large resort hotels to attract the elite; thus, the area has never been well publicized. The trailheads are not easily found, unless one has a guidebook, since they are often at the end of a long hollow, well beyond heavily traveled roads. Nevertheless, for those who seek them out, there are very nice hikes to be had in this section.

Trail in winter: The trails in this section are all nice day trips. The Seager Trail leads to several "3500" summits (summits 3500 ft. elevation or higher). The unplowed woods road leading from Mill Brook Rd. to Balsam Lake and Graham mts. is a fine route for skiing. One can ski to the summit of Balsam Lake Mt. and most of the way up Graham. The Kelly Hollow Trail is also fine for skiing.

Short Hikes:

Rider Hollow—*2.0 mi. round trip. Walk through an idyllic glen with rippling waters and beautiful trees. Turn back when the route becomes steep.*

Kelly Hollow—*3.8 mi. loop. A woods road hike to a pretty beaver pond. Smell the conifers and enjoy the land.*

Moderate Hikes:

Balsam Mt. Loop—*5.25 mi. loop. Follow the Rider Hollow and Mine Hollow trails to the Biscuit Brook–Pine Hill Trail, then turn S over Balsam*

Mt. and return via the Rider Trail. A lot of elevation change.

Pakatakan Mt.—4.15 mi. through trip. Ascend the German Hollow Trail and descend Pakatakan Mt. to Margaretville on the Dry Brook Ridge Trail.

Harder Hike:

Dry Brook Ridge Trail—9.4 mi. through trip. Climb Pakatakan Mt. and walk the Dry Brook Ridge Trail to Mill Brook Rd. Fine ridgeline views and easy walking once on top of the ridge.

Huckleberry Brook–Dry Brook Ridge Loop—10.5 mi. This trail winds up and down the Huckleberry and Dry Brook ridges for a long ramble.

Trail Described	Total Miles (one way)	Page
Burroughs Memorial Field	0.5	191
Dry Brook	13.45	192
German Hollow	1.5	194
Huckleberry Trail	7.6	196
Graham Mt.	trailless	197
Kelly Hollow	3.8	197
Rider Hollow	1.75	199
Mine Hollow	1.0	201
Seager	3.0	202

ROUTE GUIDE FOR ARKVILLE–SEAGER

This guide begins at Arkville. It follows the Dry Brook Rd. to its end in Seager. Dry Brook Rd. becomes Co. Rd. 49.

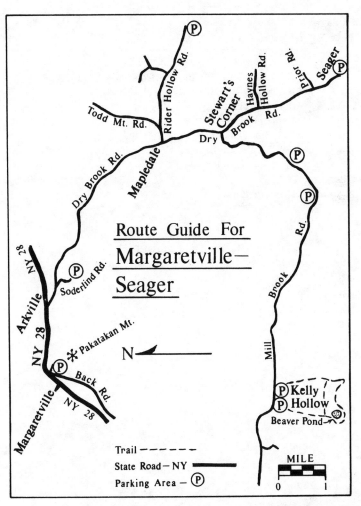

Route Guide For
Margaretville—
Seager

Trail ----
State Road—NY —
Parking Area — P

MILE
0   1

Mileage N to S	Description	Mileage S to N
0.0	Arkville. Jct. of NY 28 and Dry Brook Rd. Immediately W of Dry Brook bridge on NY 28; follow Dry Brook Rd. (Co. Rd. 49).	9.5
0.4	Jct. Soderlind Rd. on S side	9.1
3.5	Cemetery	6.0
4.3	Delaware/Ulster Co. line	5.2
4.7	Jct. Mapledale Bridge; Rider Hollow Rd. on E side (Co. Rd. 49A).	4.8

Mileage N to S	Description	Mileage S to N
6.1	Jct. Stewarts Turn; Mill Brook Rd. on W side of jct., Dry Brook Rd. goes straight ahead.	3.4
8.9	Jct. Prior Rd. on E side of road	0.6
9.5	End of road in Seager. Snowplow turnabout.	0.0

Burroughs Memorial Field

Each region develops people who in time come to represent certain aspects of that region. No one so represents the essence of nature in the Catskills as does John Burroughs.

"The most precious things of life are near at hand, without money and without price. Each of you has the whole wealth of the universe at your very door. All that I ever had, and still have, may be yours by stretching forth your hand and taking it." So said Burroughs.

"We can use our scientific knowledge to poison the air, corrupt the waters, blacken the face of the country, and harrass our souls with loud and discordant noises, or we can mitigate and abolish all these things." Does this sound like a contemporary environmentalist? This was Burroughs in 1913.

Everyone who loves the Catskills should visit Burroughs Memorial Field, a State Historical Site. See Boyhood Rock, where he is buried; look out to the mountains from the slopes high above Roxbury, perhaps walk the informal paths on the grounds. The tranquility of another age permeates the very air of this place.

Access Location: *From Roxbury, drive about a mile N of the village on NY 30 to Hardscrabble Rd. Turn W and drive 0.9 mi. to Burroughs Memorial Rd. Turn L and drive 1.4 mi. to Burroughs Memorial Field.*

(60) Dry Brook Ridge Trail

The Dry Brook Ridge Trail starts near Margaretville and climbs Pakatakan Mt. From there, it proceeds SW along Dry Brook Ridge to the Beaverkill Valley. A good backpack trail, it also provides side trips to Graham and Balsam Lake mts. The name Dry Brook is a corruption of "drei brucke," which is "three bridges" in German. At one time, three covered bridges spanned Dry Brook.

Trailhead: *Access to the trailhead is from the jct. of NY 28 and NY 30 at the E end of the bridge over the E Branch of the Delaware River in Margaretville. Drive 0.35 mi. S on NY 28/30 and turn L on the first side road (opposite a hardware store). Drive approximately 0.1 mi. on the side road and take the first L. Drive 0.15 mi. to the end of the road; this is the trailhead.*

From the trailhead (0.0 mi.), follow blue trail markers up an old logging road that was widened by the CCC (Civilian Conservation Corps) in the 1930s to make a ski trail. At 0.3 mi., the trail passes a rock overhang and small cave L. Moderate grades gain elevation quickly to 0.6 mi., where a trail enters from the L. There is a small spring at the base of a bank at 1.05 mi. and state boundary markers are seen on the R at 1.3 mi.

The route continues to ascend the old road to the "summit" of Pakatakan Mt. (2500 ft.) at 1.8 mi. The summit is more of a change in grade at the end of the ridge than a peak. From here the route is essentially level to 2.4 mi., where a gradual upgrade begins. This continues to the German Hollow Trail jct. at 2.65 mi. (Water is found on this trail at 0.4 mi.; a lean-to is at 1.0 mi., after much elevation loss. See below.)

At 3.0 mi. is the new DEC Huckleberry Brook Loop Trail jct. (see trail 62).

The trail ascends from the jct. A descent at 3.3 mi. soon ends. An unmarked trail R at 3.75 mi. drops down along Huckleberry Brook to Huckleberry Brook Rd.

The trail now goes along the ridge with some ups and downs, but it is generally easy hiking. Several excellent viewpoints look out towards distant Pepacton Reservoir. The other end of the Huckleberry Brook Loop Trail enters at 5.2 mi. (see trail 62).

The trail slowly climbs along Dry Brook Ridge at elevations near 3400 ft., with more views W. On top of a cliff at 6.7 mi., it ascends to another small summit at 7.1 mi. and then descends slightly. Flat for a while, it drops down a small cliff at 7.6 mi. and then pitches down at 7.8 mi.

Descent continues on easier grades to the Dry Brook Ridge lean-to at 8.2 mi., having lost about 750 ft. of elevation in the last mi. There is a spring here and a tributary of Mill Brook.

From the lean-to, the trail gains 350 ft. of elevation in pitches to a small summit at 8.7 mi. From there, a gradual descent to Mill Brook Rd. commences through a field of ferns. The trail (1993) approaches a private property line at 9.1 mi., but stays on state land. There is a large parking area on the N side of the road, where the trail crosses Mill Brook Rd. The trail enters the rear of this parking area at 9.4 mi.

(Stewarts Turn intersection is 2.2 mi. NE on Mill Brook Rd.; Arkville is 8.3 mi. To the R, 0.9 mi. SW is the trailhead that leads 0.25 mi. N to the Mill Brook lean-to.)

The blue-marked Dry Brook Ridge Trail goes SW, 50 ft. on Mill Brook Rd. At height of land, the trail turns L and ascends a gradual grade S along an unmaintained town road. (This section provides a quick but unspectacular route into Balsam Lake Mt. and Graham Mt. in summer, and makes an outstanding ski-shoe route in winter. Because of heavy use by hunters, it is wise to avoid this trail in deer season. Camping isn't permitted here.)

The upgrade continues to a trail register at 9.55, where the road levels. Alternating climbs and level spots lead to a spring, indicated by a sign and blue-marked side trail, at 10.6 mi. A jct. at a height of land, elevation 3250 ft. (650 ft. higher than Mill Brook Rd.), at 11.25 mi. marks the usual place to start up Graham Mt.

From here the trail gradually descends along the roadway to the Balsam Lake Mt. Trail jct. at 11.6 mi. (This trail leads an easy 0.75 mi. to the summit of Balsam Lake Mt. and then another 0.45 mi. to a new lean-to, before returning to the Dry Brook Trail. See Balsam Lake Mt. Loop, Delaware–Beaver Kill section.)

The blue-marked trail bears L from the jct. and descends in easy stages to a jct. at the other end of the Balsam Lake Mt. Trail at 12.55 mi. (It is a steep 0.45 mi. to the lean-to on this side trail.) The Dry Brook Ridge Trail continues to lose elevation slowly, crossing a bridge at 12.95 mi. It passes a few outbuildings before reaching the DEC parking area near the entrance road to the Balsam Lake Angler's Club at 13.45 mi. At the S end of the parking lot the trail ends at the jct. of the Neversink–Hardenberg Trail (trail 44) at 13.5 mi.

It is 2.0 mi. from this parking area SW along Beaverkill Rd. to the Hardenberg Trailhead.

Distances: *To Pakatakan Mt. summit, 1.8 mi.; to German Hollow Trail, 2.65 mi.; to side trail R, 3.75 mi.; to small summit, 7.1 mi.; to lean-to, 8.2 mi.; to Mill Brook Rd., 9.4 mi.; to height of land, 11.25 mi.; to first Balsam Lake Mt. Trail jct., 11.6 mi.; to second Balsam Lake Mt. Trail jct., 12.55 mi.; to parking area trailhead, 13.45 mi. (23.2 km).*

(61) German Hollow Trail

The German Hollow Trail is an access route to the Dry Brook

Ridge Trail from the N. It bypasses Pakatakan Mt. and permits the late-arriving hiker to reach a lean-to without much hiking.

Trailhead: *Trail access is off the Dry Brook Rd. (See* Route Guide *for Arkville–Seager.) Turn S onto unmarked Soderlind Rd. 0.4 mi. along Dry Brook Rd. from NY 28. The dirt road climbs a grade 0.3 mi. to a private turnabout and DEC signpost. Parking is tight. Please do not block private driveways.*

From the DEC signpost (0.0 mi.), the yellow-marked trail crosses a small brook and begins to ascend a gradual grade on a woods road to a trail register at 50 ft. Conifers are close to the road edge. A moderate upgrade at 0.1 mi. eases at 0.2 mi. but still climbs. Bear R at a road fork at 0.3 mi. and resume a moderate upgrade. Very steep pitches soon keep your attention.

A privy in poor condition is on the R when the grade finally levels at 0.55 mi. The trail leaves the woods road and bears L to the very nice German Hollow lean-to at 0.6 mi. (Avoid the trail that heads E in front of the lean-to. It leads 0.15 mi. to water at Rensselaer Creek.)

The German Hollow Trail leaves the L rear of the lean-to as a footpath through the woods until it rejoins the woods road at 0.7 mi. Turning L, the road climbs a moderate-steep grade with a brief respite at 0.8 mi. Moderate and gradual grades alternate as you ascend the ridge.

There is a spring R at 1.1 mi. A very large rock cairn marks the spot. A metal pipe has a good flow of water. At some time in the logging days of the past, considerable work was done to develop this old spring, but it is only a hiker's stop now.

One last steep grade leads you to a height of land, at 1.25 mi. A gradual slope loses a little elevation as the route swings NW and soon levels. This is an attractive section. At 1.35 mi. the route swings W again and climbs a couple of last pitches. The way levels 125 ft. before the Dry Brook Ridge Trail at 1.5 mi. (It is 2.65 mi. NW to Margaretville and 5.55 mi. SE to the Dry Brook Ridge lean-to; see above.)

Distances: To lean-to, 0.6 mi.; to spring, 1.1 mi.; to Dry Brook Ridge Trail jct., 1.5 mi. (2.4 km). Elevation at jct., 2780 ft. (834 m). Ascent, 1280 ft. (384 m).

(62) Huckleberry Brook Trail and Dry Brook Ridge Loop

Map 42: F-5
Central Catskills

The Huckleberry Trail is 7.6 mi. long, but when combined with a short road section and a section of the Dry Brook Ridge Trail (trail 60), it makes a nice 10.5-mi. outing. The trail description is of the loop route rather than just the Huckleberry Trail. The Huckleberry Brook portion of this loop is only partially completed at this time (Spring 1994). The trail has been cut and parking lots are completed. A general description of the trail is provided here, anticipating that trail signs will be in place for the 1994 hiking season. The hiker should be aware that this is an incomplete description, pending field examination, and may contain errors. The trail is a ramble up, along and down ridges, following contours wherever possible.

Trailhead: Approximately 1.9 mi. SW of Margaretville, turn L off NY 28/30 onto a road. Drive 0.1 mi. to Back River Rd. Turn R and travel 0.1 mi. on Back River Rd. to a fork. Bear L onto Huckleberry Brook Rd. (Hill Rd.). Bear R at the next fork, staying on Huckleberry Rd. At 1.6 mi. there is a 3-car parking area on the R and a trailhead on the L.

From the trailhead, the trail climbs N, crossing Hill Rd. at 0.3 mi., where there is another parking area. It continues NE, reaching a jct. with the Dry Ridge at 2.0 mi. and having gained 1450 ft. elevation from the trailhead. It then follows the Dry Brook Ridge Trail (trail 60) E for 2.2 mi., where it again intersects the Huckleberry Brook Trail at 4.2 mi.

Here it turns S and descends 1.2 mi. to Ploutz Rd. and a parking area at 5.4 mi. Crossing the road, the trail continues descent until it crosses a stream and begins climbing Huckleberry Brook Ridge. The trail gains little elevation here. It meanders W along the ridge approximately 3.0 mi. before swinging N and descending steeply 1000 vertical ft. to Huckleberry Rd., which it reaches at 9.8 mi.

The hiker has only to turn R and walk W 0.7 mi. to the starting point parking area.

Distances: To Hill Rd., 0.3 mi.; to Dry Brook Ridge Trail, 2.0 mi.; to Huckleberry Brook Trail, 4.2 mi.; to Ploutz Rd., 5.4 mi.; to Huckleberry Brook Rd., 9.8 mi.; to parking area, 10.5 m. (17.0 km).

Graham Mt. (Unmaintained Trail)

The informal route to Graham Mt. begins at a jct. at a height of land at the 11.25 mi. point of the Dry Brook Ridge Trail (see above). It is entirely on private land and hikers are encouraged to gain permission before hiking this land. The usual route is to travel 0.4 mi. SE on the old Trappen Rd. descending to a fork, and then bear R for the mountain.

(63) Kelly Hollow Trail

Map 42: F-5
Central Catskills

The Kelly Hollow Trail is a diamond in the rough. Formerly a snowmobile trail, it was recently remarked as a cross-country ski trail (yellow markers). Kelly Hollow is also a very attractive hiking area. Its lean-to makes it a good short overnight backpack trip. The Short Loop is 2.0 mi. and the Long Loop is 3.8 mi.

Trailhead: Trail access is off Mill Brook Rd. (See Route Guide for Arkville–Seager.) This is also 5.5 mi. E of the Mill Brook Rd. jct. with Old NY 30 on the S side of Pepacton Reservoir. The west access is 0.3 mi. farther W on Mill Brook Rd. Enter the east access road and drive 0.1 mi. to the picnic and parking area. A 10-car parking area was constructed on the S side of Mill Brook Rd. in 1992.

The trailhead (0.0 mi.) is at a barrier located to the L of the picnic area. The hardscrabble road climbs gradually S past apple trees and old stone walls. There is a trail register at 0.25 mi. The relatively flat route passes a woods road jct. at 0.3 mi. On the R the slope drops off into a deep ravine. The grassy lane reaches the Short Loop jct. at 0.5 mi. (This short-cut crosses a stream as it descends 0.15 mi. to a wooden bridge over a second stream at Halfway Point. It then climbs steeply to rejoin the Long Loop at its 2.6 mi. point.)

The Long Loop continues S, sometimes on rocky ground, sometimes over grass or pine needles. Tall pines surround you. It reaches a bridge at 1.0 mi., skirts a bog, and continues through the pine forest to a second bridge at 1.15 mi. Swinging W and staying on contour, the trail then winds back to the N and NW. There is a spring in a wet spot at 1.71 mi.

A climb up a moderate rise and one final pitch-up lead to the Kelly Hollow lean-to, only 450 ft. in elevation above the trailhead. It sits in an attractive spot beside Beaver Pond. A good fireplace and a privy are provided. There is evidence of past beaver activity.

The trail circles the pond, crosses its inlet at 2.05 mi., and then heads N. Soon it descends. The jct. of the Short Loop at 2.6 mi. provides two options for completing the trip.

Continuing N past the jct., the trail drops quickly and then levels to cross another bridge at 2.7 mi. It again descends steeply, over rocks that are probably flooded by spring meltoffs.

The trail finally levels at 3.1 mi. and swings NW past stone walls at 3.2 mi. It reaches a barrier and passes a small cemetery at 3.3 mi. There are several nice campsites beneath large evergreens before the west access point on Mill Brook Rd. at 3.4 mi. where the brook is crossed. The trail returns to the E access parking area in 0.25 mi. through an attractive conifer forest.

Distances: *To Short Loop jct., 0.5 mi.; to bridge, 1.0 mi.; to spring, 1.7 mi.; to lean-to, 1.9 mi.; to second Short Loop jct., 2.6 mi.; to west access point, 3.4 mi.; to parking area, 3.8 mi. (6.1 km) for Long Loop; 2.0 mi. (3.2 km) for Short Loop.*

(64) Rider Hollow Trail (W end of the Oliverea–Mapledale Trail)

Map 42: H-5
Central Catskills

The first mile of the Rider Hollow Trail is one of the prettiest in the Catskills. The trail connects to the Biscuit Brook–Pine Hill Trail, which permits a variety of hike options of varying difficulty.

Trailhead: *Access to the Rider Hollow Trail is from Mapledale on the Dry Brook Rd. (See Route Guide for Arkville–Seager.) Turn E on Rider Hollow Rd. (Co. Rd. 49A). You may notice red trail markers as you drive to the trailhead. Bear R at the Todd Hill Rd. fork at 0.5 mi. and then turn R at the Old Baker Rd. at 1.4 mi. Continue on Rider Rd. It becomes a dirt road at 2.2 mi. and narrows. Bear L at a fork at 2.4 mi. to a very large DEC parking area at the end of the road at 2.6 mi.*

A gate and trail register are found at the far end of the parking area. The level trail leaves the gate (0.0 mi.) and follows red trail markers along the S side of Rider Hollow Brook. At .07 mi. the trail turns L, crosses the brook on a series of stepping stones and continues along an old woods road, which crossed the stream at a different place. The nearly level route reaches a clearing where a lean-to once stood at 0.3 mi.

The trail continues upstream. A pipe brings spring water from the opposite side of the stream, 100 ft. before a jct. is reached at 0.35 mi. Here, the yellow-marked Mine Hollow Trail (see below) continues straight ahead from the DEC signpost. The red-marked Rider Hollow Trail crosses to the S side of the stream on a bridge, turns L, and reaches the Rider Hollow Lean-to at 0.5 mi.

The trail recrosses the stream on rocks (easy in summer, but difficult at high water) at 0.55 mi. From there it follows a wide woods road up a gradual grade until it is high above the water. It moves out of sight of the stream before descending to the water's edge.

Where a tributary joins the stream at 0.95 mi., the trail crosses the brook and starts to climb the side of the ridge. The character of the trail changes from that of an almost idyllic glen to that of a tough climb. Long pants are a good idea to protect oneself from the nettles that will be encountered along the way.

The grade is steady and moderate. It gains 750 ft. elevation before leveling again. A spring is on the R, at 1.65 mi.

The slope eases before pitching up a 10-ft. rock massif. A side trail R leads to a water source at the base of the massif. The 4-way jct. with the Biscuit Brook–Pine Hill Trail (see Big Indian–Upper Neversink section) is 100 ft. farther along the trail at 1.75 mi.

Here, from the spine of the ridge, the McKenley Hollow Trail (see Big Indian–Upper Neversink section) continues straight ahead with red trail markers, descending steeply 1.85 mi. to McKenley Hollow.

A lean-to is located at the base of the hollow. Balsam Mt. is L and Haynes Mt. is R on the blue-marked Biscuit Brook–Pine Hill Trail.

Distances: *To Mine Hollow jct., 0.35 mi.; to Rider Hollow lean-to, 0.5 mi.; to base of steep section, 0.95 mi.; to spring, 1.65 mi.; to Biscuit Brook–Pine Hill Trail jct., 1.75 mi. (2.8 km). Ridge elevation, 3050 ft. (915 m). Ascent, 1060 ft. (318 m).*

(65) Mine Hollow Trail

Mine Hollow Trail is a connector trail from the Rider Hollow Trail to the Biscuit Brook–Pine Hill Trail (trail 43). It makes possible an excellent loop for Rider Hollow to Balsam Mt. daytrippers and also gives backpackers from Rider Hollow a way around Balsam Mt. if heading N. At one time there was thought to be gold in this hollow, but a mine yielded none.

Trailhead: *Access is from a jct. at the 0.35 mi. point of the Rider Hollow Trail, below the Rider Hollow lean-to.*

The trail follows the N bank of Rider Hollow Brook to 0.1 mi., where it bears L along Mine Hollow Brook. Gradual, moderate and eventually steep grades take the trail higher and higher above the brook. The route is well designed, though strenuous with a backpack. It slabs higher, pulling away from the brook at 0.4 mi. and then swings N.

A small boulder at 0.65 mi. invites a rest; a brief respite in grade provides welcome relief. The grade becomes moderate again at 0.9 mi. The trail bears R around a large rock outcrop at 0.95 mi., pitching up to the level jct. with the Biscuit Brook–Pine Hill Trail

(trail 43) at 1.0 mi. (Go R, 1.3 mi. to Balsam Mt. and L, 0.9 mi. to Belleayre Mt.)

Distances: *To Mine Hollow Brook, 0.1 mi.; to departure from brook, 0.4 mi.; to small boulder 0.65 mi.; to rock outcrop 0.95 mi.; to Biscuit Brook–Pine Hill jct., 1.0 mi (1.6 km). Ascent from Rider Hollow jct., 800 ft (240 m).*

(66) Seager Trail

Map 42: H-6 to I-6
Central Catskills

The Seager Trail follows Dry Brook and its tributary, Shandaken Brook, up to a jct. with the Biscuit Brook–Pine Hill Trail (trail 43), between Eagle and Big Indian mts. It provides several hiking options in conjunction with other trails, and is a good winter ascent route. However, it entails several brook crossings without bridges.

Trailhead: *Access to the trailhead is at the end of the Dry Brook Rd. from Arkville. (See Route Guide for Arkville–Seager.) Park at the large turnabout at the road's end in Seager.*

The trail leaves the turnabout (0.0 mi.) passes a trail register and heads SE on private land along a woods road with yellow trail markers. The grassy lane parallels the W side of Dry Brook, making a wide bend R at 0.1 mi. The trail sidles along the bank for a short distance at 0.25 mi., where there is a washout, and crosses a rocky tributary from Drury Hollow. The trail soon reaches a wide, flat section and rejoins the old woods road as it goes through a grassy woods by the brook.

At 0.7 mi. the trail leaves the road at a ford and climbs R up a small mound to another woods road. The trail crosses Flatiron Brook just as it enters Dry Brook at 0.85 mi. A very attractive waterfall is immediately upstream on Dry Brook.

The trail levels and reaches a jct. with DEC distance signs at 1.0

mi. Here a private road crosses Dry Brook on a wooden bridge. Beautiful waterfalls cascade above and under the bridge. This is the place where many hikers begin the bushwhack up Doubletop Mt. The hiking trail stays on the W side of Dry Brook and passes a cobble section.

At 1.1 mi. the trail branches R at another ford. At 1.2 mi., it crosses the creek. (This is easy in dry weather but difficult at high-water periods.) There is a DEC sign on the far bank. Do not follow the woods road by the sign, but rather head E up the slope to a second woods road that follows above the N bank of Shandaken Brook. (Be careful not to pass this spot on the return trip.)

The grade is gradual and provides very comfortable hiking. At 1.5 mi. the route forks L above the creek. Then, at 1.6 mi., it drops down and crosses to the S side of Shandaken Brook. The woods road climbs a curving grade to 1.65 mi., where it forks R on cobble. The route becomes grassy again and enters state land at 2.0 mi. where it passes through an open birch, beech, and maple forest.

The trail returns to Shandaken Brook at 2.15 mi. and crosses it. Shandaken lean-to is on the opposite bank in an open wooded flat area above the water. A pipe with spring water comes out of the far side of the brook bank.

The trail leaves the R rear of the lean-to and starts a diagonal ascent, edging away from the water. Soon it is a steady, moderate upgrade, working its way up the ridge to the E. To this point the grades have been minimal, but over 600 ft. elevation is gained in the next 0.9 mi. The route eases in slope at 2.4 mi., actually drops a little, and then becomes a steep climb. At 2.7 mi., the path finally levels and becomes an enjoyable rolling footpath with a few short pitches.

The Biscuit Brook–Pine Hill Trail (trail 43) jct. (see Big Indian–Upper Neversink section) is reached at 3.0 mi. Big Indian Mt. is S on the blue-marked trail; Eagle Mt. is N. You may be able to locate a faint old trail that drops down to Burnham Rd. to the E.

Distances: *To Drury Hollow Brook, 0.6 mi.; to Flatiron Brook, 0.85 mi.; to lean-to, 2.15 mi.; to Biscuit Brook–Pine Hill Trail jct., 3.0 mi. (4.9 km). Jct. elevation, 3110 ft. (933 m). Ascent from trailhead, 1110 ft. (333 m).*

Delaware–Beaver Kill Section

The Delaware–Beaver Kill section of the Catskills has always been a mystery. Source of the Delaware River (named after a colonial governor of Virginia, Lord De La Warr), the region was argued over in the courts for years because various patent boundaries could not be positively identified. The Delaware's sources include the West Branch of the Delaware, Little Delaware, East Branch of the Delaware, Beaver Kill, Willowemoc Creek, Mongaup River, and East and West branches of the Neversink. Which of these is the fabled "Fish Kill" of patent arguments is not known, but the trails of this section visit many of these waters.

This is the land from which the mainmast of the ship *Constitution* (*Old Ironsides*) was cut. Here are the waters for which the great trout fisherman Theodore Gordon invented the dry fly.

Though this is a beautiful land and a wild part of the Catskills, its road network wanders from county to county, the roads changing names and numbers at each border. Hikers should study their maps well, use the Route Guides provided in this book, and have a full tank of gas. Many of the best hikes are through trips requiring two vehicles. The trails often cross ridgelines from valley to valley; the trailheads are generally much farther apart by connecting roads than by trail.

That understood, there are many excellent trails where few other hikers will disturb your solitude. Extensive backpack trips are possible on connecting short trails and what is collectively known as the Delaware Ridge Trail. (See chapter on Extended and Challenging Opportunities.) One has to work a little harder to reach many of these trailheads, but the rewards are commensurate with the efforts.

Trail in winter: These trails are somewhat isolated and thus not as utilized in winter as they might be otherwise. However, they are excellent for skiing. The trails of the Beech Mountain Nature Preserve and the Forest Preserve lands adjacent to them are especially good.

Short Hikes:

Little Pond—*3.0 mi. round trip. Walk the grounds of an abandoned farm area around ponds and open fields; turn back when the climbing gets steep.*

Long Pond Loop—*4.4 mi. loop. Take a woods walk to a lean-to along old roads and enjoy the forest.*

Alder Lake—*1.5 mi. A woods walk seldom out of view of the lake. Pleasant wildlife and good for photography.*

Frick Pond Loop—*2.2 mi. Frick Pond is a beautiful pond with many plants and birds to see.*

Moderate Hikes:

Balsam Lake Mt. Loop—*4.35 mi. loop. The trail leads up to a fire tower summit in the center of a wild forest.*

Pelnor Hollow–Campbell Mt. Trails to NY 206—*7.4 mi. through trip. Walk a wooded ridge and climb a mountain, but be sure you're up to it.*

Trout Pond–Mud Pond Loop—*3.9 mi. loop. Visit some nice ponds and do a little woods road walking over a ridge. Take a fishing pole or a camera.*

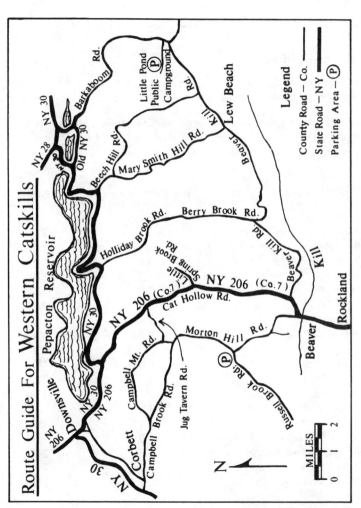

Route Guide For Western Catskills

Legend
County Road — Co. ——
State Road — NY ━━
Parking Area — Ⓟ

N

MILES
0   1   2

Big Loop—*6.3 mi. An easy woods road hike with many things to see.*

Harder Hike:

Beaver Kill Ridge Loop—*10.55 mi. loop. A marvelous woods walk over several small mountains and on parts of several trails.*

Delaware Ridge—*25.7 mi. through trip. Go from Alder Lake to Trout Pond by several connecting trails. Take your time because this one is a hard backpack.*

Trail Described	Total Miles (one way)	Page
Alder Lake Loop	1.5	213
Alder Lake to Big Pond	2.9	215
Big Pond to Touch-me-not Trail	1.1	217
Touch-me-not	3.5	218
Little Pond	1.8	220
Middle Mt.	2.0	222
Mary Smith	4.5	223
Huggins Lake	1.7	225
Pelnor Hollow	4.0	226
Campbell Mt.	5.8	228
Little Spring Brook	0.6	231
Trout Pond	5.4	232
Mud Pond	2.4	234
Trout Pond–Mud Pond Loop	3.9	235
Long Pond Loop	4.4	236
Long Pond–Beaver Kill Ridge	3.0	238
Mongaup–Hardenburgh	6.4	239
Balsam Lake Mt. Loop	4.35	241
Mill Brook Ridge	5.8	317

ROUTE GUIDE FOR MARGARETVILLE–DOWNSVILLE

Mileage W to E	Description	Mileage E to W
0.0	Traffic light, Margaretville NY 30; turn E for Pepacton Reservoir.	27.0
0.1	Turn R if driving W on NY 30; turn L if driving E on NY 30.	26.9
2.8	E. Branch Delaware River	24.2
3.6	Jct. NY 28 and NY 30. Turn L on NY 30 if driving W; turn R on NY 30 if driving E.	23.4
12.0	NY 30 bridge across Pepacton Reservoir. NY 30 continues past the bridge. Jct. on S side of bridge is Old NY 30, which runs 1.9 mi. E to Barkaboom Rd.	15.0
14.4	Beech Hill Rd.	12.6
19.0	Holiday and Berry Brook Rd.	8.0
20.9	Miller Hollow Rd.	6.1
23.8	Jct. NY 30 (Co. Rd. 7) turns S.	3.2
26.0	E. Branch Delaware River	1.0
27.0	NY 30 and NY 206; traffic light; Downsville.	0.0

ROUTE GUIDE FOR LIVINGSTON MANOR–CLARYVILLE

Mileage W to E	Description	Mileage E to W
0.0	Livingston Manor, jct. Old NY 17 (Co. Rd. 179) and DeBruce Rd. (Co. Rd. 81). DeBruce Rd. runs NE under NY 17 and passes Willowemoc Motel.	16.8
2.4	Cross bridge; DeBruce Rd. is Sullivan Co. 82.	14.4
5.6	Sign for DeBruce if driving E; Sullivan Co. 82 now Sullivan Co. 83 if driving E.	11.2
6.0	Cross bridge.	10.8
6.05	Rd. N is Mongaup Rd.; Mongaup Pond Public Campgrounds 3.9 mi. on this rd.	10.75
	DeBruce Rd. is now Willowemoc Rd. if driving E.	
9.6	Large bridge over Willowemoc Creek in hamlet of Willowemoc	7.2
9.7	Jct. Rd. S to Parksville; continue E.	7.1
9.8	Jct. Rd. S to Parksville; continue E.	7.0
10.5	Willowemoc Campsite	6.3
10.6	Bridge over Fir Brook; jct. at E end of bridge. If going to Long Pond–Beaver Kill Ridge Trail, turn N at jct. and immediately bear L again onto a second road. The second road is Flugertown Rd.; Willowemoc Rd. is now called Pole Rd.	6.2
14.2	Sullivan/Ulster Co. line	2.6
14.7	Round Pond on S side rd.	2.1
14.9	Jct. Turn R onto Round Pond Rd. if driving E; turn L onto Pole Rd. if driving W. Dirt roads.	1.9

Mileage W to E	Description	Mileage E to W
15.5	Jct. Round Pond Rd. and West Branch Rd. (Co. Rd. 47). Turn R if driving E; turn L if driving W (Round Pond Rd. is not marked and is dirt). Ulster Co. Rd. 47 becomes Sullivan Co. Rd. 157.	1.3
16.8	Claryville bridge over E Branch of Neversink River; jct. Co. Rd. 157 and Co. Rd. 19.	0.0

ROUTE GUIDE FOR BEAVER KILL RD.–QUAKER CLEARING

Unmarked Beaver Kill Rd. runs E from a jct. with NY 206 (Co. Rd.7) 2.8 mi. N of the village of Roscoe traffic light and 4.0 mi. N of the bridge over Beaver Kill Creek. It is also 3.2 mi. S of the Little Spring Rd. jct. on NY 206. Beaver Kill Rd. runs through parts of three counties to Quaker Clearing and the parking area at the Balsam Lake Mt. trailhead.

Mileage W to E	Description	Mileage E to W
0.0	Beaver Kill Rd. and NY 206 (Co. Rd. 7) jct.	22.3
0.5	Delaware/Sullivan Co. line	21.8
2.1	Jct.—do not cross bridge. Continue straight ahead; Prince Hall Masonic Home is here.	20.2
3.1	Jct. Unmarked Pelnor Hollow Rd. turns N and climbs hill on dirt rd.	19.2
4.3	Jct. Holiday and Berry Brook Rd. goes N, straight ahead. Beaver Kill Rd. makes a hard turn S if driving E, a hard turn W if driving W.	18.0

Mileage W to E	Description	Mileage E to W
5.3	Beaver Kill Public Campground on S side of rd.	17.0
5.5	Beaver Kill village. Pass through covered bridge and then turn R if going E; turn L and go through covered bridge and bear L if going W.	16.8
5.7	Jct. Turn L if going E; turn R if going W.	16.6
6.2	Jct. Co. Rd. 152. Turn L if going E; turn R, towards Beaver Kill, if going E.	16.1
6.3	Jct. Continue past Elm Hollow Rd.	16.0
9.2	Jct., Lew Beach; Mary Smith Hill Rd. goes N, from E side of Shin Creek bridge; Beaver Kill Rd. goes straight past intersection.	13.1
10.1	Sullivan/Ulster Co. line	12.2
10.8	Jct. Beach Hill Rd. goes N.	11.5
12.9	Jct. Barkaboom Rd. goes N. Little Pond Public Campground's entrance road is 0.2 mi. up Barkaboom Rd.	9.4
14.3	Jct. at Turnwood; Co. Rd. 54 N goes 2.6 mi. to Alder Lake.	8.0
16.0	Road unpaved to E; paved to W.	6.3
17.4	Hardenburgh hamlet	4.9
18.3	Huge estate, S side of rd.	4.0
19.3	Zen Studies Society International building, N side of rd.	3.0
20.3	Mongaup–Hardenburg Pond Trailhead and DEC parking area, S side rd.	2.0
21.1	Quaker Clearing; DEC signpost; Neversink–Hardenburgh Trailhead, S side of rd. (soon to be moved to below).	1.2
22.3	DEC Balsam Lake Mt. Trailhead parking area	0.0

(67) Alder Lake Loop

Alder Lake is a nice place for an afternoon walk, a picnic or perhaps some modest canoeing. It has several designated campsites that are well-spaced to provide a degree of privacy. Fishing is allowed with worms or artificial lures only.

Trailhead: *Using the* Route Guide *for Beaver Kill Rd.–Quaker Clearing on pages 211–212, turn N onto Co. Rd. 54 at the jct. at Turnwood. This is at the 14.3 mi. (W-E) point of the route guide. Drive 2.6 mi. to the road's end at the entrance of the Cross Mt. camp entrance road (Old Edwards Rd.). Bear R at this curve. A second jct. immediately confronts you. DO NOT go up the hill; bear R instead. The next 0.4 mi. is gravel road which terminates at the Alder Lake Trailhead parking area. There is room on the L for several vehicles to park.*

Beyond the barrier gate are a sign and trail register. Follow the roadway past the barrier a short distance to the remains of the old Coykendall Lodge. Turn R and follow a path down a grade to the lake shore, a dam and a DEC signpost 0.1 mi. from the barrier gate. This is the trailhead of the Alder Lake Loop Trail.

From the DEC signpost (0.0 mi.), turn N (away from the dam) and follow the shoreline path around the lake. At just under 0.1 mi., the first of three well-spaced designated campsite side trails is reached. Soon after, red trail markers are seen; these should be followed on this trail. The attractive trail continues past some high bushes to another designated campsite at 0.45 mi. before crossing a bridge at 0.5 mi. A second bridge is crossed 200 ft. farther along the trail and then the route edges away from the lake and gradually climbs.

Bear L at a narrow fork at 0.6 mi., and 20 ft. farther bear R onto a broad woods road. The woods road gradually ascends a grade and bears R again at each of two forks. The second fork is at the top of the knoll, where the trail reaches a jct. with the Mill Brook Ridge Trail (trail 83A) at 0.7 mi. (This yellow-marked trail ascends 1.5 mi. to a lean-to and then continues over Mill Brook Ridge to Balsam Lake Mt., 6.0 mi. E.) The trail then quickly drops down to a large bridge which crosses the major lake inlet at 0.75 mi.

Though hard to spot unless one is looking for it, there is a very pleasant designated campsite some 100 ft. along the trail from the bridge and R, 250 ft. in the woods toward the lake.

The level trail soon begins to climb gradually again at 0.8 mi., briefly levels, and then gradually ascends to a height of land at 1.0 mi. The route is now well above the lake level and some 200-250 ft. from the shore, though the lake is easily viewed through the trees.

Gradual descent brings you to a small bridge at 1.2 mi. Then a slight upgrade leads to a side path to the R and another designated campsite. Soon the route passes through a small woods opening and joins another woods road. Bear R, following arrow signs. The woods road curves down to the L corner of an open field, turns sharply R and follows the edge of the woods back to the lake's outlet dam.

(If one turns R just before reaching the metal railing at the dam approach and walks approximately 300 ft. across the open field to a path leading up the hill into the woods, the first of two more designated campsites will be reached.)

The route crosses the dam on a wide walkway. The trailhead DEC signpost is reached at 1.5 mi.

Trail in winter: *This is an excellent trail for skiing. There are several other woods roads along the trail which might also be interesting to explore on skis.*

Distances: *To first designated campsite, 0.1 mi.; to jct. with Mill Brook Ridge Trail, 0.7 mi.; to large bridge at dam inlet, 0.75 mi.; to height of land, 1.0 mi.; to completion of trail loop, 1.5 mi. (2.4 km).*

(68) Alder Lake to Big Pond

This trail is an extension of the series of short trails that permits a backpacker to hike across Delaware County to Trout Pond. It wanders from one to another old woods road across ridges from near Alder Lake to Big Pond.

Trailhead: *Follow the trail access directions for the Alder Lake Loop (trail 67) to the 2.6 mi. point on Co. Rd. 54, where the Cross Mt. camp entrance rd. is reached. The trail begins 75 ft. S of this entrance road. A few vehicles can be parked on a wide shoudler, just around the curve from the trailhead.*

From the trailhead (0.0 mi.) on the W side of Co. Rd. 54, red trail markers lead down a short grade and across Alder Creek to a flat path which heads downstream. At 0.1 mi., the path zig-zags and then begins a moderate ascent up a wide old woods road. It soon makes a sweeping curve NW, becoming a gradual upgrade generally to the W.

The route levels at 0.4 mi., running roughly parallel to the ridge, having gained about 250 ft. elevation from the trailhead. Posted signs are found on the uphill side of the trail at 0.5 mi. and there are also 10-15 ft. cliffs.

Bear L (W) at 0.6 mi., where arrow signs at a 3-way jct. point the way. Then, at 0.7 mi., the nearly level height of land suddenly drops down a short moderate grade, passes through a small field and, with more arrow signs, makes an abrupt L turn S in woods.

The route soon swings SSW and back to the S again, beginning a long gradual downgrade on a woods road. Another small clearing is seen R as the route continues descent to an arrow sign very near the bottom of the grade in a tributary valley of Alder Creek. Here, the arrow sign points R and the trail crosses a brook at 1.15 mi. on a rock bridge made of immense rock slabs. Another woods road leads WSW up a gradual and then moderate grade. Having lost over 200 ft. elevation in the descent, the trail now regains it and more until it nearly levels out at about 1.5 mi. Several stone walls are seen during the ascent, suggesting an agricultural past for this land.

The SW route curves slightly R at 1.7 mi., where the unobservant hiker may unwittingly follow a fork road L and head back downhill. AVOID THIS.

The trail becomes a path again and begins to swing from SW to NW at 1.9 mi. Ascending a gentle grade, height of land is finally reached at 2.0 mi. and 2550 ft. elevation. Here, the trail begins a downgrade toward Barkaboom Rd. and Big Pond. The path direction is now WNW, becoming moderate in grade.

The remainder of the trail is unusual in two respects. First, there are two small groves of spruces, which are relatively rare in Delaware County. Second, the person who designed the trail took advantage of the even slope and built a series of long switchbacks. Such lengthy switchbacks are common on trails in the western United States but are quite rare in the East. This excellent design makes a stubborn grade into a pleasant stroll to Big Pond.

The trail winds N and then W before heading NW through a spruce grove at 2.2 mi. It then heads N through open deciduous forest, where the hiker must keep the trail markers in sight. Another spruce grove is found at 2.3 mi. and the NW route swings W, NW and finally SW. At 2.4 mi. the trail joins a woods road where it makes an acute turn R and gradually descends to the N.

At 2.6 mi., the trail curves to the SW and descends a moderate grade along a deeply worn rocky woods road. (If traveling in the opposite direction, be careful to avoid going onto a narrow path NE at this curve.)

At the bottom of the grade, the trail turns R, crosses a small creek valley floor and climbs quickly to an open field. The level trail now follows the L edge of the field to another field and then down a small grade to the rear of a large parking area at 2.9 mi. Big Pond can be seen through the trees to the N. Two faint trails lead from the NE corner of the parking area, near the yellow metal barrier gate, to designated campsites at Big Pond.

A gravel road leads 350 ft. to Barkaboom Rd. There is a second parking area 500 ft. N on the road at the shore of Big Pond. The Big Pond to Touch-me-not Trail (trail 69) begins along Barkaboom Rd., 100 ft. N of the trail register at this parking area.

Distances: *To first arrow jct., 0.6 mi.; to first height of land, 0.7 mi.; to rock bridge in tributary valley, 1.15 mi.; to second height of land, 2.0 mi.; to acute jct. where woods path meets woods road, 2.4 mi.; to parking area near Big Pond, 2.9 mi. (4.7 km).*

(69) Big Pond to Touch-me-not Trail

Map 44: E-6
Western Catskills

This short trail steeply ascends the shoulder of Touch-me-not Mt. to join the Touch-me-not Trail (trail 70).

Trailhead: *Follow the* Route Guide *for Beaver Kill Rd.–Quaker Clearing (see pages 211–212) to the Barkaboom Rd. jct. at the 12.9 mi. (W-E) point of the route. Turn N and travel 0.9 mi. to a large parking area at Big Pond. There is a trail register and exhibit board at this parking area. The trailhead is 100 ft. farther N on the W side of Barkaboom Rd. (A gravel road 0.1 mi. S on Barkaboom Rd. leads 350 ft. to a second parking area for the Alder Lake to Big Pond Trail [trail 68] trailhead.)*

From the trailhead (0.0 mi.), the route climbs 175 ft. up a very steep slope with red trail markers before turning sharply R. For the remainder of the climb, the trail is mostly NW with occasional swings NNW or W. The climbing is continuous, alternating from gradual to moderate in slope.

At 0.4 mi., the open trail narrows to a path and the hiker must pay more attention to trail markers. Then, at 0.6 mi., the route heads W for a short distance and becomes steep. From this point to 1.0 mi., climbing is either steep or moderate, until the trail finally levels on the ridge crest.

Heading NW from the crest, the path gradually descends and reaches the Touch-me-not Trail (trail 70) jct. at 1.1 mi. The tree-covered summit of Touch-me-not Mt. is 0.1 mi. S from this jct. Cabot Mt. summit is 1.3 mi. NW along the Touch-me-not Trail.

Distances: *To where trail narrows, 0.4 mi.; to where trail becomes steep, 0.6 mi.; to ridge crest, 1.0 mi.; to Touch-me-not Trail jct., 1.1 mi. (1.8 km).*

(70) Touch-me-not Trail

Map 44: E-6
Western Catskills

This is a rugged trail that makes a nice hike. Often, part of it is combined with the Little Pond Trail (trail 71) to make a loop route from the Little Pond Public Campground. A swim and a picnic can climax the day.

Trailhead: *Trail access is at the Little Pond Public Campground. The campground is 0.9 mi. off Barkaboom Rd., 0.2 mi. N of Beaver Kill Rd. (See Route Guides for this chapter.) About 0.1 mi. beyond the campground toll booth, and just beyond the pond's outlet dam, is a parking area. From the N end of the parking area, walk along the macadam path between the showers and the bath house to a trail register at the rear of the bath house.*

From the trail register (0.0 mi.), go R 30 ft. to a red-marked trail that enters the woods. The trail immediately climbs a moderate grade to the NE. The slope continues for 0.3 mi. and then gets steeper until it nears the ridgeline.

The trail becomes rock, ascending through cuts in rock outcrops at 0.6 mi. At 0.7 mi., the route flattens out on the 2760-ft. summit of Touch-me-not Mt. Little Pond can be seen through the trees to the S, but viewing is not good. The trail descends slightly to a jct. at 0.8 mi. where the trail from Big Pond enters.

The path is generally flat until it drops through a cleft in a cliff edge at 1.05 mi. Stay to the L as you descend and then bear L at the base. At 1.1 mi. the trail turns sharply R and then L. Take care to watch trail markers in this section.

The trail drops over another ledge at 1.15 mi. and continues to descend to 2450 ft. before climbing over a small rise at 1.45 mi. The yellow-marked Little Pond Trail (trail 71) (see below) enters from the L at a jct. at 1.5 mi. (A loop hike can be made by returning to the campground on this trail.)

Beyond the jct. the trail is nearly level, with interspersed pitch-ups. It follows contour at 1.65 mi. and then begins to ascend Cabot Mt. at 1.75 mi. The route then turns R and becomes relatively steep. Becoming very steep at 1.85 mi., the trail climbs around a cliff face.

Finally, at 2.05 mi., the mountain levels. As the trail heads SW along the edge of the ridge, a rock outcrop at L at 2.1 mi. provides a panoramic view S. Touch-me-not Mt., Little Pond and countryside all the way to Slide Mt. stand out. Cabot Mt.'s summit is at 2970 ft. elevation. At one time, it was called Hunt Hill. This is a good place for a long rest.

From the lookout, the wide trail curves around the mountaintop to the NW. From time to time, it meets and leaves another, wider, unmarked trail. The hiking trail descends at 2.4 mi. while the other trail stays on a level track. At 2.9 mi., the trail drops steeply into the

Beech Hill Rd. valley.

The trail moderates at 3.1 mi., entering a narrow public land corridor that is posted on each side. The rate of descent lessens before the Beech Hill Rd. trailhead sign at 3.5 mi. (It is difficult to see this sign from vehicles if coming from the S. There is a wide spot here where cars can be parked.) NY 30 is 3.7 mi. N; Beaver Kill Rd. is 2.6 mi. S. The Middle Mt. (trail 72) trailhead is 0.2 mi. N on Beech Hill Rd.

Distances: *To summit of Touch-me-not Mt., 0.7 mi.; to jct. of Big Pond to Touch-me-not Trail, 0.8 mi.; to jct. of Little Pond Trail, 1.5 mi.; to lookout at Cabot Mt., 2.1 mi.; to moderate descent off mt., 2.4 mi.; to Beech Hill Rd. trailhead, 3.5 mi. (5.7 km).*

(71) Little Pond Trail

Map 44: D-5
Western Catskills

The first part of the Little Pond Trail is a lovely woods road walk through an abandoned farm, by fields that have yet to turn back into woods. The many ferns to enjoy, stone walls to admire, berries to pick, and excellent views of Touch-me-not Mt. enhance your day. Myriad different flowers and trees welcome the hiker.

Many hikers travel only in this section. Those seeking more rugged climbing can continue up the last section of this trail and return to the campgrounds via part of the Touch-me-not Trail (see above). This description begins with a path around the E side of Little Pond, joining the Little Pond Trail at its 0.2 mi. point.

Trailhead: *For access to the trailhead, use the same directions given for the Touch-me-not Trail (trail 70), above. From the trail register (0.0 mi.) at the rear of the bath house mentioned in that trail description, walk L, following* *yellow trail markers. The trail winds around the E side of Little Pond, passing near campsites. It avoids wet spots by moving away from the shoreline when necessary. Campsites on the E shoreline must be reached by boat.*

At 0.4 mi., the trail crosses the inlet of Little Pond on a bridge. Then yellow arrow signs point R. (Yellow trail markers also go L, 0.2 mi. to the official starting point of the Little Pond Trail at the NW corner of the pond.)

A short pitch-up quickly becomes a gradual grade along the W side of the inlet stream, still following yellow trail markers. An old beaver pond R at 0.7 mi. is evidence of past beaver activity, but no beaver house is seen.

The woods road continues uphill to a series of meadows and tree plantations. Becoming grassy, the roadway runs N along the W side of a meadow whose side is bordered by spruce.

The route climbs a gentle slope, now with a pine plantation L. At one point, Touch-me-not Mt. can be seen to the rear. Past a stone wall near 1.2 mi. the old roadway continues through another meadow. There is a pond L at 1.3 mi. Then, at 1.5 mi., the trail leads through a grassy area up to a higher viewing spot, where a sweeping vista of almost 180 degrees greets the hiker.

The trail curves NE and abruptly changes its character. Soon swinging back NW, it becomes steep and then very steep before reaching the Touch-me-not Trail (trail 70) jct. at 1.8 mi. (Turning R, this trail climbs Touch-me-not Mt., and returns 1.5 mi. to the campground trail register, where your trip began (if following this route, be careful to avoid the Big Pond Trail L, near the summit of Touch-me-Not); turning L, it ascends Cabot Mt. and reaches Beech Hill Rd. in 2.0 mi. See above.) Though short, both sections of the Touch-me-not Trail are rugged. Experienced hikers should have no trouble, but novices may find the trail more strenuous than anticipated.

Distances: *To pond inlet, 0.4 mi.; to beaver pond, 0.9 mi.; to stone wall, 1.2 mi.; to lookout vista, 1.5 mi.; to Touch-me-not Trail jct., 1.8 mi. (2.9 km). Ascent, 540 ft. (162 m).*

(72) Middle Mt. Trail

Map 44: D-6
Western Catskills

This is a short trail probably best done in conjunction with connecting trails to make a full day's outing.

Trailhead: *The trailhead is at the jct. of a dirt road on the W side of Beech Hill Rd. From NY 30, it is S 3.5 mi. (partially unpaved) along Beech Hill Rd.; from Beaver Kill Rd., it is N 2.8 mi. (See Route Guides for this chapter.) There is room to park on the shoulder of the road at this jct. or you can drive 0.1 mi. W on the trailhead dirt road to park. The Middle Mt. trailhead is 0.2 mi. N of the Touch-me-not Mt. (trail 70) trailhead.*

From the Beech Hill Rd. trailhead (0.0 mi.) walk W, following red trail markers. Bear L at a trail sign at 0.05 mi. and continue over the level, loose rock route.

Steep climbing begins at 0.3 mi. and continues to the summit of Beech Hill (2884 ft.) at 0.5 mi. Ascent from the trailhead is 594 ft. There are no beech and there is no view.

A gradual downgrade leads to a flat col at 0.7 mi. Level terrain pitches up at 0.8 mi. to a lookout point S at 0.9 mi., now mostly obscured by tree growth. The grade eases from there to the summit (2975 ft.) at 1.1 mi. Ascent from the col is 200 ft.

The summit is flat and through a berry patch to 1.35 mi., where the trail bears R and pitches downward. At 1.5 mi. it goes along the top of a rock outcrop, then turns and descends a small cliff. Descent resumes at a more moderate rate on loose rock.

Finally leveling out at 1.8 mi., the trail heads SW. It reaches the small parking area trailhead on Mary Smith Hill Rd. at 2.0 mi. Across the road, the Mary Smith Trail (trail 73) heads W. NY 30 is N, 2.2 mi. on partially unpaved Mary Smith Hill Rd. and then L, 1.1 mi. on Beech Hill Rd. Beaver Kill Rd. is S, 3.2 mi. on Mary Smith Hill Rd. (See *Route Guides* for this chapter.)

Distances: *To Beech Hill, 0.5 mi.; to Middle Mt. summit, 1.1 mi.; to Mary Smith Hill Rd., 2.0 mi. (3.2 km).*

(73) Mary Smith Trail

Map 44: C-6
Western Catskills

This trail runs E-W from the Middle Mt. Trail (trail 72) to the Pelnor Hollow Trail (trail 74). It crosses one road.

Trailhead: *Trail access is from the W side of the Mary Smith Hill Rd. From NY 30, travel 1.1 mi. up Beech Hill Rd., then fork R onto Mary Smith Hill Rd. and drive another 2.2 mi. on partially unpaved road to the trailhead. From Beaver Kill Rd., it is 3.2 mi., N on Mary Smith Hill Rd. (See the* Route Guides *for this chapter.) There is a small parking area on the E side of the road. (The Middle Mt. trail leaves the rear of this parking area.)*

The Mary Smith Trail is on the W side of the road across from the parking area. Leave the trailhead (0.0 mi.) and head W, following red trail markers through evergreen forest.

The trail soon turns L and begins a steep upgrade. Switchbacks climb to 0.3 mi., where the trail makes a sharp R. It moderates and reaches a viewing point S at 0.4 mi. in a fern-covered flat area. A series of alternating pitches and level zones leads up to a height of land at 0.8 mi.

The path then loses elevation to a flat area and, at 1.3 mi., pitches down. There is evidence of rock work on the trail at 1.5 mi. The trail is on the W edge of the ridge and presents good views in winter, when the leaves are off the trees.

The route drops nearly 150 ft. and makes a sharp L. Minor upgrades take it over another height of land near the summit of Mary Smith Hill.

The path swings L. A small spur trail at 2.2 mi. leads to a rock overlook. The route becomes nearly flat to a slight upgrade at 2.6 mi. The trail then goes down between rocks. There are sharp switchbacks L and R at 2.8 mi., leading to the top of a ledge, and then the path drops down a rocky area with loose rocks on the trail. The rate of descent moderates at 2.9 mi., but steepens again before leveling at 3.2 mi.

Holliday and Berry Brook Rd. intersect the trail at 3.3 mi., at the high point of the pass. There is room to park several vehicles on the E side of the Road. NY 30 is 3.0 mi. N; Beaver Kill Rd. is 3.6 mi. S (See the *Route Guides* for this chapter.)

The trail continues SW across the road. It crosses under a high power line at 3.4 mi.; the hiker is also walking over the East Delaware Aqueduct, which is far under the ground surface.

The trail re-enters the Forest Preserve at the woods line. The route bears R on a grassy road at 3.5 mi. and begins a gradual ascent which pitches upward at 3.6 mi. It flattens at 3.7 mi., runs through a young woods, and then passes a berry bramble at 3.9 mi. An arrow sign points R at 4.0 mi.

There is more berry bramble and the pathway climbs again. The terrain becomes more hilly at 4.3 mi. and remains steep to a jct. with the Pelnor Hollow Trail (trail 74) at 4.5 mi. Pelnor Hollow Rd. is 3.2 mi. S. A 3-way jct. with the Little Spring Brook Trail (trail 76) and the Campbell Mt. Trail (trail 75) is 0.8 mi. NW.

Distances: *To viewing point, 0.4 mi.; to first height of land, 0.8 mi.; to pitch down, 1.3 mi.; to lookout on Mary Smith Hill, 2.2 mi.; to Holliday and Berry Brook Rd., 3.3 mi.; to Pelnor Hollow jct., 4.5 mi. (7.3 km).*

Huggins Lake Trail (Unmaintained Trail)

Map 44: C-6
Western Catskills

The woods road to Huggins Lake makes a pleasant afternoon's walk to an attractive body of water. It makes a good cross-country ski trail.

Trailhead: *The trailhead is on the E side of Holliday and Berry Brook Rd. 4.5 mi. S of NY 30 and 1.8 mi. N of Beaver Kill Rd. (See the Route Guides for this chapter.) Any posted signs refer to land bordering the trail corridor near the start of the hike. The corridor to the lake and the lake itself are state-owned.*

Do not block the trailhead road. Park on the opposite side of the road.

The unmarked woods road leaves the trailhead (0.0 mi.) and gradually climbs 100 yds. to a gate in an open spot. Passing through the opening in the gate, continue along the grassy lane, which swings L at 0.1 mi. The young hardwood forest has many ferns.

The trail ascends gradually. At 0.4 mi. a woods road comes in sharply from the L and the hiking route also bears L. Leveling off at 0.7 mi., it has curved SE. It reaches a height of land at 1.15 mi., after some more easy climbing. There is a grassy spot at this point.

Beyond, the woods road is a gently rolling route from which Huggins Lake can be seen below to the L. The road swings sharply N at 1.5 mi. and descends to the S end of the lake. There is a dam (1993) at R and a bridge across Huggins Hollow Brook at 1.7 mi. A woods road runs along the W side of the brook. There are grassy areas beside the lake on the other side of the bridge and informal campsites around the shoreline. Another road runs around the E side of the lake and continues N. (In time, proposals may result in a trail along this road to connect with the Mary Smith Trail [see above].)

Distances: To height of land, 1.15 mi.; to descent to lake, 1.5 mi.; to Huggins Lake, 1.7 mi. (2.8 km).

(74) Pelnor Hollow Trail

Map 44: C-7 to C-6
Western Catskills

The Pelnor Hollow Trail is little used, except by hunters in autumn. This is unfortunate, because much of the route is attractive and Pelnor Hollow lean-to is one of the best in the Catskills. The trail makes a good day trip (through to NY 206) in conjunction with the Campbell Mt. Trail (trail 75).

Trailhead: Trailhead access is off the N side of Beaver Kill Rd. (See Route Guide for Beaver Kill Rd.–Quaker Clearing.) Unmarked and unpavd Pelnor Hollow Rd. climbs N at a fairly steep grade before nearly leveling. Best parking is on the road shoulder before reaching the official DEC trailhead, about 1.1 mi. from Beaver Kill Rd. just beyond a small farmhouse and large barn. It might be best to check with the landowner before leaving the vehicle. The remaining 0.4 mi. to the trailhead is first over a narrow loose rock section and then up a rough grade. The trailhead signpost and state land are just beyond the Dorset Sporting Club's camp, 1.5 mi. from Beaver Kill Rd.

From the trailhead (0.0 mi.),a grassy lane leads N, following blue trail markers. The level roadway reaches a small clearing at 0.3 mi., where a barrier gate blocks further advance. The trail bears L, angles up a slope from a DEC sign, and enters the woods. The route soon levels again, ascending only occasionally on very easy grades. The open sugar maple forest is most attractive.

Two stone cairns at 0.8 mi. mark a side trail R that leads down-slope to a very large pond (not shown on most maps). The trail continues N and reaches the Pelnor Hollow lean-to at 0.9 mi. Located in open woods, with the pond visible about 0.1 mi. downslope, this is a very pleasant spot. A trail leads E from the lean-to to a spring.

The trail beyond the rear of the lean-to is less maintained, but is still easy to follow. It ascends a short, moderate slope that soon becomes a gradual grade.

At 1.2 mi., the trail makes abrupt L and R turns. At 1.4 mi. a sign indicates snowmobiles should go no farther. The footpath climbs a short steep pitch, easing before a height of land at 1.8 mi. on an unnamed hill of 2672 ft. elevation. From there, it descends a moderate grade to 2.35 mi., where the route becomes a rocky woods road and soon levels. The hiker needs to watch trail markers at 2.5 mi. at a brief blowdown section.

Widely varying grades gain elevation before the trail reaches the Mary Smith Trail (trail 73) jct. at 3.2 mi. (The Mary Smith Trail heads NE, 1.2 mi. to Holliday and Berry Brook Rd.; see above.)

The trail turns NW, soon losing elevation on moderate and steep grades. At 3.35 mi. it makes a sharp R turn and is again level. There is a lookout W at this turn, but be careful on the rock outcrop.

The trail continues N, gradually losing altitude as it curves W and then S. Turning W again, the route pitches down and enters a beautiful pine and spruce plantation at 4.1 mi.

Watch the trail markers for a sharp L turn halfway through the stand. The route crosses a brook at 4.4 mi. before reaching a clearing with a 3-way jct. at 4.45 mi. Little Spring Brook Trail (trail 76) enters from the S; the Campbell Mt. Trail (trail 75) heads N towards NY 206 (see below). This large, open clearing sprinkled with apple trees is a good place to take a break and enjoy watching the butterflies and birds awhile.

Distances: *To clearing, 0.3 mi.; to lean-to, 0.9 mi.; to top of hill, 1.8 mi.; to Mary Smith Trail jct., 3.2 mi.; to steep loose rock descent, 3.45 mi.; to 3-way jct., 4.45 mi. (7.2 km).*

(75) Campbell Mt. Trail

Map 44: C-6 to B-6
Western Catskills

The Campbell Mt. Trail runs from valley to valley, climbing over Brock and Campbell mts. It is good hiking on a fairly rugged but well-maintained trail.

Trailhead: *The trail starts at the 3-way jct. with the Little Spring Brook and Pelnor Hollow trails. The easiest approach to the trailhead is N via the 0.6-mi. Little Spring Brook Trail (trail 76) (see below).*

The trail heads N from the DEC signpost (0.0 mi.), following blue trail markers. The nearly level grassy road soon begins a gradual descent, with fine stone walls bordering each side of the roadway. Don't miss the abrupt L-turn arrow sign at 0.3 mi., where the trail cuts through an opening in the wall and enters a conifer plantation.

The route climbs NW through pleasant forest at varying but comfortable grades. It levels for awhile at 0.55 mi. and then climbs again to 0.8 mi. where it turns S. At a high point at 1.1 mi., some 350 ft. elevation above the woods road with stone walls, Buck Mt. Club signs are affixed to trees.

The footpath now turns WNW, descending somewhat before it climbs a short, gradual grade to an intersection with the snowmobile trail from Miller Hollow at 1.4 mi. A sharp turn L is the beginning of a gradual ascent on a woods road. At 1.45 mi. the trail turns R, leaves the woods road, and pitches up a moderate grade. (A sign states that the Buck Mt. Viewpoint is another 0.1 mi. along the snowmobile trail road.)

The ascent of Brock Mt. continues steeply, with short level stretches, to 1.7 mi. The trail then bears L through a flat wet spot, where the top of Brock Mt. can be seen. Take care to watch trail markers in this section. Bearing R again, the route soon becomes very steep. Leveling off at a high point of ascent, some 50 ft. below the wooded top of Brock Mt. (2760 ft.), the trail passes through a thorny berry patch at 2.0 mi.

A moderate and then gradual grade drops down to a col and unmarked jct. at 2.4 mi. (The side trail L descends to NY 206.) The blue trail swings N and heads towards the other summit of Brock Mt., which it reaches by easy grades at 2.65 mi.

The last descent on the way to NY 206 now begins. Turn L at a woods road jct. at 2.7 mi. At 2.75 mi., a sign points to a downgrade that is gradual at the start but soon becomes steep. There are fewer trail markers but more orange paint blazes. At 3.1 mi., after a steep descent for 100 yds., the trail swings R. The path angles down a slope for the last 200 ft. to NY 206, at 3.4 mi. (This path is difficult to spot from the highway.) Across the road at a small signpost there is enough room for several vehicles to park, well off the road.

This trailhead is on the N side of a height of land on NY 206 (Co. Rd. 7). From NY 30 it is S, 2.2 mi. on NY 206. (See *Route Guide* for Margaretville–Downsville.) It is 3.0 mi. N of Little Spring Brook Rd. on NY 206. On some maps, NY 206 is called Cat Hollow Rd.

From the small trailhead post marker (3.4 mi.) on the W side of NY 206, the trail goes L down a woods road to a gate with a stop sign on it. Blue trail markers show the way as the descent continues to a stream crossing at 3.7 mi. After a second stream, the trail becomes grassy as it turns NW. Informal campsites in this section show considerable litter.

The trail crosses a log bridge and then passes a rock wall at 4.2 mi. At 4.3 mi., there is an unmarked trail jct. The unmarked trail continues N, but the marked trail swings W. It begins a gradual climb, passing three small streams with 10-ft. cascades in the next 10 minutes.

The trail turns S. At 4.55 mi. the roadway divides, with the marked trail bearing R. Easy to moderate grades bring you to the Campbell Mt. Lean-to at 4.7 mi. The divided trail rejoins the marked trail here. Again, there is considerable litter.

Beyond the lean-to, elevation continues to increase as the trail gradually swings from SW to NW and back to W. The height of land (2430 ft.) on Campbell Mt. is reached at 5.2 mi., after a gain of 680 ft. elevation from the first creek W of NY 206.

The trail is relatively flat to 5.5 mi., and then descends. After making a sharp L, the roadway swings SE on moderate downgrades. It passes a cabled gate at 5.65 mi., and then reaches another gate, at the Campbell Mt. Rd trailhead, at 5.8 mi.

The quickest way to the Campbell Mt. Rd. trailhead, if roads are dry, is via Jug Tavern Rd. Turn W on this road 0.8 mi. S of the Campbell Mt. trailhead on NY 206 (Co. Rd. 7). Drive 1.6 mi. to Campbell Mt. Rd. Turn R and drive 0.7 mi. to the parking area at the trailhead on the E side of the road.

The trailhead can also be reached from Downsville by driving S 3.6 mi. on NY 30 to Campbell Brook Rd. Turn E, drive through Corbett and at 2.3 mi. turn L and then R onto Campbell Mt. Rd. Drive 2.9 mi. to the trailhead. The Trout Pond Trail (trail 77) is on the opposite side of the road from the Campbell Mt. Trail. (This access route was not usable in 1994 due to a closed bridge.)

Distances: To stone wall turn, 0.3 mi.; to turn S, 0.8 mi.; to height of land, 1.15 mi.; to Miller Hollow snowmobile trail, 1.4 mi.; to high point on Brock Mt., 2.0 mi.; to lower summit of Brock Mt., 2.65 mi.; to NY 206, 4.4 mi.; to Campbell Mt. lean-to, 4.7 mi.; to height of land on Campbell Mt., 5.2 mi.; to Campbell Brook Rd., 5.8 mi. (9.4 km).

(76) Little Spring Brook Trail

Map 44: B-6
Western Catskills

Little Spring Brook Trail is a short connector trail that meets the ends of both the Pelnor Hollow and Campbell Mt. trails (see above) at a 3-way jct. It allows the hiker to modify the length of hikes on these trails.

Trailhead: Trailhead access is off the E side of NY 206 (Co. Rd. 7) at the end of Little Spring Brook Rd., which is 6.2 mi. N of the traffic light in Roscoe and 5.2 mi. S of the NY 30 jct. (See Route Guides for this chapter.) Park at the turnabout 1.1 mi. down Little Spring Brook Rd.

From the unmarked trailhead (0.0 mi.), head N on a grassy track, soon passing a house on the R. At 100 ft., there is a spring with a pipe. A trail sign is another 50 ft. along the way, where state land begins. Yellow trail markers guide you up a gradual grade beside the bank of Little Spring Brook, which the trail crosses at 0.3 mi.

The trail reaches the L side of a pond at 0.35 mi. and stays between it and a stone fence on the L. The trail enters mixed forest at 0.45 mi., as it swings NE and levels just before reaching a jct. Here, at 0.6 mi., Pelnor Hollow Trail (trail 74) and Campbell Mt. Trail (trail 75) meet in a clearing having nice old apple trees. (The Campbell Mt. Trail runs 2.4 mi. W to NY 206 and beyond; the Pelnor Hollow Trail runs 4.0 mi. S to Pelnor Hollow Rd.; see above.)

Distances: To pond, 0.35 mi.; to 3-way jct., 0.6 mi. (1.0 km).

(77) Trout Pond Trail

Map 44: A-7 to A-6
Western Catskills

The Trout Pond Trail offers a good overnight backpack trip, especially for the angler. Unfortunately, heavy use of the area has resulted in a large amount of litter. Please do not add to the probem. If you can carry it in full, certainly you can carry it out empty.

Trailhead: To reach the northern trailhead, use the access directions for the Campbell Mt. Rd. parking area in the Campbell Mt. Trail (trail 75) description above. From the trailhead (0.0 mi.) on the S side of Campbell Mt. Rd., follow blue trail markers S. (The Campbell Mt. Trail, on the N side of this road also has blue trail markers.)

The Russell Brook Rd. trailhead can be reached from NY 206 (Co. Rd. 7). From the traffic light in Roscoe, it is 2.4 mi. N on NY 206 to Morton Hill Rd. Immediately past the Beaver Kill bridge, turn W onto Morton Hill Rd., bear R at 0.2 mi., and drive to a jct. 3.2 mi. from NY 206. Turn L onto unmarked Russell Brook Rd. and drive 0.5 mi. to the trailhead parking area. There is an attractive waterfall 0.2 mi. farther along Russell Brook Rd.

The trail descends to a DEC sign at the N Branch of Campbell Brook at 0.3 mi. A pipe from a sometimes flowing spring protrudes from the bank near where a wooden bridge crosses the brook.

The route swings NW, climbs a little, and levels off. Then a broad loop back to the SE begins as the trail levels at intervals while continuing to ascend Campbell Mt. The hiker needs to be sure to follow small blue hikers' trail markers rather than the larger snowmobile trail markers, since snowmobile trails criss-cross the hiking trail occasionally.

A snowmobile trail branches L at 0.9 mi.; an old road crosses the trail at 1.0 mi. Arrow signs point the way at 1.35 mi. After a little more climbing, the trail reaches its high point of 2525 ft. at 1.5 mi., 475 ft. above Campbell Brook.

The trail heads SSE on a slight downgrade. A herd path R at 1.6 mi. leads to an open field full of many kinds of berries. The trail continues S, descending 350 ft. in elevation before reaching Campbell Brook Rd. at 2.1 mi.

(To reach this trailhead from Downsville, drive S, 3.6 mi. on NY 30, to Campbell Brook Rd. Turn E and drive 4.9 mi. to the trailhead, which is on a dirt road. (In 1994 this route was not possible due to a closed bridge.) The trailhead can be reached from NY 206 via Jug Tavern Rd. [See *Route Guide* for Margaretville–Downsville.] Jug Tavern Rd. is 3.3 mi. S of NY 30. Turn W and drive 1.6 mi. to Campbell Mt. Rd. Turn L and drive 0.4 mi. to Campbell Brook Rd. Turn R and drive 0.55 mi. to the trailhead.)

From the DEC sign, the trail turns L and runs E 175 yds. along Campbell Brook Rd., then turn R at 2.2 mi. and heads SSE through a gate. A gradual descent leads to the bridge over the S Branch of Campbell Brook at 2.45 mi.

The trail heads WSW and soon crosses another brook on a bridge before turning SE. A moderate-to-steep grade climbs over a hill. The grade eases at 2.9 mi., but continues to ascend some more before the trail veers SE and starts to descend.

At a trail sign at 3.4 mi., a snowmobile trail bears L and circles back to Campbell Brook Rd. The blue-marked trail bears R and drops SW down a moderate pitch. It eventually levels and reaches a jct. at the N end of Trout Pond at 4.0 mi. A large body of water, it was once called Cables Lake.

(The Mud Pond Trail [trail 78] heads W from the jct., crossing the pond inlet bridge to the Trout Pond lean-to. [It has been relocated farther to the W, away from the inlet water.] There is a spring near the old site.)

The Trout Pond Trail continues S from this jct. along the E side of Trout Pond. At 4.1 mi., the trail passes the small dam of a tributary stream. The route continues to a jct. at the outlet of the pond at 4.5 mi. Here, a side trail crosses the pond dam to a clearing. The lean-to that once occupied this spot no longer exists. Crossing the dam is no problem in dry weather, but high water can make it fairly dangerous.

The roadway continues S, descending on gradual grades to another jct. at 5.3 mi. Here, a snowmobile trail comes in from Mud Pond to the W. Still heading S, the route crosses a bridge. A gradual upgrade ends at the trailhead on Russell Brook Rd. The very large parking area is at 5.4 mi., immediately NE of the gated trailhead.

Distances: *To N branch Campbell Brook, 0.3 mi.; to height of land, 1.5 mi.; to open field, 1.6 mi.; to Campbell Brook Rd., 2.1 mi.; to turn from Campbell Brook Rd., 2.2 mi.; to S branch Campbell Brook, 2.45 mi.; to second height of land, 3.0 mi.; to Mud Pond jct. and Trout Pond Lean-to, 4.0 mi.; to Mud Pond snowmobile trail jct. 5.3 mi.; to Russell Brook Rd. trailhead, 5.4 mi. (8.7 km).*

(78) Mud Pond Trail   Map 44: A-6 to A-7

The Mud Pond Trail provides the hiker of the Trout Pond Trail with a loop option. (See trail 79.) In recent years, trail modifications have taken place (1995).

Trailhead: *The Mud Pond Trail description begins at the junction of the Mud Pond Trail and the Trout Pond Trail at the north end of Trout Pond. For trailhead access to this location, see the trailhead descriptions given for the Trout Brook Trail (trail 77).*

The blue-marked Mud Pond Trail heads generally W from the trail jct. at the N end of Trout Pond (0.0 mi.). It crosses the inlet of Trout Pond and passes the former lean-to site. A spur path L beyond the inlet bridge leads 0.1 mi. to the relocated lean-to. Red snowmobile trail markers are also present on the main trail, which ascends about 450 ft. to the top of Cherry Ridge, swinging S and reaching a height of land at 0.8 mi. The trail now descends on moderate to gradual grades, swinging W through a young hardwood forest to a jct. at 1.9 mi. near Mud Pond. The trail turns R (W) for 0.1 mi. to a spur path L to Mud Pond. It then turns L, ascends gradually to a height of land at 2.0 mi. and rejoins the Trout Pond Trail at 2.9 mi. (A turn R at this jct. leads to Russell Brook Rd. trailhead in 0.1 mi.)

Distances: To lean-to, 0.1 mi.; to jct. near Mud Pond, 1.9 mi.; to jct. with Trout Pond Trail, 2.9 mi.; to Russell Brook Rd., 3.0 mi. (4.8 km).

(79) Trout Pond–Mud Pond Loop   Map 44: A-6
Western Catskills

This loop provides a nice day trip to some attractive bodies of water, with several types of terrain to keep your interest.

Trailhead: Start from the Russell Brook Rd. trailhead. (Refer to Trout Pond Trail [trail 77] and Mud Pond Trail [trail 78] above.)

Walk 1.4 mi. to the lean-to at the N end of Trout Pond and then continue to Mud Pond at 3.3 mi. Retrace to the jct. Ascend gradually for 0.2 mi. to a height of land, then descend 350 ft. on varying grades down a broad woods road past an impressive stand of evergreens to the Trout Brook Trail jct. at 4.2 mi. From here it is 0.1 mi. on the Trout Brook Trail to the Russell Brook Rd. trailhead.

Distances: To Trout Brook Lean-to, 1.4 mi.; to Mud Pond, 3.3 mi.; to Trout Brook Trail, 4.2 mi.; to Russell Brook Rd. trailhead, 4.3 mi. (6.9 km).

(80) Long Pond Loop

The Long Pond Loop provides an interesting day trip or some variation on a short overnight trip to the Long Pond Lean-to. The hiker should expect to do some wading across Willowemoc Creek and should probably not try it in times of high water.

Trailhead: *Trail access is from the trailhead to Long Pond, off Flugertown Rd., 2.45 mi. from Willowemoc Rd. (See* Route Guide *for Livingston Manor to Claryville.) The hiker should read the description of the Long Pond– Beaverkill Ridge Trail, Willowemoc Rd. to Flugertown Rd., before starting this hike.*

The trail leaves the trailhead and heads SE, following red foot trail markers as well as orange snowmobile markers. It crosses Willowemoc Creek on a bridge, turns N and follows the Willowemoc upstream to another bridge, which crosses an intermittent channel of the Willowemoc. From here the trail swings E and climbs, first steeply, then gradually, as it winds around a bit, and then continues on to the Long Pond spur trail and trail register at 0.85 mi. Turning R, the spur trail arrives at the Long Pond Lean-to at 1.05 mi., some 150 yds. from Long Pond. The spur trail continues SW 1.4 mi. to the Long Pond Trailhead parking area on Flugertown Rd.

Hikers can simply retrace their steps back to the trailhead, and probably should do so in times of wet weather or high water. However, the loop route returns back to the jct. with the Long Pond– Beaver Kill Ridge Trail (trail 81) and turns R. It follows red trail markers E. Avoid a side trail R at 1.6 mi.

The route swings NE and reaches a parking spot at 2.4 mi. Continuing on, the route arrives at the Basily Rd. jct. at 2.8 mi. There are DEC signposts here.

The loop follows an unmarked section of Basily Rd. straight

ahead, NW. (The red-marked trail makes a sharp R and goes on to Willowemoc Rd.)

The road soon starts descending to a stream, which it reaches at 3.25 mi. The 20-ft.-wide stream must be waded. Then, 150 yds. farther, the 30-ft.-wide Willowemoc Creek must also be waded. Swinging S, the woods road passes through a meadow at 3.6 mi. and then curves around the R side of a swampy area.

Basily Rd. becomes Flugertown Rd. as it enters Sullivan Co. at 4.1 mi. (If approaching from Flugertown Rd., one can probably drive to this point.) After an unmarked path L the trail crosses a bridge and bears L at a jct. at 4.3 mi. The road reaches the Long Pond–Beaver Kill Ridge trailhead N on the R side of road at 4.35 mi.; the DEC signpost for the S half of the trail, where the trip began, closes the loop at 4.4 mi.

Distances: *To Long Pond spur trail, 0.85 mi.; to Long Pond lean-to, 1.05 mi.; to spur trail jct. from lean-to, 1.25 mi.; to last legal parking spot, 2.4 mi.; to Basily Rd. jct., 2.8 mi.; to Willowemoc Creek, 3.25 mi.; to original trailhead, 4.4 mi. (7.1 km).*

(81) Long Pond–Beaver Kill Ridge Trail (Flugertown Rd. to Beaver Kill Ridge)

This description begins at the 4.8 mi. point of the Long Pond–Beaver Kill Ridge Trail. (See trail 45, Long Pond–Beaver Kill Ridge Trail [Willowemoc Rd. to Flugertown Rd.], Big Indian–Upper Neversink Section.) It climbs to the Beaver Kill Ridge, where it joins the Mongaup–Hardenburgh Trail (trail 82). It can be used in combination with other trails to make some very enjoyable backpack trips.

Trailhead: *The trailhead is on the W side of Flugertown Rd., 2.5 mi. N from Willowemoc Rd. (See* Route Guide *for Livingston Manor to Claryville.)*

The trail leaves a DEC signpost [0.0 mi.] and follows red foot trail markers as well as orange snowmobile trail markers up a gradual grade. After some rolling terrain, the route levels at 0.2 mi. and remains so to a jct. at 0.45 mi. Here, the Long Pond–Beaver Kill Ridge Trail turns N (R), leaving the snowmobile trail, still following red markers. (The L fork, with yellow markers, is the continuance of the Mongaup–Willowemoc Trail [trail 84].)

The level red-marked trail runs along an old woods road. Avoid a woods road R at 0.85 mi. The almost flat, wide route swings NE and passes through attractive deciduous forest.

The route becomes a footpath. At 1.3 mi., the trail starts NW up a moderate grade. In a series of pitches, it ascends a spur of Beaver Kill Ridge, reaching the crest of the spur at 1.8 mi. Here, at 2754 ft. elevation, the trail turns N and follows the spur crest to Beaver Kill Ridge.

The grade eases considerably. The woods are fairly open. With only a few short pitches, the hiker can relax and enjoy this excellent forest. In several places, the trail is essentially flat.

Partially blocked views can be seen off the E side of the ridge at 2.9 mi. At a T-jct. in a small clearing at 3.0 mi., the trail joins the Mongaup–Hardenburgh Trail (trail 82). (Mongaup Pond is 3.2 mi. W; Beaver Kill Rd. is 3.2 mi. N.)

Distances: *To Mongaup Pond–Willowemoc Trail jct., 0.45 mi.; to base of spur, 1.3 mi.; to crest of spur, 1.81 mi.; to Mongaup-Hardenburgh Trail jct. 3.0 mi. (4.9 km) (7.8 mi. from Willowemoc Rd.). Elevation, 3025 ft. (907 m); ascent from Flugertown Rd., 1025 ft. (307 m).*

(82) Mongaup–Hardenburgh Trail

Map 43: F-7 to G-6

The trail climbs Mongaup Mt. and then goes along Beaver Kill Ridge before reaching Beaver Kill Rd. near Quaker Clearing. Few views reward the hiker until the leaves have fallen off the trees in autumn. However, as a woods ramble, it is "par excellence." Not many trails pass through such high-quality forest. Spotting vehicles requires extensive driving, so the hiker may wish to use just part of this trail for a loop hike, in conjunction with other trails. (See Beaver Kill Ridge Loop Trail [trail 91], below.)

Trailhead: *Trail access is off DeBruce Rd. 6.05 mi. E of Livingston Manor. (See Route Guide for Livingston Manor to Claryville.) Turn N on Mongaup Rd. and drive 2.8 mi. to the jct. of Mongaup Pond Rd. Turn R here and drive 1.1 mi. to the toll booth at Mongaup Pond Public Campground. Bear L from the toll booth and drive another 1.1 mi. to a T-jct. at Areas G-F. Turn L into Area G.*

The trailhead is on the N side of the paved "G" Loop Rd. Travel about 0.3 mi. into Area G to the new parking area, R, up a slope.

Walk back to the trailhead at the barrier rocks (0.0 mi.). Follow blue hiking trail markers and red snowmobile markers. The grassy perimeter road parallels the shoreline of Mongaup Pond, reaching a jct. at 0.3 mi. Turn L on a rocky pathway and head NNE to a trail register at 0.35 mi.

The route is by the W side of a small brook for a short distance before turning L again at an unmarked jct. at 0.45 mi. The blue-marked trail climbs gradual grades with short moderate pitches through a beech-birch forest. It is a steady but easy ascent through a section of blowdown caused by a microburst windstorm in the mid-'90s.

After another half mile, the pitches become steeper. The path swings NE at 1.55 mi. and reaches the wooded middle summit of 2980-ft.-high Mongaup Mt. at 1.6 mi., having ascended 800 ft. from Mongaup Pond.

The footpath turns E and is nearly level before starting a series of moderate and steep downgrades to a small col at 2.05 mi. Gradual upgrades to the next high point begin immediately. Another series of pitches leads up past boulders at moderate to steep grades. The slope eases just before the flat E summit (2928 ft.) of Mongaup Mt. at 2.6 mi. Ascent from the col is 380 ft.

After a few initial short pitches, long pleasant downgrades lead to the next low spot of the ridge. The trail is well marked. At 3.1 mi., a short steep pitch up starts an ascent after a descent of only about 100 ft. from the summit.

At 3.2 mi., the red-marked Long Pond–Beaver Kill Ridge Trail (trail 81) enters from the R at a jct. clearing. (This trail runs 3.0 mi. to Flugertown Rd.; see above.) The blue-marked Mongaup–Hardenburgh Trail continues ENE at moderate grades, reaching another high point (3062 ft.) at 3.3 mi.

The ridgeline is fairly level. A slight descent begins, bottoming out at 3.8 mi. A short ascent then flattens out at 4.0 mi., near 2850 ft.

elevation. A spring is sometimes flowing at 4.2 mi. Ascending again, a moderately steep grade reaches an unnamed high point (3224 ft.) at 4.8 mi.

The trail turns NE and descends slightly before following the nearly flat ridge top. It swings NW at 5.4 mi. and then N at 5.8 mi. The descent resumes with varying grades; it becomes quite steep at 6.2 mi. before leveling again.

Private property signs mark the Balsam Lake Angler's Club at 6.3 mi. The trail crosses the Beaver Kill on a suspension bridge at 6.35 mi. and returns to state land. The 150-ft.-wide Beaver Kill corridor is privately owned. Fishing is strictly prohibited. One last short upgrade must be climbed to the DEC signpost and parking area at Beaver Kill Rd. at 6.4 mi. (The Balsam Lake Mt. parking area is 2.0 mi. E; Little Pond Public Campground is 7.6 mi. W.)

Distances: *To Mongaup Pond, 0.3 mi.; to middle summit of Mongaup Mt., 1.6 mi.; to Long Pond–Beaver Kill Ridge Trail jct., 3.2 mi.; to 3224-ft. elevation high point, 4.8 mi.; to Beaver Kill suspension bridge, 6.35 mi.; to Beaver Kill Rd., 6.4 mi. (10.4 km).*

(83) Balsam Lake Mt. Loop

Map 42: G-6
Central Catskills

This hike uses the southern end of the Dry Brook Ridge Trail and all of the 1.6-mi. Balsam Lake Mt. Trail. Balsam Lake Mt., sometimes called Balsam Roundtop Mt., can be done in conjunction with Graham Mt. to make a full day's outing.

Trailhead: *Trailhead access is from the Balsam Lake Mt. DEC parking area at the end of Beaver Kill Rd. (See Route Guide for Beaver Kill Rd.–Quaker Clearing.)*

The blue-marked Dry Brook Ridge Trail (trail 60) heads NNE from the parking area trailhead (0.0 mi.). (Avoid the road that enters the Balsam Lake Angler's Club in a NW direction.) It passes a few buildings and climbs at easy, steady grades before crossing a small stream on a bridge at 0.5 mi. It reaches the Balsam Lake Mt. Trail jct. at 0.9 mi., having gained about 400 ft. elevation from the trailhead.

Turn L and follow the red trail markers of the Balsam Lake Mt. Trail NW. The route becomes moderately steep and rocky. At 1.2 mi., the trail veers L to avoid a ledge. A pipe coming from the base of a rock at 1.35 mi. marks a spring at R of trail. A new lean-to has been constructed here.

The Balsam Lake Mt. Trail passes the 3500-ft. elevation sign beyond the old spur trail to two former lean-tos. The last stretch to the summit clearing seems almost flat. It reaches the Mill Brook Ridge Trail jct. at 1.65 mi. (Consider following this yellow-marked trail W 0.1 mi. to a fern glade with a wonderful view of the western Catskills.) The summit is at 1.75 mi. A picnic table is found in the small clearing. The thicket of trees around the clearing prevents ground viewing. The tower was reopened in June 2000. Views unfold spectacularly as you begin to climb above the tree tops. Graham and Doubletop Mts. loom to the E. Between these peaks is Hunter Mt. Graham Mt. is directly E. Summit elevation, 3723 ft. Ascent, 1193 ft.

The trail heads E from the clearing on a jeep road. The gradual downgrade has short pitches. Fine views are found at 2.0 mi., before moderate grades lose elevation quickly. The jeep road grade eases and then flattens before a barrier gate is reached at 2.45 mi. A second jct.

with the Dry Brook Ridge Trail (trail 60) occurs at 2.5 mi. (The unmarked jct. for the Graham Mt. Trail is 0.35 mi. E of here at height of land.)

Turn R and follow the blue-marked Dry Brook Ridge Trail (trail 60) SW. Gradual grades take you along a dirt roadway to the first jct. with the Balsam Lake Mt. Trail at 3.45 mi. It is another 0.9 mi. back to the parking area, at 4.35 mi.

Distances: To jct. of Balsam Lake Mt. Trail, 0.9 mi.; to lean-tos, 1.4 mi.; to Mill Brook Trail jct., 1.65 mi.; to Balsam Lake Mt. summit, 1.75 mi.; to Dry Brook Ridge Trail jct., 2.5 mi.; to Balsam Lake Mt. jct., 3.45 mi.; to parking area, 4.35 mi. (7.0 km).

(83A) Mill Brook Ridge Trail (see p. 317)

(84) Mongaup–Willowemoc Trail   Map 43: F-7
Southern Catskills

This trail runs from the Mongaup Pond Public Campground to the Long Pond–Beaver Kill Ridge Trail (trail 81). It can be combined with that trail or the Neversink–Hardenburgh Trail (trail 44) to make multi-day backpack trips.

Trailhead: Access is via Mongaup Pond Public Campground. (See Route Guide for Livingston Manor–Claryville.) From the campground toll booth, bear R towards Area B and almost immediately turn L into the parking lot for the beach and picnic area. Park here.

Hike 0.2 mi. to Area B. Enter Area B, turn R at site 38, and follow the red-marked snowmobile trail from the rear of site 38. When this connector trail reaches the camp perimeter snowmobile trail at a T-jct., turn L. Follow the snowmobile trail N approximately 0.8 mi. to the Mongaup–Willowemoc Trail trailhead jct. The M–W trail follows yellow trail markers E. Gradual inclines wind up to the col of a ridgeline at 0.8 mi. A long gradual-to-moderate downgrade descends

A typical Catskill woods road

generally E towards Butternut Creek. There is a small bridge over a brook at 1.3 mi. The Wild Azalea Trailhead (to S) is at Butternut Jct. at 1.45 mi. The route levels and then traverses rolling terrain before crossing a large wooden bridge over Butternut Creek at 1.85 mi.

Across the bridge, the route immediately turns R at a T-jct. This is an attractive section, with the rippling brook, mosses, and rocks holding the hiker's attention as the trail follows the top of a high bank. Turning SE at 2.0 mi., the path continues through an interesting hemlock grove and then ascends gradually to cross another small bridge at 2.45 mi. Gradual climbing resumes and the trail crosses a wide woods road at 2.6 mi. (It runs from Flugertown Rd., N to Sand Pond, which is privately owned.)

Soon heading N on level ground, the trail comes to the Long Pond–Beaver Kill Ridge Trail (trail 81) jct. at 2.95 mi. Here, the Mongaup–Willowemoc Trail and the Long Pond–Beaver Kill Ridge Trail merge, following both yellow and blue trail markers for the remainder of the way to Flugertown Rd. (The Long Pond–Beaver Kill Ridge trail runs 2.65 mi. N to join the Mongaup–Hardenburgh Trail [trail 82]).

Bear R and head E. A level trail continues to 3.2 mi. and then gradually descends to Flugertown Rd. at 3.4 mi. (The continuation of the Long Pond–Beaver Kill Ridge Trail [trail 81] is 0.05 mi. E on Flugertown Rd.; Willowemoc Rd. is 2.5 mi. E and then S on Willowemoc Rd.)

Distances: To col, 0.8 mi.; to Butternut Creek, 1.85 mi.; to Sand Pond woods road, 2.6 mi.; to Long Pond–Beaver Kill Ridge Trail jct., 2.95 mi.; to Flugertown Rd., 3.4 mi. (5.5 km). (This is 4.2 mi. from Mongaup Pond Parking area.)

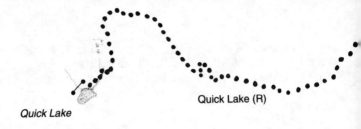

Quick Lake

Quick Lake (R)

Ʌ
N

⬛ Private Land

▨ Beech Mountain Nature Preserve
Private land with an easement allowing for limited public use:
  • No hunting or trapping
  • Foot travel only, stay on marked hiking trail
    unless fishing at Hodge Pond

Frick Pond Loop Trip (85), Big Loop Trip (86),
Quick Lake Trail (87), Flynn Trail (88),
Big Rock Trail (89) & Loggers Trail (90)
Based on Livingston Manor and Willowemoc quadrangles

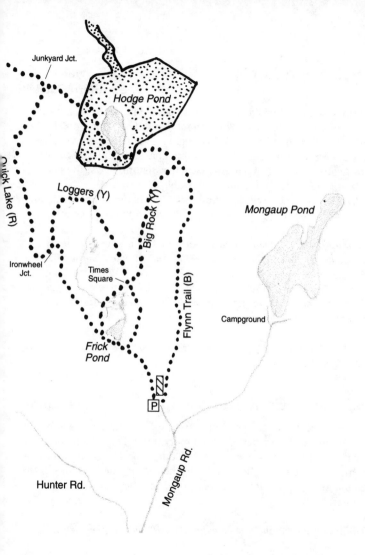

Frick Pond Region

The Frick Pond trailhead provides access to a 13.8-mi. network of relatively new trails in the Willowemoc–Long Pond Wild Forest. A series of old roads were seeded with grasses and now are wonderfully open routes for easy day trips, backpacking and especially cross-country skiing. While there are few distant views, the ponds, flora and open routes are most enjoyable to travel.

Each of the four trail descriptions in this network has additional information for skiing, provided in a "Trails in Winter" section.

Trailhead: Refer to the 6.05 mi. (W-E) point of the Route Guide *for* Livingston Manor–Claryville *(pp. 210–211). Turn N onto Mongaup Rd. and drive 2.7 mi. to a road junction where there is a Mongaup Public Campsite signpost. Turn L onto Beech Mt. Rd. and travel 0.4 mi. to a double parking area at the Frick Pond trailhead. (Do not travel onto the posted private property beyond the parking area.)*

There are actually two trailheads, on opposite sides of this road, a trail register and an exhibit board.

(85) Frick Pond Loop Trip Map: see p. 246

The Frick Pond Loop combines sections of several trails to permit a good outing of rather modest difficulty. Frick Pond is one of the most attractive bodies of water in the Catskills. The general route is given here. The hiker should refer to the detailed descriptions of the trails making up the loop that are found in other parts of this book chapter.

Trailhead: Refer to the trail access of the Frick Pond Region (see above).

Follow the Quick Lake Trail (trail 87) from the Frick Pond Region trailhead until it reaches the Big Rock Trail jct. Then, take the Big Rock Trail (trail 89) to Times Square jct. Turn R and travel the Loggers Trail SE until it rejoins the Quick Lake Trail. From there, turn L and return to the Frick Pond Region trailhead.

Trail in winter: This loop makes a short but very enjoyable outing for skiers of nearly all abilities.

Distances: To Big Rock Trail jct., 0.7 mi.; to Times Square jct., 1.2 mi.; to Quick Lake Trail jct., 1.75 mi.; to Frick Pond Region trailhead, 2.15 mi. (3.5 km).

(86) Big Loop Trip

Map: see p. 247

The Big Loop makes a good day trip of moderate difficulty. It combines the Flynn Trail (trail 88) with part of the Quick Lake Trail (trail 87). A general description of the route is given here. The hiker should refer to the detailed descriptions of the trails making up this loop that appear in other parts of this book section.

Trailhead: Refer to the trail access for the Frick Pond Region (see above).

Follow the Flynn Trail (trail 88) from the Frick Pond Region trailhead all the way to its end at Junkyard Junction at 3.2 mi.
(Here, the hiker may wish to continue 0.9 mi. N on the Quick Lake Trail (trail 87) to the Western Vista and then return to this jct. This will add a total of 1.8 mi. to the trip.)
From Junkyard Junction, turn L and follow the Quick Lake Trail SW back to the Frick Pond Region trailhead, which is reached at 6.3 mi.

Trail in winter: This is an ideal ski route for intermediate skiers. Grades are very easy on the Flynn Trail (trail 88) and to Western Vista. From Junkyard Junction to Ironwheel Junction, there are more challenging downgrades. The remainder of the trail to Frick Pond Region trailhead has gentle to gradual grades.

Distances: To Big Rock Trail jct., 1.7 mi.; to Hodge Pond, 2.4 mi.; to Junkyard Junction, 3.2 mi.; to Ironwheel Junction (Loggers Trail), 4.8 mi.; to second Big Rock Trail jct., 5.6 mi.; to second Loggers Trail jct., 5.9 mi.; to Frick Pond Region trailhead, 6.3 mi. (10.2 km).

(87) Quick Lake Trail (via Frick Pond)

Map: see p. 246–247

Quick Lake is a destination well-suited for an overnight backpacking trip or as part of a long loop trail in conjunction with the Flynn Trail (trail 88). It follows old woods roads and has some challenging long grades past Junkyard Junction.

Trailhead: Refer to the trail access in the Frick Pond Region (see above).

The Quick Lake Trail follows red DEC trail markers from the NW corner of the parking area (0.0 mi.). After descending steps, the grade soon levels and the forest route circles a home on the W side of private property.

At 0.1 mi., a wide woods road is reached and the trail abruptly turns L and follows it. The nearly level roadway heads N, reaching a signpost at the first jct. with the Loggers Trail (trail 90) at 0.4 mi. Loggers Trail bears R.

The Quick Lake Trail continues straight ahead along the S edge of a meadow and then drops down a moderate grade. Good views are gained of Frick Pond during the descent. The pond's shore is reached at 0.5 mi. Here, the route makes a L turn and crosses the pond outlet on a wide 50-ft.-long bridge. It bears R, climbing a small grade and then follows the shore.

A second small bridge is crossed just before the Big Rock Trail (trail 89) jct. is reached at 0.7 mi. Frick Pond is slightly below your elevation to the R and is a very attractive body of water.

The Quick Lake Trail continues straight ahead to the NNW. The surrounding terrain is open meadow that has many young trees gradually filling in the open space. The grade gradually ascends with occasional leveling zones. A small hemlock grove is passed through at 1.0 mi. and the route crosses a small meadow at 1.2 mi.

The second jct. with Loggers Trail (trail 90) is found at 1.5 mi. at Ironwheel Junction. The iron wheels and axle of an old wagon are found here.

The trail leaves the jct., heading S, and becomes a nearly moderate upgrade. Bear R at the jct. at 1.7 mi. where an arrow sign indicates the way toward Junkyard Junction. The route has curved to the NW.

Though the woods road changes direction often, ranging from NW to NNE, its general direction is N on moderate and gradual grades.

Height of land is reached at 2.4 mi. The elevation is 2750 ft., a gain of 610 ft. from the trailhead.

After a slight descent, the route bears R at an arrow sign at 2.45 mi. Alternating level and gradual grades eventually reach Junkyard Junction at 3.1 mi. (The Flynn Trail [trail 88] enters this jct. from the E.)

From this jct., the Quick Lake Trail winds NW 150 ft. to where the actual junkyard is found. Mostly level woods road brings you to what is generally referred to as the Western Vista at 4.0 mi. The distant view W, across the Shin Creek Valley and beyond, is particularly impressive in autumn, when multicolored leaves cover the distant ridge.

From here the trail loses about 800 ft. in elevation before reaching Quick Lake. Gradual and moderate grades descend SSW. There is a 4-way jct. with an arrow sign which points the way to Quick Lake at 4.3 mi., where the trail turns R and descends to the W. Soon, the route bears R at another jct. and then passes straight through a third and fourth jct. Follow trail markers carefully. Finally, at 4.9 mi. the route turns abruptly L at yet another jct., where a "Trail to Quick Lake" sign with directional arrow is found.

A level stretch over bare rock on the roadway is crossed at 5.3 mi. and the trail swings N and NW. Then the roadway curves W and descends with moderate grade in a very widely cleared section at 5.6 mi. The trail makes a sweeping R turn NNW and continues descending with lessening steepness, finally leveling and turning W and SW with more gradual downgrades. Pass by a side road at the L at 6.8 mi. The trail continues a winding descent until it reaches Quick Lake.

At 7.1 mi., a side path L leads steeply down a slope to the shore of the lake, but the trail continues straight ahead, leveling at its closest point to Quick Lake at 7.15 mi. (The trail continues to 7.22 mi., where a yellow barrier gate is reached.)

Quick Lake is 125 ft. off the trail and has a few fire rings and a picnic table. Beavers have greatly cut trees around the shoreline.

Trail in winter: *Quick Lake Trail is an excellent trail for intermediate ability skiing as far as Western Vista at 4.0 mi. Beyond this point to Quick Lake requires expert skills and good stamina.*

Distances: *To first Loggers Trail jct., 0.4 mi.; to Frick Pond and Big Rock Trail jct., 0.7 mi.; to Ironwheel Junction, 1.5 mi.; to Junkyard Junction, 3.1 mi.; to Western Vista, 4.0 mi.; to wide downgrade, 5.6 mi.; to Quick Lake, 7.2 mi. (11.7 km).*

(88) Flynn Trail Map: see p. 247

This trail gradually increases in vertical ascent until 610 ft. of elevation has been gained over its 3.2 mi. of distance to the Quick Lake Trail (trail 87) at Junkyard Junction. It follows a wide gravel road to Hodge Pond in the Beech Mt. Nature Preserve and then more grassy woods roads to Junkyard Junction.

Trailhead: Refer to the trail access in the Frick Pond Region (see above).

The Flynn Trail leaves the E edge of the road (0.0 mi.) opposite the parking area, following blue DEC trail markers. It passes the E side of a private home and then rejoins the road, which is now state land, at 0.1 mi. There is a barrier at L. The trail turns R (N) and runs up a steady grassy road grade. The route levels at 0.4 mi., but soon resumes climbing. The road curves NNE and views of the valley can be seen to the NW at 0.7 mi. The trail levels briefly again at 1.0 mi. and once more at 1.1 mi. Avoid any side roads into the woods. Views are no longer apparent by the time the Big Rock Trail (trail 89) is reached at 1.7 mi. in another level zone. (This trail drops off steeply to the L.) The snowmobile trail to Mongaup Pond is to the R.

The level stretch curves W. The trail reaches another jct. at 2.0 mi., just after passing the boundary of Beech Mt. Nature Preserve. (No camping is permitted on this property or at Hodge Pond. Public transit is granted only for use of the DEC trail and for fishing at Hodge Pond. Please do not disturb any scientific equipment you may see, since long-term studies are in progress.) The trail turns L and descends a nearly flat route that curves S. A barn is seen at R at 2.3 mi.

The roadway continues around the bend to the N, entering a large meadow at the edge of Hodge Pond at 2.4 mi. Turn L and follow a grassy road past the pond outlet and up a gradual slope. Hodge

Pond is seen very well, 100 yds. downslope R at 2.5 mi.

Continuing up the roadway, the route passes a series of small fields. Direction arrow signs are seen at 2.7 mi. Avoid the grassy lane that forks R. Follow the L side of the fork uphill, where it soon curves L (NW) at 2.8 mi.

Increasing grades lead to another jct. and the trail swings L again with arrow signs at 2.9 mi. From there, generally level terrain is found until Junkyard Junction is reached at 3.2 mi. Here, the Quick Lake Trail (trail 87) enters from Frick Pond to the SW and leaves for Quick Lake to the NW.

Trail in winter: *This is an excellent intermediate ski trail that can be combined with other trails to make a very nice outing.*

Distances: *To barrier, 0.15 mi.; to viewpoint, 0.7 mi.; to Big Rock Trail jct., 1.7 mi.; to Hodge Pond, 2.4 mi.; to first arrow jct., 2.7 mi.; to Quick Lake Trail at Junkyard Junction, 3.2 mi. (5.2 km).*

(89) Big Rock Trail

Map: see p. 247

This is a short, steep trail until it reaches Times Square jct. From there to the Quick Lake Trail (trail 87) jct. it becomes a flat walk in what is perhaps the most attractive part of the whole region. Most people will hike only this second part in conjunction with other trails. (See Frick Pond Loop [trail 85]). However, a few stalwart trampers may combine it with sections of the Flynn Trail (trail 88) and Quick Lake Trail (trail 87) to make a larger loop.

Trailhead: *Trailheads for this trail are at the 1.7-mi. point of the Flynn Trail (trail 88) and the 0.7-mi. point of the Quick Lake Trail (trail 87).*

Following yellow trail markers, the Big Rock Trail leaves the Flynn Trail (trail 88) and quickly loses elevation to the W. Bear R at a pair of woods road forks at 0.05 mi. and 0.1 mi. as the trail turns NNW.

Moderate grades become steep at 0.3 mi. and turn SSE. Only a few level zones are found as the winding trail descends through deciduous forest. A big swing W occurs at 1.0 mi., before the woods road levels off at a 4-way jct. called Times Square. There has been a loss of 600 ft. in elevation in this 1.1-mi. distance.

From this point forward, the character of the terrain changes radically and the walk becomes a flat stroll through exceptional woodland. Leaving Times Square, the trail heads SW through deciduous forest until a magnificent hemlock stand is entered at 1.25 mi. Ferns, mosses and other vegetation will occupy your curiosity. Two attractive bridges cross over inlets of Frick Pond before a 285-ft.-long raised boardwalk at 1.45 mi. takes you through a small wetland area. The immense hemlock grove is finally exited at 1.5 mi. Interesting views of Frick Pond are enjoyed as the route takes you along the W shore of the water. The Quick Lake Trail (trail 87) is reached at 1.6 mi.

Trail in winter: Only very skilled skiers should attempt the section of trail from the Flynn Trail to Times Square. The route here is quite wide but becomes progressively steeper over its course. The section from Times Square to Quick Lake is suitable for nearly all skiers and can be combined with other trails to make a delightful loop. (See the Frick Pond Loop [trail 85].)

Distances: To steep zone, 0.3 mi.; to Times Square, 1.1 mi.; to raised boardwalk, 1.45 mi.; to Quick Lake Trail jct., 1.6 mi. (2.6 km).

(90) Loggers Trail

Map: see p. 247

This generally flat trail has a few easy grades and the route can be combined with the Quick Lake Trail (trail 87) to make what is sometimes called the Loggers Loop.

Trailhead: *This trail may be accessed at jcts. along the Quick Lake Trail (trail 87) at 0.4 mi. and 1.5. mi.*

The trail bears R from the Quick Lake Trail (trail 87) at 0.4 mi., climbing a small grade. It then crosses an open field. Yellow trail markers guide you up a gradual grade at 0.1 mi. on a wide woods road. The way levels and Frick Pond can be partially seen in the distance L through trees.

Times Square jct. is reached at 0.55 mi. and the trail passes through it without turning. The trail is now a somewhat more narrow woods road that curves N as it climbs a moderate grade. Height of land is at 0.8 mi. amongst black cherry and yellow birch.

At 1.3 mi., the route bends to the NW and eventually W. A woods road fork is found at 1.4 mi. and the trail continues L to the SW. (The R fork leads to a low shelf in an open field. A brook flows past the far edge of the clearing, making this a nice camp spot for backpackers.) The L fork you follow passes beneath the low shelf and gradually descends.

There is an interesting sedimentary rock outcrop at 1.7 mi. Ironwheel Junction is reached at 1.8 mi., where the trail rejoins the Quick Lake Trail.

Trail in winter: *This trail is suitable for skiers of nearly all levels of ability and can be combined with other trails to make interesting loop routes.*

Distances: *To Times Square, 0.55 mi.; to height of land, 0.8 mi.; to Quick Lake Trail jct., 1.8 mi. (2.9 km).*

(91) Beaver Kill Ridge Loop

Map 43: F-7
Southern Catskills

The Beaver Kill Ridge Loop permits very nice day trips for the hiker, using parts of several trails in the Beaver Kill Ridge region. It offers both flatland and ridgeline scrambling. There are no outstanding views, but the forest is one of the nicest in the Catskills. It is a good idea to refer to the descriptions of the various trails making up this loop before starting the trip.

Trailhead: *Trail access is off DeBruce Rd. at Mongaup Pond Public Campground. (See* Route Guide *for Livingston–Claryville.) Bear R from the campground's entrance toll booth, driving toward Area B. Almost immediately turn L into the beach and picnic parking area. Start your hike from here.*

From the parking area (0.0 mi.) walk 0.2 mi. E, entering Area B. Turn R from the Area B road at Campsite 38. Follow the red-marked snowmobile connector trail from the rear of Campsite 38. This joins the Mongaup Pond snowmobile trail at 0.25 mi.

Turn L at this jct. and follow the snowmobile trail N 1.1 mi. to a jct. with the blue-marked Mongaup–Hardenburgh Trail (trail 82) at 1.35 mi. A picnic table and fireplace are at this jct.

Turn R and follow this trail N 1.3 mi. to the middle peak summit of Mongaup Mt. at 2.65 mi. Then go E along the trail to the jct. of the Long Pond–Beaver Kill Ridge Trail (trail 81) at 4.25 mi.

Turn R, following the red-marked Long Pond–Beaver Kill Ridge Trail (trail 81) S to its jct. with the Mongaup–Willowemoc Trail at

6.8 mi.

Turn R and follow the yellow-marked Mongaup–Willowemoc Trail (trail 84) SW and then W, 3.3 mi. back to the Mongaup Pond snowmobile trail. The jct. with this trail is at 10.1 mi.

Turn L at this jct., returning 0.45 mi. to the parking area where the trip originated. The parking area is at 10.55 mi. A nice swim and possibly a picnic put a great finish to the day.

Distances: *To Area B, 0.2 mi.; to Mongaup Pond snowmobile trail, 0.25 mi.; to Mongaup–Hardenburgh Trail jct., 1.35 mi.; to summit of Mongaup Mt., 2.65 mi.; to jct. with Long Pond–Beaver Kill Ridge Trail, 4.25 mi.; to jct. with Mongaup–Willowemoc Trail, 6.8 mi.; to Mongaup Pond snowmobile trail jct., 10.1 mi.; to parking area, 10.55 mi. (17.1 km).*

Prattsville–Shandaken Section

The northwest Catskills, described in this section, include Spruceton Valley, with its approaches to Hunter and West Kill mts. Routes to eight 3500-ft. peaks are found here.

When the Palatine Germans, earlier saved by Queen Anne and sent to the colonies, took flight from their Hudson River landlords, it was in the Schoharie Valley that they sought refuge. It was also in this region that Zadock Pratt later built one of the great tanneries of the Catskills.

Today, this is a quiet rural area where deciduous forests cover mountains that challenge your skills in land navigation. Trust your compass! Where private land must be crossed, please seek permission and do not litter. Spruceton Rd. is a long walk, so be sure you go in with a full gas tank. The last part of Spruceton Rd. is dirt. In winter, turning around is tricky and the DEC parking areas are not normally plowed, excepting the Spruceton trailhead.

Trails in winter: All trails in this section are frequently climbed in winter. Bear Pen and Vly are generally done together. However, skiing Bear Pen from NE is a fine trip.

North Dome and Sherrill are also often done together, but make a long trip in winter. A very early start is required.

Diamond Notch is good for skiing. The upper parts of the notch are often crusty and require good skills.

Spruceton Rd. parking is often difficult in the winter. Try to get your parked vehicle off the road. The unmarked North Dome parking area at 2.9 mi., Mink Hollow parking area for West Kill Mt. at 3.8 mi. and parking area at 6.9 mi. are not usually plowed. Do not park at the snowplow turnaround at the end of the road at 7.0 mi. The large Spruceton Trail parking area at 6.7 mi. is generally plowed.

The parking area for Halcott Mt. on the W side of NY 42 is generally plowed. In the occasional event it is not, the next safe parking area is 1.3 mi farther S on NY 42, at the Forest Preserve access area at the E side of NY 42. This will increase the length of the climb somewhat.

Short Hikes:

Pratt's Rock—1.0 mi. round trip. Casual hike full of interesting history. This is a good break on a long trip.

Diamond Notch Falls—1.6 mi. round trip. Almost level walk on an attractive woods road along Diamond Notch Brook to very nice waterfalls.

Moderate Hikes:

Spruceton Trail to Hunter Mt.—6.8 mi. round trip. Follows a jeep road up a steady moderate grade to the fire tower on Hunter Mt.

Halcott Mt.—approx. 6 mi. round trip. This is moderate for bushwhack trips, requiring good compass work. Good jaunt for experienced hikers.

Harder Hikes:

North Dome–Sherrill Mts.—approx. 6 mi. through trip. This is a trailless hike with a variety of challenges.

West Kill Mt.—7.8 mi. through trip; requires two vehicles. The trip has some nice brooks to follow, some steep climbing on the Devil's Path, and a variety of terrain.

ROUTE GUIDE FROM PRATTSVILLE TO SHANDAKEN

Mileage N to S	Description	Mileage S to N
0.0	Schoharie Creek bridge., N end of Prattsville	17.8
1.1	Pratt's Rock	16.7
1.5	NY 23 turns E, NY 23A continues straight.	16.3
7.3	Take side road to Lexington at NY 23A jct.	10.5
7.5	Cross Schoharie Creek bridge at NY 42 jct.	10.3
9.5	Gas station	8.3
10.4	West Kill hamlet and Spruceton Rd. (See separate route guide for Spruceton Rd.)	7.4

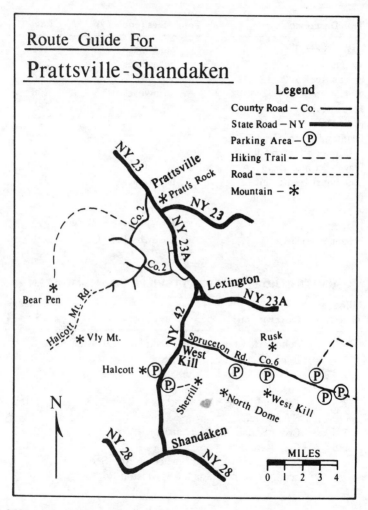

Route Guide For

Prattsville-Shandaken

Legend

County Road — Co. ————
State Road — NY ━━━━━
Parking Area — Ⓟ
Hiking Trail — — — —
Road - - - - - - - - - -
Mountain — *

NY 23
Prattsville
* Pratt's Rock
NY 23
Co. 2
NY 23A
Co. 2
Lexington
NY 23A
* Bear Pen
Halcott Mt. Rd.
NY 42
* Vly Mt.
Spruceton Rd.
Rusk
*
Co. 6
West Kill
Halcott * Ⓟ
Ⓟ
Ⓟ
Ⓟ
Ⓟ
Ⓟ
Ⓟ
* Sherrill
*
* North Dome
* West Kill
N
Shandaken
NY 28
NY 28

MILES
0 1 2 3 4

11.8	Height of land in Deep Notch	6.0
12.8	Unmarked parking area, W side of road; starting point for Halcott Mt.	5.0
14.1	Forest Preserve access parking; alternate starting point for Mount Sherrill.	3.7
17.8	Jct. NY 42 and NY 28 at Shandaken	0.0

ROUTE GUIDE FOR SPRUCETON ROAD

Mileage W to E	Description	Mileage E to W
0.0	Spruceton Rd. (Co. Rd. 6) and NY 42 jct. at hamlet of West Kill (look for flag pole).	7.0
0.05	Post Office	6.95
1.8	Bridge over West Kill	5.2
1.9	Shoemaker Rd. (good starting point for Mt. Sherrill)	5.1
2.8	Bridge over West Kill	4.2
2.9	Unmarked DEC parking area, S side (good starting point for North Dome Mt.)	4.1
3.8	Mink Hollow trailhead for West Kill Mt.	3.2
5.3	Sunshine Valley House (overnight lodging and meals by reservation)	1.7
6.0	Paved road narrows and becomes dirt.	1.0
6.7	Very large DEC parking area; N side	0.3
6.9	DEC parking area, S side; Use for West Mt., Diamond Notch, Devil's Path, Hunter Mt.; not plowed in winter.	0.1
7.0	Barrier cable, end of road.	0.0

Bearpen Mt. Bushwhack

No Map

Bearpen Mt. has no marked trail all the way to its summit. And, despite the maze of wood roads and old ski trails on this newly acquired (1999) state reforestation area, no cannister has been placed at the summit. It is possible to get very close to the summit via Ski Run Rd.

Ski Run Rd. leads up a pleasant hardscrabble route to the abandoned Bearpen Mt. Ski Area. In no place is it difficult; there is only one short steep grade on the whole route. This route is easy for snowshoers and excellent for skiers of intermediate to expert skills.

Trailhead: Access to Ski Run Rd. is off NY 23 immediately N of the Schoharie Creek Bridge in Prattsville. Turn W on Co. Rd. 2. Proceed along the narrow paved road through exquisite farmland vistas. Near height of land at 1.9 mi., pass Harry Peckham Rd. on the L. Unidentified Ski Run Rd. is on the R at 2.1 mi. Park at the beginning of Ski Run Rd. In winter, since Ski Run Rd. is not plowed, care must be taken in locating it.

The route is unmarked, but easy to follow. Gradual grades of a tree-lined lane take you generally W. Avoid side trails. At 1.0 mi., the road leaves private land in Greene Co. and enters state reforestation land in Delaware Co. It winds in and out of state land for the next two mi.

At 1.5 mi., the route begins a general swing S. Leveling off, it reaches a jct. at 2.3 mi. (The hiker who bushwhacks N from this jct. will reach the summit of 3440-ft. Roundtop Mt. after walking approximately 0.5 mi.)

Avoid the level R fork, which leads to the Roxbury Ski Area, at this junction. Bear L up the small grade that soon levels again. The route occasionally passes through small clearings as it swings SE, passing a pond on the R at 3.8 mi. A short way farther, the jeep road drops down a small grade, with the ruins of the former ski lodge and old ski slopes in view.

Curving R, the way to the summit leaves the road 100 ft. beyond the lodge ruins and climbs steeply to a lookout bluff at 4.0 mi. Excellent viewing is possible here. Roundtop Mt. is NNW and the ridge that Ski Run Rd. ascends is directly across the valley. Hunter Mt. stands out on the horizon to the SE, with West Kill, Rusk, North Dome and Sherrill in lesser dominance. Pratt Rock can be seen at the edge of Prattsville.

Most hikers end their hike here. To reach the true summit requires crossing a downed tree zone, following a bearing of approximately 145 degrees. The route enters open deciduous woods with many ferns covering its floor. It is difficult to discern the nearly level summit at 4.2 mi.

Another route up Bearpen Mt. is from the col between Bearpen and Vly mts. along the Halcott Mt. Rd. (See Vly Mt., below.) That route presents an opportunity to climb both mountains for a nice day trip. However, one has to find ways through some minor cliff fronts. Cliffs can be avoided by following woods roads on the E side of the ridge for 0.5 mi. before ascending the ridge.

Distances: *To junction, 2.3 mi.; to lookout bluff, 4.0 mi.; to summit, 4.2 mi. (6.7 km). Ascent from Ski Run Rd., 1600 ft. (489 m.); ascent from end of pavement on Halcott Mt. Rd., 1940 ft. (582 m); ascent from col on Halcott Mt. Rd., 790 ft. (237 m). Summit elevation, 3600 ft. (1308 m).*

Vly Mt. (Bushwhack) (No Map)

The word vly *(vlei, vlai)* is a Dutch term for marsh or swamp. Vly Valley is S of the peak and Vly Creek originates high on the shoulder of Vly Mt., but there are no marshes in the immediate area of the mountain.

The ascent of Vly Mt. is probably best made from the Halcott Mt. Rd. (See *Route Guide* for Prattsville to Shandaken.) This old road is paved up the N side approach to the col between Vly and Bearpen mts. to within 1.3 mi. of the col.

Trailhead: Beginning at the NY 23 bridge of Schoharie Creek, just N of the village of Prattsville, proceed 2.7 mi. along Co. Rd. 2 to its jct. with Don Irwin Rd. at the bottom of a steep hill. Turn L and continue along narrow Co. Rd. 2 another 2.0 mi. to a 4-way jct. Co. Rd. 2 swings L; Truesdell Rd. bears R; Halcott Mt. Rd. bears R and then immediately L. Jeager Rd. at L is passed at 0.2 mi. The pavement ends 0.5 mi. along Halcott Mt. Rd. Parking space is hard to find here. Care should be taken to park well off the road to avoid blocking the way.

Hiking begins from end of pavement (0.0 mi.) Now hardscrabble, Halcott Mt. Rd., bounded by private lands on each side, continues steeply up the mountain. It is another 1.3 mi. to the col. A compass bearing taken from a point just beyond the hunting camp in the col will guide one to the summit. Alternating steep and level terrain are found before the last steep pitch to the summit. One may be fortunate enough to locate a herd path for the last 0.2 mi. The summit is wooded.

Ascent from end of pavement, 1870 ft. (561 m). Ascent from col, 720 ft. (216 m). Summit elevation, 3529 ft. (1059 m).

(92) Pratt's Rock Trail   (No map)

The short climb around Pratt's Rock, created by Zadock Pratt to memorialize his life, is more a step back into history than a hike. But it's good exercise and provides a fascinating glimpse into another era. One soon learns why his employees revered him and changed the name of their little settlement, Schoharieskill, to Prattsville. It is particularly remarkable because Pratt was a tanner baron—a breed of businessman not often regarded with fondness. In a more quiet time, Prattsville was called "the Gem of the Catskills."

In 1825, Pratt's tannery worked 60,000 hides, burned 1,500 cords of wood, and extracted tannin for tanning from 6,000 cords of hemlock bark. He was proud of the fact that his factory tanned a million hides in 20 years. In time, he became a U.S. Congressman, founded the National Bureau of Statistics, and pushed for the completion of the Washington Monument.

Trailhead: *Pratt's Rock, listed in the State Register of Historic Places, is a short distance SE of Prattsville on NY 23, 0.4 mi. N of the jct. of NY 23 and NY 23A. From the parking area, steps lead up to a covered exhibit area, where interesting information and photos can be found. Beyond, a path parallels the highway, passing picnic tables and ending at a monument commemorating one of Pratt's favorite horses. (Pratt owned over a thousand horses in his lifetime.)*

A branch path winds up the hill towards Pratt's Rock, passing sculptured rocks. A small shelter cut into a boulder was originally intended to be Pratt's grave.

Five minutes of climbing brings you to Pratt's Rock, a high cliff into which are sculptured white-washed figures and writings that symbolize Zadock Pratt's life. An arm representing work, a hemlock (necessary for tanning), the family motto and shield, a horse, and Pratt's face stand out. Do not go farther along this trail, since the way is dangerous.

On the descent, a side path R curves upward to the top of the cliff face you just left. This lookout offers a splendid view down the Schoharie valley towards Deep Notch and Halcott Mt.

Distances: *Round trip approximates 1.0 mi. if all sections are walked. Vertical ascent, about 200 ft. Elevation, 1500 ft. (450 m).*

North Dome Mt. (Bushwhack)

Map 42: K-4
Central Catskills

North Dome Mt. is part of the West Kill–North Dome Wilderness area. The mountain was formerly called Blue Bell Mt.

Trailhead: *Access is from the 2.9-mi. point of Spruceton Rd., where a small DEC parking area (unplowed in winter) is located. It has no sign, but Forest Preserve Wilderness signs are on the trees. (See Route Guide for Spruceton Rd., p. 263.)*

Climb S up the ridge spur until near the summit. Then bear E somewhat. The summit is fairly open but nearly flat. Some care is required to discern the true high point and the canister.

In summer, Mt. Sherrill is often done with North Dome, but climbers in winter frequently find it impossible to complete both peaks as a day trip. If heading for Sherrill, travel W into the col between the two mountains. The climb out of the col up the side of Sherrill is very steep. A descent off Sherrill back to Spruceton Rd. can be made almost entirely on state land if the hiker drops down the spur ridge crest from the summit, W of Bennett Brook. Stay W of any yellow paint blazes on trees or stone fences. There is a very narrow band of private property near Spruceton Rd. It may be difficult to cross the West Kill at roadside in times of high water.

Ascent, 1910 ft. (573 m). Summit elevation, 3610 ft. (1083 m).

(93) Spruceton Trail

The Spruceton Trail follows the Hunter Mt. fire tower jeep road all the way to the summit. Relatively easy to climb, this route is most attractive and enjoyable to hike.

Trailhead: *The DEC parking area trailhead is at the 6.7 mi. point on Spruceton Rd. (See Route Guide for Spruceton Rd.) The level trail leaves the NE end of the parking area with DEC blue trail markers. A yellow barrier gate blocks vehicles, and the route soon parallels the E side of Hunter Brook, reaching a trail register at 0.3 mi.*

At an open campsite on the R at 0.4 mi., the trail turns L and crosses Hunter Brook on a wide bridge. A steady moderate upgrade reaches a sharp switchback at 0.5 mi. (This is the starting point for Rusk Mt.; see below.) Occasional switchbacks and steady grades end at a height of land at 1.7 mi., where the trail turns R. (Avoid continuing straight ahead on the old Hunter Rd. down through Taylor Hollow towards Deming Rd.)

The trail now becomes a twisting moderate grade. This is suitable for expert skiers only; skishoers can easily snowshoe the next 0.3 mi of difficult ski trail before redonning their skis to ski the rest of the relatively flat mountain top.

A yellow-marked spur trail R, with a log fence, at 2.2 mi. leads 100 ft. to an open area with a stone fireplace. Beyond the fireplace 200 ft. is a good spring, with water gushing from a metal pipe. This is a very pleasant camping spot.

Gradual grades continue to the John Robb lean-to, 30 ft. L of the trail at 2.3 mi. It receives much use. There are good views W and NW across the trail from the lean-to. This lean-to is at 3500 ft. elevation, marking the highest point where camping is permitted on the mountain in nonwinter conditions.

At a jct. at 2.4 mi. the yellow-marked Colonel's Chair Trail (trail 28) (see Stony Clove section) heads N 1.1 mi. to the Hunter Mt. Ski Lodge and ski chairlift, at the Colonel's Chair. (This is a good emergency escape route.)

The trail essentially levels at 2.5 mi., with only an occasional short upgrade. A brook runoff at 2.9 mi. leads 40 ft. to the top of an old glacial meltoff waterfall. Almost dry now, it shows evidence of once having had more water.

At a trail jct. at 3.0 mi. an unidentified but yellow-marked trail L descends towards the Becker Hollow Connector Trail (trail 30). It is little used and is not recommended.

The Spruceton Trail climbs a moderate grade at 3.3 mi., reaching the Hunter Mt. fire tower at 3.4 mi. The trail crosses the W edge of the very large summit clearing to the fire tower and fire observer's cabin. It is necessary to climb the fire tower for a view, but for those who do, a 360-degree panorama awaits. The Blackhead Range is to the NE; Kaaterskill High Peak can be seen to the E; the Devil's Path mountains are S; West Kill Mt. is W.

The Becker Hollow Connector Trail (trail 30) (see Stony Clove section) leaves the SE edge of the clearing.

The Spruceton Trail was built to end at the fire tower. However, when the trail was constructed, the fire tower was S of its present site. The Spruceton trail, continuing from the NW side of the clearing, swings to the SE along the flat ridge and ends at the jct. of the Becker Hollow Trail (trail 29) and Hunter Mt. Spur Trail at 3.6 mi., where the original fire tower stood. (Because it is above 3500 ft. elevation, the former Hunter Mt. lean-to has been removed and the scattered open sites around this jct. are no longer used for camping. This is necessary to protect the fragile summit vegetation from destruction.)

Distances: To Hunter Brook bridge, 0.4 mi.; to height of land, 1.7 mi.; to spring and open campsite, 2.1 mi.; to John Robb lean-to, 2.3 mi.; to jct. of Colonel's Chair Trail, 2.4 mi.; to unmarked jct., 3.0 mi.; to summit fire tower and jct. of Becker Hollow Connector Trail, 3.4 mi.; to jct. of Becker Hollow Trail and Hunter Mt. Connector Trail, 3.6 mi. (5.8 km). Summit elevation, 4040 ft. (1235 m); ascent, 1950 ft. (585 m).

Rusk Mt. (Bushwhack)

Map 41: L-3
NE Catskills

Rusk Mt. is the fourth of five peaks which make up the Lexington Chain. It is named for Samuel E. Rusk, an assistant of the early mapmaker, Arnold Guyot. Rusk wrote one of the first guidebooks for this section of the Catskills.

The Rusk Mt. that appears on today's USGS maps is not the mountain Guyot actually named Rusk. Guyot's Rusk was one peak to the E. Guyot's names for the peaks, W to E, were Lexington (3100 ft.), Pine Island (3240 ft.). Bee Line (3360 ft.), Evergreen (3680 ft.), and Rusk (3640 ft.). Today's USGS maps list them, W to E, nameless (3100 ft.) (though climbers call it Packsaddle Mt.), nameless 3140 ft.), Evergreen (3360 ft.), Rusk (3680 ft.), and nameless (3640 ft.). The whole chain makes an interesting day's outing, though most hikers head just for the USGS Rusk Mt.

Trailhead: The easiest approach to Rusk Mt. is via the Spruceton Trail up Hunter Mt. (See above; see Route Guide for Spruceton Rd.) The most direct route leaves the Spruceton Trail at 0.5 mi., at a notable switchback. Leave the trail here and head R up Ox Hollow for the summit. Near the top one needs to negotiate a way around some ledges. Good views look out to the Spruceton Trail and Southwest Hunter Mt.

Another approach to Rusk Mt. is from the old Taylor Trail jct. at 1.7 mi., where the Spruceton Trail levels and turns E. For Rusk Mt., head NW along the ridge from this spot. Ascent from Spruceton Rd., 1577 ft. (473 m). Summit elevation, 3680 ft. (1004 m).

(94) Diamond Notch Trail to Diamond Notch Falls

Map 41: L-4
NE Catskills

This short section of the Diamond Notch Trail connects to the Devil's Path and is often used by hikers ascending Hunter Mt. or Southwest Hunter Mt. Those who wish to hike the whole Diamond Notch Trail should refer to the Diamond Notch Trail (trail 34) (see Stony Clove Section).

Trailhead: The Diamond Notch Trail begins at a barrier cable at the end of Spruceton Rd. (See Route Guide to Spruceton Rd., p. 263.) From the barrier cable (0.0.), walk SE along a gradually uphill woods road following the NE bank of the West Kill. Pleasant deciduous forest surrounds you, and blue DEC trail markers guide your way.

The route continues easily to a 4-way trail jct. in a large clearing at 0.7 mi. A large trail bulletin board, a trail register, and several informal campsites are found here. The Diamond Notch Trail crosses the West Kill over Diamond Notch Falls and then bears immediately L, proceeding SE. The trail up West Kill Mt. via the Devil's Path (trail 96) turns R, just over the bridge, and follows the S bank of the creek W, with red DEC trail markers. The Hunter Mt. section of the Devil's Path (trail 95) does not cross the brook, but heads straight ahead (W) past the bulletin board and immediately begins to ascend the mountain.

Distances: To first open campsite, 0.3 mi.; to second open campsite, 0.6 mi.; to 4-way jct. with Devil's Path, 0.7 mi. (1.1 km).

(95) Devil's Path to Devil's Acre Lean-to

This section of the Devil's Path is often hiked by those ascending Southwest Hunter Mt. or Hunter Mt. The lean-to makes a good starting point for Southwest Hunter Mt., and those going to Hunter Mt. can reach the Hunter Mt. Spur Trail (trail 32), 300 ft. farther along the trail from the lean-to.

Trailhead: The trailhead is at the 4-way jct. with the Diamond Notch Trail (trail 94), 0.7 mi. from the end of Spruceton Rd. (see above).

From the trailhead (0.0 mi.) proceed W, following red DEC trail markers. The gradual grade is comfortable here. A large brook at 0.15 mi. dominates a section that can be wet during inclement weather. More climbing brings you to another stream at 0.45 mi.

The grade varies from this point, but generally steepens. An unmarked path at 0.75 mi. leads R to an informal campsite and then to a large flat boulder from which a view of the valley is possible. At 0.9 mi., rushing water can be heard in the ravine below.

After steady climbing to 1.45 mi., the trail levels and swings sharply S. Another spur trail R at 1.5 mi. leads to Geiger Point, an overhang with good viewing. Walking is comfortable in this section. A downgrade is followed by a pitch up to a height of land, where the herd path to Southwest Hunter Mt. begins. Look for the path where the main trail begins its descent to the Devil's Acre lean-to. The trail passes several informal campsites on a knoll at 1.8 mi., and then crosses a good spring outflow at 1.9 mi. This is a nice site, providing a base camp for many climbs. Southwest Hunter Mt. is along the ridge to the W. The Devil's Path continues 300 ft. to the jct. of the Hunter Mt. Spur Trail (trail 32). This can be followed to the Spruceton Trail (trail 93) and summit of Hunter Mt. 1.75 mi. from the lean-to; see above. Devil's Tombstone Public Campground is 2.2 mi. farther along the Devil's Path (trail 31) on NY 214 in Stony Clove.

Distances: *To first brook, 0.15 mi.; to second brook, 0.45 mi.; to Geiger Pt., 1.45 mi.; to spring, 1.9 mi.; to Devil's Acre lean-to, 1.95 mi. (3.2 km), 2.65 mi. from Spruceton Rd. Ascent, 1150 ft. (345 m).*

Southwest Hunter Mt. (Bushwhack)

Clearly higher than 3500 ft. in elevation, the peak SW of Hunter Mt. was not placed on the Catskill 3500 Club's original list of 3500-ft. peaks. It seems to meet at least one of the other criteria; being at least one-half mile from any other 3500-ft. summit or having a drop between it and neighboring peaks of at least 250 ft. Why was it left off the list?

As with many things in the climbing world, we'll probably never know the whole answer. Current maps are more accurate than the maps originally used. Standards for designation have shifted through time. The peak had no official name on USGS maps. It has been surmised by at least one of the original compilers that some Catskill 3500 Club founders didn't agree that the peak was separate, but rather felt it was a spur ridge of Hunter Mt. Rather than cause friction in the newly forming group, the matter was not pressed.

The name Southwest Hunter is beginning to show up on maps. In 1987 the Catskill 3500 Club voted to include the mountain in its climbing list for membership, and it has been officially required by all climbers accepted after April 1, 1990.

Trailhead: *The easiest approach to the mountain is from Spruceton Rd. (See the Spruceton Rd. to Devil's Acre Lean-to trail description, above.)*

Leave the Devil's Path. Continue about 0.3 mi. beyond Geiger Point Lookout. After a long, gradual downgrade, the Devil's Path climbs to a height of land. Follow around this flat area to the point where the trail begins to descend, and look for the prominent herd path to Southwest Hunter Mt. Sometimes it is marked by a cairn. Follow the nearly level grade of the old railroad for nearly 20 minutes, passing a couple of paths upward, to a good path which heads up via a drainage for about 0.2 mi. to the summmit area. It may be possible to locate an old railroad bed to follow for some distance before ascending the mountain.

Ascent from Spruceton Rd., 1560 ft. (468 m); summit elevation, 3740 ft. (1122 m).

(96) Devil's Path (West Kill Mt. Section)

Map 41: L-4 to K-4
NE Catskills

This section of the Devil's Path provides two routes to the summit of West Kill Mt., or a nice through trip for hikers with two vehicles. The trail passes through the West Kill Mt.–North Dome Wilderness Area. Most climbers ascend West Kill Mt. from the Diamond Notch end of the trail.

Trailhead: Starting from the DEC parking area at the 6.9 mi. point of Spruceton Rd. in summer, walk 0.8 mi. to the 4-way Diamond Notch Falls jct. (This parking lot is not plowed in winter. Use the parking area at 6.7 mi.). The trailhead is at the SW corner of the bridge over Diamond Notch Falls.

From the bridge (0.0 mi.), the Devil's Path follows the S bank of the West Kill downstream. The red-marked DEC route veers away from the water at 0.1 mi. and begins alternating moderate and gradual upgrades to the SW. Lush ferns and other ground cover make this an attractive walk through open deciduous forest.

The trail enters remnants of an old forest road at 0.15 mi., but this may not be readily evident to the hiker. The way is more gradual. A small outcrop on the L at 0.7 mi. has a wet-weather spring.

Leaving the old roadway course at 0.9 mi., the trail becomes moderate to steep as it climbs the E ridge. As the ridge line comes close, the grade becomes more gradual.

A sign indicating the 3500-ft. elevation mark appears at 1.4 mi. As the route begins to climb the rock outcrop at 1.4 mi., it passes a large rock overhang on the R. Capable of holding a small party of hikers, this makes a good emergency shelter. A wind-protected rock wall and fire ring add to the benefits of the location.

Beyond the overhang a slight loss of elevation is followed by nearly level rolling terrain to another downgrade. There are two more knolls to cross before the last climb to the summit.

At the Buck Ridge Lookout at 2.1 mi., a large, flat, rock ledge L provides excellent open views to the SE over Diamond Notch Hollow towards Indian Head and Overlook mts. On the R, a path leads 100 ft. to a low, flat boulder that offers views NE towards Hunter Mt. and N to Rusk Mt. It is another 0.1 mi. of gradual grade to the wooded summit. The summit offers no view.

As one begins to descend beyond the summit, it is evident that this section of trail is less used than that already described. The nearly level ridge trail has berry bushes pressing in at several places, but the way is nevertheless still easy to follow. A spring R in a wet spot at 2.5 mi. marks the start of a gradual downgrade. The 3500-ft. elevation sign is at 2.9 mi.

From 3.0 mi., the route is again nearly level. The trail is wide and clear from this point onwards. A short, moderate rocky downgrade at 3.6 mi. is followed by a steady gradual descent. At 3.9 mi. a steep rocky upgrade leads you over a ridge spur. Beyond this point varying grades lead to a trail sign at 5.2 mi.

Bearing R, the remaining 1.8 mi. of trail gradually descends N through Mink Hollow to Spruceton Rd. The trail reaches the E bank of Mink Hollow Brook at 5.6 mi., where many burnt tree stumps tell of a past forest fire. At 6.1 mi., great glacial erratics dot the slope. A significant hemlock grove gives evidence of what the early Catskills were like before the tannery industry left the forest denuded of this magnificent tree in the mid-1800s.

A slight upgrade ends at a trail sign pointing straight ahead. (Avoid a side trail on the E.) A final downgrade leads to a DEC trail register, 100 yds. before the Spruceton Rd. trailhead at 7.0 mi. (This trailhead is 3.8 mi. from West Kill hamlet and has parking for several vehicles.)

Distances: To beginning of moderate to steep grades, 0.9 mi.; to 3500 ft. point and to rock overhang, 1.4 mi; to Buck Ridge Lookouts, 2.1 mi.; to West Kill Mt. summit, 2.2 mi.; to 3500 ft. sign, 2.9 mi.; to steep rocky upgrade, 3.9 mi.; to trail sign, 5.2 mi.; to Mink Hollow Brook, 5.6 mi.; to boulder field, 6.1 mi.; to Spruceton Rd., 7.0 mi. (11.3 km) (7.8 mi. from DEC parking area). Summit elevation, 3880 ft. (1187 m). Ascent from Diamond Notch Falls bridge, 1500 ft. (450 m).

Halcott Mt. (Bushwhack)

Map 42: J-4
Central Catskills

The village of Halcott Center was named after George W. Halcott, an early settler. So, it seems, was Halcott Mt. This peak is part of the Forest Preserve's 4900-acre Halcott Mt. Wild Forest.

Trailhead: The usual starting point on state land is an unmarked parking area off the W side of NY 42, 2.4 mi. S of the hamlet of West Kill. This point is also 5.0 mi. N of the NY 42-NY 28 jct. in Shandaken and just S of the height of land in Deep Notch. The parking area is usually plowed in winter.

From the parking area, a path leads SW up a small grade and after 100 ft. turns abruptly R to continue up a steep bank to the top of a nice waterfall. Of the two streams shown on the map, this stream is the one farthest N. Cross it and head for the ridge. Good compass work is needed.

Though this is a straightforward climb through fairly open deciduous forest, you will travel a long way up moderately steep grades before any leveling occurs. Depending on your initial course, you will probably have to bear S or SW on top of the ridge.

Other approaches, which require gaining permission to cross short stretches of private land, are from Upper Birch Creek Rd. out of Pine Hill and from Brush Ridge Rd. (Townsend Hollow Rd.) out of Fleischmanns.

Ascent, 1760 ft. (527 m). Summit elevation, 3537 ft. (1061 m).

Mt. Sherrill (Bushwhack)

Map 42: K-4
Central Catskills

Mt. Sherrill is part of the West Kill Mt.–North Dome Wilderness Area. The mountain is named after Col. Sherrill, a Shandaken tannery owner, who lost his life at Gettysburg during the Civil War.

Trailhead: A good access point for the mountain is on the E side of NY 42 at the DEC Forest Preserve Access parking area, 3.7 mi. S of the hamlet of West Kill and 3.7 mi. N of the jct. of NY 42 and NY 28 at Shandaken. (See Route Guide from Prattsville to Shandaken.)

Typically, parties climb an old woods road until it runs out and then continue along the crest of the spur ridge to the summit. The mountain can also be climbed from North Dome for a long day trip. (See the North Dome description above.)

Ascent, 1980 ft. (595 m). Summit elevation, 3540 ft. (1062 m).

Buttermilk Falls

Extended and Challenging Opportunities

Fine opportunities for both extended and challenging outings exist in the Catskills. Extended trips in particular are often overlooked, because the extensive road network of the Catskills makes day trips possible in almost any section. This guidebook is designed so as to group trips found in the same local road network. Consequently, trips that overlap chapters can be difficult to discern.

One of the purposes of this chapter is to provide complete sequencing of extended outings for the hiker. Where an extended outing overlaps more than one guidebook chapter, the sections are listed with mileages. The hiker should refer to each separate chapter for a description of the specific trail section.

Different types of challenges require different skills, degrees of physical stamina, and experience. Enjoyment, appreciation, aesthetics, and self-renewal are fundamental parts of the "recreating" involved in recreation. These are best obtained when the outing is commensurate with the hiker's abilities. Sometimes, adding a day to the length of a trip or knowing when to quit a bushwhack can make the difference between a marvelous experience and a bad memory. Good planning makes good trips.

Long Hikes and Extended Outings

Backpacking in the Catskills can be enhanced if the planning anticipates certain factors. Trails in the Catskills tend to start climbing almost immediately and then level off on ridge tops, where they become long enjoyable rambles. Take your time in the early stages of a hike with a heavy backpack until the terrain levels.

Carry plenty of water; little water is found on the ridges. It will often be necessary to drop down off a ridge to lower elevations to a lean-to for water. Remember that camping is not permitted above 3500 ft. elevation, except in winter. Carry a light rope; occasionally you may wish to lower a heavy pack down a short vertical section, rather than descend with it on your back.

Although trails frequently cross roads, don't expect to find general stores for supplies or immediate help in emergencies on these roads. Rural roads are generally isolated and houses are far apart.

The Devil's Path

The Devil's Path is an E-W trail offering some of the most challenging and interesting hiking in the Catskills. It extends 23.2 mi. from Platte Clove in the E to Spruceton Rd. in the W. In the process, it keeps to ridgelines, going over Indian Head, Twin, Sugarloaf, Plateau, most of Hunter, and West Kill mts. Its intermontane descents drop into Jimmy Dolan, Pecoy, Mink Hollow, Stony Clove and Diamond notches. These can be dangerous when wet or icy.

The trails of the extreme eastern section date back to Colonial days, but they were not officially designated as hiking trails until 1930. The Hunter Mt. section was built in 1935 and the West Kill section was constructed in 1973-74.

Sections of Devil's Path	Miles
Plateau–Indian Head Wilderness Section	13.05
Hunter Mt. Section	4.15
West Kill Mt. Section	7.0
Total	24.2

Escarpment Trail

The Escarpment Trail can be completed in a single day by good hikers, but it is usually done in sections. It makes a splendid three-day backpack trip. The long ridge trail runs S-N from North/South Lake Public Campgrounds to NY 23, near Windham. First development as a trail began in 1932 with the work of A. T. Shorey around North Lake. The Northern section was completed in 1967. In 1987 a portion of the original trail, which climbed past Kaaterskill Falls from NY 23A, was deleted. The trail now starts from the DEC parking area at Schutt Rd., just outside the main gate to North/South Lake Public Campground.

Sections of Escarpment Trail	Miles
Southern Section	7.2
Northern Section	15.9
Total	23.1

Delaware Ridge Trail

Many of the individual trails found in the Delaware–Beaver Kill section of the Catskills connect and are collectively known as the Delaware Ridge Trail. These trails are not heavily used, and thus are not maintained as well as might be desired. However, they are well marked and provide the hiker with a wilderness experience not often gained on other trails which have more hiking pressure. For the experienced backpacker, they provide a rugged and thoroughly interesting network of trails.

Delaware Trail Sections, from E-W	Miles
Alder Lake to next trailhead	0.4
Alder Lake to Big Pond Trail	2.9
Connecting road section	0.15
Big Pond to Touch-me-not Trail	1.1
Touch-me-not Trail section	2.7
Connecting road section on Beech Hill Rd.	0.2
Middle Mt. Trail	2.0
Mary Smith Trail	4.5
Pelnor Hollow (connecting section only)	0.8
Campbell Mt. Trail	5.8
Trout Pond Trail	5.4
Total	25.95

The Finger Lakes Trail connects with the Delaware Ridge Trail from the W. Road sections are being decreased yearly. Write to Finger Lakes Trail Conference, Inc., P.O. Box 18048, Rochester, NY 14618-0048 for maps and information.

The recently completed Mill Brook Ridge Trail has connected the Delaware Ridge Trail to the Dry Brook Ridge Trail and that, in turn, links directly with the Neversink–Hardenburgh Trail. It is possible to hike all the way from New York City to western New York State on a sequence of interconnecting trails.

The Long Path

The Long Path is a dream transformed only partially into reality. In the 1930s members of the Mohawk Valley Hiking Club proposed a "long path" that would compare to Vermont's Long Trail. It would start at the George Washington Bridge in New York City and end in the Adirondacks. For many years the trail went only to NY 23, N of Windham Peak. In the last few years, however, renewed interest has extended the trail to John Boyd Thatcher State Park near Albany (1995). From time to time, new sections of trail are opened and a little more of the dream becomes reality.

The Long Path follows established trails in the Catskills. The listing below is only for the Catskill sections covered in this guidebook. Those interested in trail descriptions for the whole Long Path should see the *Guide to the Long Path*, published by the NY/NJ Trail Conference.

Long Path sections S-N, as covered in this guide	Miles
Long Path (Upper Cherrytown Rd.–Peekamoose Rd.)	8.7
East on Peekamoose Rd.	0.5
Peekamoose–Table Trail (from Peekamoose Rd.) to summit of Table Mt.	4.3
Table–Peekamoose Trail (from Denning–Woodland Trail) Table Mt. summit to Denning–Woodland Valley Trail	2.75
Denning–Woodland Valley Trail (jct. Table–Peekamoose Trail to Curtis-Ormsbee Trail)	1.75
Curtis-Ormsbee Trail	1.6
Slide–Cornell–Wittenberg Trail (jct. of Curtis-Ormsbee Trail to summit Wittenberg Mt.)	3.8
Wittenberg–Cornell–Slide Trail (Wittenberg summit to Woodland Valley Public Campground)	3.9

Woodland Valley to Phoenicia via Woodland Valley Rd., NY 28 and NY 214	5.75
Phoenicia to Mt. Tremper Trailhead via Co. Rd. 40, which is Old NY 30	1.4
Phoenicia Trail to Mt. Tremper Trail	2.75
Willow Trail to Mt. Tremper Trail	3.2
Jessup Rd. and NY 212 (Willow to Lake Hill)	2.3
Mink Hollow Rd. to Mink Hollow Trail	2.85
Mink Hollow Trail (South of Devil's Path)	3.05
Devil's Path (Plateau–Indian Head Wilderness Area) (Mink Hollow to Jimmy Dolan Notch	3.45
Jimmy Dolan Notch Trail	2.3
Devil's Path (Plateau–Indian Head Wilderness Area) (Jimmy Dolan Notch to Prediger Rd.)	0.5
Prediger Rd. NE to Platte Clove Rd.	0.4
Platte Clove Rd. (Prediger Rd. jct. SW to Kaaterskill High Peak Trail)	0.9
Kaaterskill High Peak Trail to Long Path jct.	3.5
Long Path Jct. to Buttermilk Falls	1.5
Buttermilk Falls Trail	4.0
Malden Ave. to NY 23A	0.35
NY 23A E to Harding Rd. Trail	0.3
Harding Rd. Trail	3.3
Sleepy Hollow Trail (Harding Rd. Trail to Escarpment Trail)	0.1
Escarpment Trail (Southern Section)	4.65
Escarpment Trail (Northern Section)	15.9
NY 23 (East Windham) to Greene Co. Rd. 10	6.95
Total	97.25

Dry Brook Ridge Trail

The Dry Brook Ridge Trail runs from Margaretville to the Beaverkill Valley. This long trail has relatively easy hiking once the ridge above Pakatakan Mt. has been reached. It is 13.45 mi. long.

Appendix I

Glossary of Terms

Azimuth	A clockwise compass bearing swung from N.
Bushwhack	An off-trail hike, usually requiring compass and map.
Col	A pass through a low spot in a ridge at right angles to the line of the ridge.
Clove	A narrow valley. (In the Catskills, said to be caused by the slap of God's hand or the swish of the Devil's tail.)
Corduroy	Logs laid side by side across a trail to assist travel in wet areas.
Fire ring	A rough circle of stones used as a site in which to build small fires.
Hollow	A small valley.
Kill	A Dutch word for waterway, creek, or river.
Lean-to	A three-sided shelter with an over-hanging roof and one open side.
Notch	A narrow pass.
Summit	The top of a mountain.
Vly *(vlai, vlei)*	Dutch for swamp or marsh.
Woods road	An old road in a woods that could have been a highway, logging road, or tote road.

Appendix II

Catskill Mountains 3000 Feet and Higher in Elevation

This list of mountains having an elevation of 3000 ft. or higher is presented here to make hikers aware of the many possibilities for interesting and worthwhile climbs and explorations in all parts of the Catskill Park. Some of these peaks are within the Forest Preserve and are open to the climbing public. Others are on private property or are surrounded by private property. Always obtain permission from landowners before hiking these lands.

Peaks 3500 ft. elevation or higher are referred to as major peaks of the Catskills. There are thirty-five of these mountains. Two of them, Slide Mt. and Hunter Mt., have elevations higher than 4000 ft. The criteria for distinguishing one 3500 ft.-summit from another (as opposed to being the shoulder of the same mountain) are that there must be at least a 250-ft. drop between it and its neighbors or it must be at least one-half mile away from them. From time to time these criteria are challenged, and ways to correct early mistakes or erroneous interpretations are presented. Be that as it may, the following list of mountains is thought to be correct.

An asterisk in the roster indicates a footnote; the number corresponds to the number on the roster. Under *remarks*, "Tr" indicates that there is a standard, maintained trail to the summit. An extra "T" means there is a fire tower on the summit. These towers are not manned and should be climbed only at the climber's own risk.

No.	Name	Elev. (ft.)	Remarks	U.S.G.S. Topographic Map
1	Slide	4180	Tr	Peekamoose Mt.
2	Hunter	4040	TrT	Hunter
3	Black Dome	3980	Tr	Freehold
4	Blackhead	3940	Tr	Freehold
5	Thomas Cole	3940	Tr	Hensonville
6	West Kill	3880	Tr	Lexington
7	Graham	3868		Seager
8	Cornell	3860	Tr	Phoenicia
9	Doubletop	3860		Seager
10	Table	3847	Tr	Peekamoose Mt.
11	Peekamoose	3843	Tr	Peekamoose Mt.
12	Plateau	3840	Tr	Hunter
13 *	Sugarloaf	3800	Tr	Hunter
14	Wittenberg	3780	Tr	Phoenicia
15	Southwest Hunter	3740		Hunter
16	Lone	3721		Peekamoose Mt.
17 *	Balsam Lake	3720	TrT	Seager
18	Panther	3720	Tr	Shandaken
19	Big Indian	3700		Shandaken
20	Friday	3694		West Shokan
21	Rusk	3680		Lexington
22	High Peak	3655		Kaaterskill
23	Twin	3640	Tr	Bearsville
24	Balsam Cap	3623		West Shokan
25	Fir	3620		Shandaken
26	North Dome	3610		Lexington
27	Balsam	3600	Tr	Shandaken

*13. Sometimes called Mink Mt.
17. Sometimes called Balsam Roundtop.

No.	Name	Elev. (ft.)	Remarks	U.S.G.S. Topographic Map
28	Bearpen	3600		Prattsville
29	Eagle	3600	Tr	Seager
30	Indian Head	3573	Tr	Woodstock
31	Sherrill	3540		Lexington
32	Vly	3529		West Kill
33	Windham High Pk.	3524	Tr	Hensonville
34	Halcott	3520		West Kill
35	Rocky	3508		West Shokan
36	Mill Brook Ridge	3480	Tr	Arena
37	Dry Brook Ridge	3460	Tr	Seager
38	Woodpecker Ridge	3460		Seager
39	Olderbark	3440		Bearsville
40	Roundtop	3440		Prattsville
41	Roundtop	3440		Kaaterskill
42	Huntersfield	3423		Ashland
43 *	Belleayre	3420	Tr	Fleischmanns
44	Stoppel Point	3420	Tr	Kaaterskill
45	West Kill	3420	Tr	Lexington
46	South Bearpen	3410		West Kill
47	Northeast Halcott	3408		West Kill
48	Spruce	3380		Shandaken
49	Beaver Kill Range	3377	Tr	Claryville
50	South Vly	3360		West Kill
51	Pisgah	3345		Margaretville
52	East Wildcat	3340		Peekamoose Mt.
53	North Plattekill	3340		Hobart
54	Shultice	3280		Roxbury
55	South Plattekill	3260		Hobart

*43. Summit is on NW end of mountain, not at old fire tower site.

No.	Name	Elev. (ft.)	Remarks	U.S.G.S. Topographic Map
56 *	Unnamed	3260		Shandaken
57	Northwest Moresville Range	3240		Roxbury
58 *	Unnamed	3224		Willowemoc
59 *	Narrow Notch	3220		Roxbury
60	Onteora	3220		Hunter
61	Richmond	3220		Ashland
62	Utsayantha	3214		Stamford
63 *	Unnamed	3211		Claryville
64	Van Wyck	3206		Peekamoose Mt.
65	Giant Ledge	3200	Tr	Shandaken
66	Burnt Knob	3180	Tr	Freehold
67	Mongaup	3177	Tr	Willowemoc
68	Cradle Rock Ridge	3160		Arena
69	West Wildcat	3160		Peekamoose Mt.
70	East Jewett Range	3140		Hunter
71	Overlook	3140	TrT	Woodstock
72 *	Unnamed	3140		Lexington
73	White Man	3140		Roxbury
74	Acra Point	3100	Tr	Freehold
75	Barkaboom	3100		Arena
76	Cave	3100		Hensonville
77	Cowan	3100		Hobart

* 56. *Located W of Winnisook Lake.*
  58. *E of Mongaup Mt. at headwaters of Willowemoc Creek.*
  59. *Located E of Narrow Notch.*
  63. *Located NW of High Falls.*
  72. *Called Pine Island by Guyot.*

No.	Name	Elev. (ft.)	Remarks	U.S.G.S. Topographic Map
78 *	Unnamed	3100		Lexington
79	Plattekill	3100		Woodstock
80	Red Kill Ridge	3100		Fleischmanns
81	West Stoppel Pt.	3100		Kaaterskill
82	Rose	3090		West Kill
83	High Point	3080	Tr	West Shokan
84 *	Unnamed	3062		Willowemoc
85	Churchill	3060		Stamford
86	Irish	3060		Roxbury
87	Round Top	3060		Hobart
88	Denman	3053		Claryville
89 *	Unnamed	3040		Roxbury
90	SW Moresville Range	3040		Roxbury
91	West Cave	3040		Ashland
92	Woodhull	3040		Peekamoose Mt.
93 *	Little Pisgah	3020		Margaretville
94	Southeast Warren	3020		Hobart
95 *	Little Rocky	3015		West Shokan
96 *	Unnamed	3000		Margaretville
97 *	Old Clump	3000		Roxbury
98 *	Unnamed	3000		Bearsville

*78. *Climbers call it Packsaddle.*

84. *Located N of Sand Pond.*

89. *Located S of Montgomery Hollow.*

93. *Located SE of Pisgah; name is local, not USGS.*

95. *Sometimes called Gulf Mt.*

96. *Located N of Hubbell Hill Hollow.*

97. *Located NW of Roxbury; USGS gives another peak this name on Hobart Quadrangle.*

98. *Located N of Silver Hollow.*

Appendix III

Table of Short Hikes

The following table lists outings having for the most part a distance of less than 2.5 mi. (one way). This table can serve to introduce short hikes in the Catskills to enthusiasts. It is especially helpful in making outing choices for people with young children. Each separate destination is listed with the *one-way* distance, name and number of the trail and any significant terrain data. In some cases, the destination suggested is reached on part of a much longer trail. Therefore, the hiker must use the trail guide carefully.

The hiker must still determine if a given outing is proper for each member of the hiking party. Physical condition, hiking skills and previous experience should be considered.

Many of these hikes are ideal for children. If you are planning to hike with children, you may wish to review information provided on page 14 in the section "Hiking with Children."

Mi.	Objective	Trail Name & Number	Notes on Terrain
BLACK DOME VALLEY–NORTH POINT SECTION			
1.1	Elm Ridge Lean-to	Elm Ridge (3)	Gentle upgrades
1.6	Acra Point	Acra Point/ Burnt Knob (4)	Fairly steep to ridge
1.5	Camel's Hump	Blackhead Range (11)	Open terrain

Mi.	Objective	Trail Name & Number	Notes on Terrain

PALENVILLE–NORTH LAKE SECTION

Mi.	Objective	Trail Name & Number	Notes on Terrain
0.4	Kaaterskill Falls	Kaaterskill Falls (15)	Easy, but rocky
1.1	Sunset Rock	Escarpment (South) (18) & yellow side trail	One short steep section

PLATTE CLOVE SECTION

2.4	Huckleberry Point	Kaaterskill High Peak (26) & Huckleberry Point	A few moderate grades

STONY CLOVE SECTION

1.0	Orchard Point	Plateau Mt. from Stony Clove (33)	Some long steep grades
2.5	Diamond Notch Falls	Diamond Notch (34)	Some long grades

BIG INDIAN–UPPER NEVERSINK SECTION

3.0	Rochester Hollow	Rochester Hollow	Easy grades
1.8	Giant Ledge	Giant Ledge–Panther Mt. (40)	Moderate grades
2.75	Slide Mt.	Slide–Cornell Wittenberg (41)	Excellent views
1.5	East Branch Neversink River	Denning–Woodland Valley (46) & Table–Peekamoose (47)	Pleasant walk

WOODSTOCK–SHANDAKEN SECTION

2.5	Overlook Mt.	Overlook Mt. (48)	Gravel road

PEEKAMOOSE SECTION

1.8	Vernooy Falls	Long Path (Cherrytown Rd.) (59)	A few steep grades
1.0	Kanape Brook	Ashokan High Point (57)	Pleasant woods walk; old road

Mi.	Objective	Trail Name & Number	Notes on Terrain

ARKVILLE–SEAGER SECTION

Mi.	Objective	Trail Name & Number	Notes on Terrain
1.0	Burroughs Memorial Field	Burroughs Memorial Field	Historical walk
2.0	Short Loop	Kelly Hollow (63)	Woods road walk

DELAWARE–BEAVERKILL SECTION

Mi.	Objective	Trail Name & Number	Notes on Terrain
1.5	Alder Lake	Alder Lake Loop (67)	Old carriage road
1.7	Huggins Lake	Huggins Lake	Easy walk
1.75	Balsam Lake Mt.	Balsam Lake Mt. Loop (83)	Fire tower
1.1	Frick Pond	Frick Pond Loop (85)	Old woods roads

PRATTSVILLE–SHANDAKEN SECTION

Mi.	Objective	Trail Name & Number	Notes on Terrain
0.5	Pratt's Rock	Pratt's Rock	Historical, steep
0.7	Diamond Notch Falls	Diamond Notch (94)	Woods road
2.65	Devil's Acre Lean-to	Devil's Path to Devil's Acre Lean-to (95)	Long upgrades

Appendix IV

Opportunities in the Catskill Region for Physically Impaired Recreationists

The following is a list of outing opportunities in the Catskill region for recreationalists who are physically impaired. **These trails and access points do not conform to formal accessibility standards and are subject to changes in weather conditions.**

Most people enjoy the out-of-doors in part because of the challenges that are found there. Those who lead trips must carefully consider the capabilities of the participants in their party and the degree of challenge desired. This is particularly important for leaders of the physically impaired. If you are considering being a leader of physically impaired recreationists, you may wish to read the section "Hiking with the Physically Impaired," which is found on page 16.

Scenic Vistas and Drives

There are many scenic vistas in the Catskills. However, few are readily accessible by vehicle. Some of the outstanding ones are listed below.

North/South Lake Public Campsite Vista. From the picnic area near the beach swimming area parking lot, walk S 0.2 mi. on roadway to the site of the old Catskill Mt. House hotel. Magnificent views of the Hudson River valley and five states.

Lookout Point Vista. Located on NY 23, 8.2 mi. W of its jct. with

NY 145, this vista is truly spectacular. There is a parking pull-off part way up the mountain.

Ashokan Reservoir Vista. A spectacular view of the mountains surrounding Ashokan Reservoir gained from the spillway bridge crossing the reservoir. This is 1.6 mi. S of the village of Ashokan on the road to Olivebridge.

NY 23A–Palenville to Haines Falls Drive. This is a very nice drive up the historic Kaaterskill Clove with its waterfalls, ledges and lookouts.

Beaver Kill Rd. to Quaker Clearing. Off NY 206 near Rockland, this rural road winds along the Beaver Kill River for 22 mi. to Quaker Clearing.

NY 30 from Grand Gorge to Downsville Drive. This drive shows the best of the East Branch of the Delaware valley and Pepacton Reservoir.

Trail Access

The nature of the Catskills is that its eroded plateau creates many very steep, rugged trails that make climbing to summits difficult for the physically impaired. On the other hand, this same geological downcutting has created many interesting valleys and hollows where woods roads seemingly wander on forever. These woods roads can be excellent avenues for walks. Check maps for flat areas. The trails listed below are actually old roadways and are good examples of what the Catskills can offer the physically impaired hiker.

Sleepy Hollow Trail. The hiker may not wish to do the whole 4.45 mi. of this famous old stage coach route to the Catskill Mountain House. However, the gradual slopes for the first 1.5 mi. to a picnic area are a reasonable trip.

Rochester Hollow. This woods road through very attractive forest runs for 3.0 mi. on state land. Rippling brooks, birds and easy grades make this a very nice area for walks in any season of the year.

Overlook Mt. Trail. This 2.4 mi. gravel road gains 1400 ft. in elevation. However, the broad lane is open and easy to climb.

Alder Lake Loop Trail. A very pleasant day can be spent at this former estate. The remains of the old Coykendall Lodge, a beautiful lake and camping areas with fire rings for cooking, offer many possibilities for an outing. The 1.5 mi. loop follows good woods roads around the lake.

Diamond Notch. This short, 0.7 mi. walk is along an essentially flat woods road beside Diamond Notch Brook to the very attractive Diamond Notch waterfall.

Boat Access

Due to the direction of slope of Catskill rocks in relation to the direction of past glacier movement, very few natural lakes ever formed in this region. To make matters worse, the many reservoirs of the region have strict regulations that prevent casual use of these bodies of water. However, it is possible to get permits for seasonal use of these reservoirs for the purpose of fishing if the boat is left at the reservoir and not removed.

Alder Lake. This is a small lake but can provide good fishing (worms or lures only) and very nice paddling. See Alder Lake Loop (above) for other activities that can provide a full day or even a weekend of outdoor enjoyment.

North/South Lake Public Campsite. This campsite has two large lakes. Rental boats; no motors.

Big Pond. Hand launch. No motors; electric O.K.

Colgate Lake. Hand launch. No motors, no electric.

Crystal Lake. Hand launch. No motors; electric O.K.

Huggins Lake. Hand launch. No motors; electric O.K.

Little Pond. Hand launch. No motors, no electric.

Mongaup Pond. Hand launch. No motors; electric O.K.

Waneta Lake. Hand launch. No motors; electric O.K.

Wilson Park. Hand launch. No motors, no electric.

The Department of Environmental Covnservation (DEC) produces a brochure, "Opening the Outdoors to People with Disabilities," available from the DEC, 50 Wolf Rd., Albany, NY 12233.

DEC also provides a free permit for physically impaired people who want to take a motor vehicle onto a normally restricted access road in Wild Forest areas. Allow three to four weeks' lead time for obtaining this permit. There is no restriction on the use of motorized wheelchairs (as long as they are the kind used in the home) in Wilderness areas. Consult DEC at the above address for further information.

Appendix V

Lean-tos in the Catskills

The following is a listing of all lean-tos within the area covered by this guidebook. They are listed according to the guidebook sections, with information on USGS map and location. Unlisted sections did not have any lean-tos at time of publication. As Unit Management Plans (UMP) are completed, relocation, removals or additional lean-tos may alter this listing (1994).

Shelter	USGS Map	Location
BLACK DOME VALLEY–NORTH POINT SECTION		
Elm Ridge	Hensonville	Escarpment Trail; 1.15 mi. from NY 23, towards Windham High Peak
Batavia Kill	Freehold	Batavia Kill Trail, 0.25 mi. from Escarpment Trail jct.
PLATTE CLOVE SECTION		
Devil's Kitchen	Lexington	Old Overlook Rd. Trail; 0.15 mi. S of Indian Head Mt. jct. off Devil's Path
STONY CLOVE SECTION		
Devil's Acre	Hunter	Devil's Path; 0.05 mi. W of Hunter Mt. Trail jct.

Shelter	USGS Map	Location
Diamond Notch	Lexington	Diamond Notch Trail; N side of notch, 0.7 mi. from Devil's Path jct.

BIG INDIAN–UPPER NEVERSINK SECTION

Belleayre	Shandaken	Belleayre Mt. Trail; 0.45 mi. E of old fire tower clearing
Hirschland	Seager	Belleayre Ridge Trail; 0.45 mi. NW of old fire tower site
McKenley Hollow	Shandaken	McKenley Hollow Trail; 0.65 mi. from trailhead
Biscuit Brook	Shandaken	Biscuit Brook–Pine Hill Trail; 1.9 mi. N of West Branch Rd. jct.
Fall Brook	Seager	Neversink–Hardenburgh Trail; 1.55 mi. from DEC parking area, 4.35 mi. from Quaker Clearing
Long Pond	Willowemoc	Long Pond–Beaver Kill Ridge Trail spur; 1.05 mi. SE of Flugertown Rd.
Bouton Memorial	Peekamoose Mt.	Table–Peekamoose Trail; 2.4 mi. E of Denning–Woodland and Valley Trail

Shelter	USGS Map	Location

WOODSTOCK–SHANDAKEN SECTION

Echo Lake	Woodstock	Echo Lake Trail; Echo Lake
Mink Hollow	Hunter	Mink Hollow Trail; 0.1 mi. S of Devil's Path jct.
Baldwin Memorial	Phoenicia	Phoenicia Trail to Mt. Tremper; 1.95 mi. E from trailhead
Tremper Mt.	Phoenicia	Phoenicia Trail to Mt. Tremper; at summit
Terrace Mt.	Phoenicia	Terrace Mt. Trail; 0.9 mi. N of jct. with Wittenberg–Cornell–Slide Trail
Fox Hollow	Shandaken	Panther Mt. Trail; 0.4 mi. W of Fox Hollow trailhead

DELAWARE–BEAVER KILL SECTION

Pelnor Hollow	Lewbeach	Pelnor Hollow Trail; 0.9 mi. N of trailhead; 2.3 mi. S of Mary Smith Trail jct.
Campbell Mt.	Downsville	Campbell Mt. Trail; 1.3 mi. from NY 206, 1.1 mi. from Campbell Mt. Rd.
Trout Pond	Downsville	Trout Pond Trail; Trout Pond inlet, 1.4 mi. N from Russell Brook Rd. trailhead

Shelter	USGS Map	Location
Balsam Lake Mt. #1	Seager	Balsam Lake Mt. Trail; 1.4 mi. from Quaker Clearing, via Dry Brook Ridge Trail to Balsam Lake Mt. Trail (0.5 mi. to spur trail R on Balsam Lake Mt. Trail)
Balsam Lake Mt. Mt. #2	Seager	Same as Balsam Lake Mt. #1, but 50 yds. farther on spur trail
Beaver Meadow	Arena	Mill Brook Ridge Trail; 2.25 mi. E of Alder Lake Trailhead

ARKVILLE–SEAGER SECTION

Shelter	USGS Map	Location
Dry Brook	Seager	Dry Brook Ridge Trail, 1.2 mi. N of Mill Brook Rd.
Mill Brook	Seager	Located at end of 0.25 mi. trail, N side of Mill Brook Rd., 0.9 mi. SW of Dry Brook Ridge Trail jct.
German Hollow	Fleischmanns	German Hollow Trail; 0.6 mi. from trailhead
Kelly Hollow	Arena	Kelly Hollow Trail; at Beaver Pond, 1.9 mi. point of trail
Rider Hollow	Seager	Rider Hollow Trail; 0.5 mi. E of trail
Shandaken Brook	Seager	Seager Trail; 2.15 mi. point of trail on Shandaken Brook

Shelter	USGS Map	Location
John Robb	Hunter	Spruceton Trail; 2.3 mi. point of trail
Devil's Acre	Hunter	See above
Turk Hollow	West Kill	0.25 mi. from end of Turk Hollow Rd., via Co. Rd. 37/3 off NY 28 at Fleischmanns

Appendix VI

State Campgrounds and Day Use Areas in the Catskill Park

Public campgrounds have been established by the DEC at many attractive spots throughout the state. Listed below are those that might be useful as bases of operations for hiking in the Catskill Park. The DEC publishes individual campground brochures and a complete listing of all campgrounds is contained in a brochure of New York State Forest Preserve Public Campgrounds titled "Camping in the New York State Forest Preserve." These brochures are available from the DEC, 50 Wolf Rd., Albany, NY 12233.

Beaverkill. Off NY 17, 7.0 mi. NW of Livingston Manor. (See *Route Guide* for Beaver Kill Rd.–Quaker Clearing.)

Mongaup Pond. Off NY 17, 3.0 mi. N of DeBruce. (See *Route Guide* for Livingston Manor–Claryville.)

Kenneth L. Wilson Public Campground. Off NY 28 near Boiceville.

Woodland Valley. Woodland Valley Rd., off NY 28 near Phoenicia. (See *Route Guide* for Woodstock–Shandaken.)

Little Pond. Off NY 17, 14.0 mi. NW of Livingston Manor. (See *Route Guide* for Beaver Kill Rd.–Quaker Clearing.)

Bear Spring Mountain. Off NY 206, 5.0 mi. SE of Walton.

Devil's Tombstone. Off NY 214, 4.0 mi. S of Hunter.

North/South Lake. Off NY 23A, 3.0 mi. NE of Haines Falls. (See *Route Guide* for Palenville–Haines Falls.)

Belleayre Mountain Day Use Area. Off NY 28, just SE of Pine Hill, Ulster County. Includes Pine Hill Lake, a 6-acre man-made lake with a swimming area, fishing and picnic facilities.

Day Use Area. Off NY 28, 1.0 mi. N of Boiceville, Ulster County (site of the proposed Catskill Interpretive Center). Includes two short interpretive foot trails.

Index

Note: Lakes are listed under their names instead of under "Lake."

Addendum

(83A) Mill Brook Ridge Trail   Map 42: F-6 to G-6
Central Catskills

Constructed in 1997, this trail links Alder Lake with Balsam Lake Mt., providing an ambitious day hike over Mill Brook Ridge. A new lean-to midway along the route lends this trail to an enjoyable overnight experience as well.

Trailhead: *Follow the trail access directions for the Alder Lake Loop (Trail 67). Follow the red-marked Alder Lake Loop Trail E around Alder Lake to its jct. with the Mill Brook Ridge Trail, 0.75 mi. E of the Alder Lake Trailhead Parking Lot.*

From the trailhead (0.0 mi.) on the E side of Alder Lake, yellow foot trail markers lead E up a short grade along an old woods road. At 0.15 mi. the trail crests a hill and briefly descends before resuming its gradual ascent at 0.25 mi. The trail crosses a small stream at 0.4 mi. and then passes through an old log landing. At 0.5 mi. the trail begins a short, steep climb after which the grade moderates. A herd path forks R at 0.9 mi., leading to the first of three beaver meadows that the trail passes.

The woods road that the trail has been following ends at a stream crossing at 0.1 mi.; the hiking trail turns L and continues as a footpath.

At 1.1 mi. another stream is crossed by way of a single log hewed flat. The trail turns L at 1.2 mi. and begins a moderate ascent, following a brook to the R. At 1.3 mi. the grade eases. The brook is now at the bottom of a steep ravine on the R.

At 1.4 mi. the trail turns L as it reaches a second beaver meadow.

The trail skirts around the N side of the meadow and reaches a jct. with two paths at 1.5 mi. The path on the R leads 80 ft. to a lean-to overlooking the beaver meadow. The path to the L leads 100 ft. to a pipe spring. This lean-to is 2.25 mi. E of the Alder Lake trailhead, and 4.5 mi. W of Balsam Lake Mt.

After leaving the lean-to, the trail turns N, climbing to a beaver pond and crossing its outlet on large rocks at 1.6 mi. After crossing a seasonal watercourse, the trail begins to climb moderately, following a drainage up Mill Brook Ridge. After a rather steep ascent near the top of the drainage, the trail reaches the top of the ridge at 2.1 mi. and turns E. It soon passes a rock ledge on the L, and swings ESE, passing a modest vista at 2.5 mi.

At 2.6 mi. the trail climbs steeply with a switchback before reaching a vista to the W at 2.8 mi. Just beyond the vista, the trail crosses over the highest point on the ridge (3480 ft.) and then begins a moderate descent as it follows the ridge E.

At 3.2 mi. the trail levels. It swings S and passes the first view of Beecher Lake (through the trees) at 3.5 mi. The trail climbs gradually, turning sharply L at 3.6 mi. and passing through a rocky ledge before switching back S. At 4.0 mi. the trail reaches the top of a large rock ledge with a wonderful view of Beecher Lake and the Beaverkill Range to the S.

Leaving the vista, the trail turns back E, easily climbs over another high point on the ridge (3420 ft.) at 4.1 mi. and then gradually descends, crossing a very small seasonal drainage at 4.4 mi. Continuing E on a nearly level traverse, the trail reaches a vista of Balsam Lake Mt., including the firetower, at 4.6 mi.

Turning sharply N, the trail begins a steep descent to the col between Mill Brook Ridge and Balsam Lake Mt. At 4.7 mi. the grade moderates as the trail swings gradually E.

Reaching the col at 4.8 mi., the trail turns ESE, climbing gradually until reaching a short but steep ascent at 5.0 mi. After turning sharply R and ascending a ledge, the trail turns E and follows along the top of the ledge, a sort of shelf from which are nice views of a mature hardwood forest. The trail turns S and passes a vista of a pair of beaver ponds in the Balsam Lake drainage at 5.15 mi.

Continuing S along the shelf, the trail crosses a seasonal spring at 5.3 mi., after which it begins a moderate ascent of Balsam Lake Mt. After a few switchbacks and occasional steep climbs, the trail reaches a jct. with a path to the most scenic vista on the mountain at 5.7 mi. Straight (N) 50 ft. is the view of the western Catskills from a fern glade.

The trail turns sharply R and heads E over level ground to join the red-marked Balsam Lake Mt. Trail (Trail 83) at 5.8 mi. Turn L to reach the summit of Balsam Lake Mt., 0.1 mi. N. The Balsam Lake Mt. lean-tos and spring are 0.25 mi. S, and the Balsam Lake Mt. Trailhead parking lot at the end of Beaverkill Rd. is 1.65 mi. S.

Distances: To lean-to at Beaver Meadow, 1.5 mi.; to highest point on Mill Brook Ridge (3480 ft.), 2.8 mi.; to Beecher Lake Vista, 4.0 mi.; to Balsam Lake Mt. Trail, 5.8 mi.; to summit of Balsam Lake Mt. (3720 ft.), 5.9 mi. (6.7 mi. from Alder Lake Trailhead Parking Area). Ascent from Alder Lake, 1520 ft.

(47A) Red Hill Trail   Map 43: H-8

Red Hill in southern Ulster County was selected in 1920 as the southernmost Catskill site for a steel fire lookout station, bypassing the slightly higher Denman Mt. nearby. It was staffed by a DEC observer until 1991, the last manned tower in the Forest Preserve. From the late 1930s to the mid-70s, observers, along with the general public, used an access road from the S. But then the private land over which it ran was sold and the new owner denied access.

No official easement had ever been obtained by the state for this road. So access today is over state Forest Preserve land by way of a new yellow-blazed foot trail from the N built in 1996 by members of the NY-NJ Trail Conference and DEC.

A slice of Forest Preserve land, an isolated piece of the Sundown Wild Forest in the town of Denning, encompasses the summit of Red Hill and connects to Dinch Road. Provision of the Sundown Wild Forest Unit Management Plan calls for building a parking lot close to the trailhead when state funding materializes. Adirondack hikers will be interested to learn that DEC Forest Rangers Pete Fish (ret.) and Steve Ovitt served the Red Hill area before transfer to the Adirondacks.

A volunteer group of local citizens under leadership of Helen and George Elias is in the process of renovating Red Hill's tower in cooperation with DEC and the Catskill Center for Conservation and Development. The group hopes for a summer 2000 official tower reopening and the resources to finish restoration of the observer's cabin and to hire a summit guide (interpreter) in future years. For more information and to contribute to the effort, write the Red Hill Fire Tower Committee, PO Box 24, Grahamsville, NY 12740.

Trailhead: If coming from the N, take Kingston Exit 19 of the NYS Thruway, following Route 28 signs to the west, then S on NY 209 toward Ellenville. Proceed SW 26 mi. on NY 209, turning R (W) on NY 55. After 6 mi., keep R on NY 55A. Continue another 7 mi., passing N of Roundout Reservoir and dam, to a T intersection. Turn R on Co. Rt. 153 (Peekamoose Road) marked to Sundown and Shokan. After 0.2 mi., turn L on Sugar Loaf Road. Continue uphill 4.2 mi., making an abrupt L turn on Red Hill Rd. After 100 yds. Dinch Rd. goes R, but on the L is a gravel lot that makes a convenient meeting spot. Reset your trip odometer to 0.0 here. Drive up unpaved Dinch Rd. past a height of land and the unmarked Rudolph Rd. to the R at 0.55 mi. Continue downhill along Dinch Rd. despite a "Dead End" *sign. Avoid a L turn into a private driveway at 0.7 mi. At 0.9 mi. a wide spot on the R provides turn-in parking for 3–4 cars. The trailhead is still farther downhill, but parking and turnaround space is more difficult there. Walk down Dinch Rd. After 360 yds. surveyor's flagging and DEC signs mark the beginning of state land on the L side. Ninety yds. farther along, yellow DEC disks mark the trail veering L into the woods.*

If coming from the S, *the intersection of NY 209 and NY 55 can be reached from NY 17 by driving 15 mi. N along NY 209 through Ellenville.*

If coming from the W, *leave NY 17 at Liberty, following NY 55 E to its jct. with 55A just past Grahamsville, thence L (N) on 55A to its jct. with Co. Rt. 153 (Peekamoose Rd.), and straight ahead on Rt. 153 to Sugar Loaf Rd. as indicated above.*

Leaving Dinch Rd., the trail traverses attractive mature second-growth hardwoods of maple, beech, cherry, poplar and ash. Watch carefully for yellow DEC trail markers in the first half of the route where the footway is still ill-defined. At 0.1 mi., cross an often-dry creek bed and begin a steeper ascent. At 0.2 mi., the trail angles up R with exposed bedrock ledges L. It passes a small hemlock grove at 0.5 mi. on the R.

At 0.7 mi., the route bears R where the trail merges with an old wagon road coming in from the L. Along this section, rock piles and uniform tree size on the R indicate an old farm.

The trail leaves the wagon road at 0.8 mi., following yellow markers L more steeply uphill. The trail alternates between uphill and level sections for the next half mile until at 1.3 mi. it levels off for the last time and the fire tower can be glimpsed between the trees ahead. The observer's cabin is on the R and a smaller utility building and outhouse on the L. The 60-foot tower is reached at 1.4 mi. in a pleasant clearing surrounded by large maple and red spruce, the latter thought to have been planted.

Views from the tower, the most southerly such outpost in Catskill

Park, are impressive. **To the S,** the three bodies of water are all sections of Roundout Reservoir, part of the complex NYC water supply system. Water flows here from reservoirs on the East and West Branches of the Delaware River and from the Neversink drainage through underground aqueducts. Above Roundout Reservoir, the Shawangunk ridge is on the horizon. Looking far leftward to the SE, with small binoculars one can pick out Mohonk's Sky Top Tower. **To the E,** R to L, one sees Peekamoose, Table and Lone Mts. Left of Lone Mt. in the distance are Balsam Cap and Friday. The next peak L and the apparent highest is Slide Mt., which is indeed the highest point in the Catskills. **Looking N** are three summits; the rightmost one with a distinctive flatish top is Doubletop. In the middle is Graham, and to its left Balsam Lake Mt., whose summit fire tower is visible with low-power binoculars or even the keen naked eye on a clear day. **To the SW** the horizon is dominated by the nearby and slightly higher Denman Mt., at 3053 ft.

Distance: *To old wagon rd., 0.7 mi.; to fire tower on summit, 1.4 mi. Summit elevation, 2990 ft. (911 m). Ascent, 890 ft. (297 m).*

Trail in Winter: *The route to the trailhead, especially the last 1.2 mi. along Dinch Rd., is not likely plowed. Having walked or skied to the trailhead, the climber may well prefer snowshoes to skis. The first half of the route is narrow and not well-enough defined to recommend for skiing.*

Notes

Notes

Notes

The Adirondack Mountain Club, Inc.
814 Goggins Road, Lake George, NY 12845-4117
(518) 668-4447/Orders only: 800-395-8080 (M–S, 8:30–5:00)

BOOKS

85 Acres: A Field Guide to the Adirondack Alpine Summits
Adirondack Canoe Waters: North Flow
Adirondack Mt. Club Canoe Guide to East-Central New York State
Adirondack Mt. Club Canoe Guide to Western & Central New York State
An Adirondack Passage: The Cruise of the Canoe *Sairy Gamp*
The Adirondack Reader
An Adirondack Sampler I: Day Hikes for All Seasons
An Adirondack Sampler II: Backpacking Trips
Catskill Day Hikes for All Seasons
Classic Adirondack Ski Tours
Climbing in the Adirondacks: A Guide to Rock & Ice Routes
Forests & Trees of the Adirondack High Peaks Region
Guide to Adirondack Trails: High Peaks Region
Guide to Adirondack Trails: Northern Region
Guide to Adirondack Trails: Central Region
Guide to Adirondack Trails: Northville–Placid Trail
Guide to Adirondack Trails: West-Central Region
Guide to Adirondack Trails: Eastern Region
Guide to Adirondack Trails: Southern Region
Guide to Catskill Trails
Kids on the Trail! Hiking with Children in the Adirondacks
Our Wilderness: How the People of New York Found,
Changed, and Preserved the Adirondacks
Trailside Notes: A Naturalist's Companion to Adirondack Plants
Views from on High: Fire Tower Trails in the Adirondacks and Catskills
Winterwise: A Backpacker's Guide

MAPS

Trails of the Adirondack High Peaks Region
Trails of the Northern Region
Trails of the Central Region
Northville–Placid Trail
Trails of the West-Central Region
Trails of the Eastern Region
Trails of the Southern Region
Trails of the Catskill Region
(see p. xiii)

THE ADIRONDACK MOUNTAIN CLUB CALENDAR

Price list available on request.

Backdoor to Backcountry

ADKers choose from friendly outings, for those just getting started with local chapters, to Adirondack backpacks and international treks. Learn gradually through chapter outings or attend one of our schools, workshops, or other programs. A sampling includes:

- Alpine Flora
- Ice Climbing
- Rock Climbing
- Basic Canoeing/Kayaking
- Bicycle Touring
- Cross-country Skiing
- Mountain Photography
- Winter Mountaineering
- Birds of the Adirondacks
- Geology of the High Peaks
  ... and so much more!

For more information about the Adirondacks or about ADK:

ADK's Information Center & Headquarters
814 Goggins Rd., Lake George, NY 12845-4117
Tel. (518) 668-4447   Fax: (518) 668-3746
Exit 21 off I-87 ("the Northway"), 9N south

Business hours: 8:30 A.M.–5:00 P.M., Monday–Saturday

For more information about our lodges:

ADK Lodges
Box 867, Lake Placid, NY 12946
Tel. (518) 523-3441, 9 A.M.–7:00 P.M.

Visit our Web site at www.adk.org

Join a Chapter

Three-quarters of ADK members belong to a local chapter. Those not wishing to join a particular chapter may join ADK as members-at-large.

Chapter membership brings you the fun of outings and social activities or the reward of working on trails, conservation, and education projects at the local level. You can still participate in all regular Club activities and receive all benefits.

Adirondak Loj .... North Elba
Albany .... Albany
Algonquin .... Plattsburgh
Black River .... Watertown
Cold River .... Long Lake
Finger Lakes .... Ithaca–Elmira
Genesee Valley .... Rochester
Glens Falls–Saratoga .... Glens Falls–Saratoga area
Hurricane Mountain .... Keene
Iroquois .... Utica
Keene Valley .... Keene Valley
Knickerbocker .... New York City area
Lake Placid .... Lake Placid
Laurentian .... Canton-Potsdam
Long Island .... Long Island
Mid-Hudson .... Poughkeepsie
Mohican .... Westchester and Putnam Counties
New York .... New York City area
Niagara Frontier .... Buffalo
North Jersey... Bergen County
North Woods .... Saranac Lake–Tupper Lake
Onondaga .... Syracuse
Ramapo .... Rockland & Orange Counties
Schenectady .... Schenectady
Shatagee Woods .... Malone
Susquehanna .... Oneonta

Membership
To Join

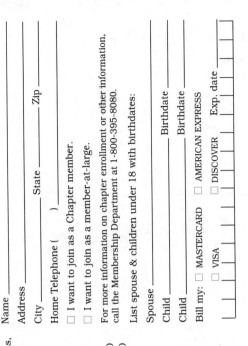

Adirondack
ADK
Mountain Club

Call **1-800-395-8080** (American Express, Mastercard, Visa, or Discover) or send this form with payment to
Adirondack Mountain Club
814 Goggins Road
Lake George, NY 12845-4117.

Check Membership Level:

☐ Life Family	$1,800
☐ Life Individual	$1,200
☐ Family	$55
☐ Adult	$45
☐ Senior Family	$45
☐ Senior (65+) or Student	$35

School _____

Fees subject to change.

Name _____

Address _____

City _____ State _____ Zip _____

Home Telephone (____) _____

☐ I want to join as a Chapter member.

☐ I want to join as a member-at-large.

For more information on chapter enrollment or other information, call the Membership Department at 1-800-395-8080.

List spouse & children under 18 with birthdates:

Spouse _____

Child _____ Birthdate _____

Child _____ Birthdate _____

Bill my: ☐ MASTERCARD   ☐ AMERICAN EXPRESS
         ☐ VISA   ☐ DISCOVER   Exp. date _____

☐☐☐☐ ☐☐☐☐ ☐☐☐☐ ☐☐☐☐

_____
Signature (required for charge)

ADK is a non-profit, tax-exempt organization. Membership fees are tax deductible, as allowed by law. Please allow 6-8 weeks for receipt of first issue of **Adirondac.**

GCAT

Membership Benefits

- **Discovery:**
  ADK can broaden your horizons by introducing you to new places, recreational activities, and interests.

- **Enjoyment:**
  Being outdoors more and loving it more.

- **People:**
  Meeting others and sharing the fun.

- *Adirondac Magazine.*

- **Member Discounts:**
  20% off on guidebooks, maps, and other ADK publications; 10% off on lodge stays; reduced rates for educational programs.

- **Satisfaction:**
  Knowing you're doing your part and that future generations will enjoy the wilderness as you do.

- **Chapter participation:**
  Brings you the fun of outings and other social activities and the reward of working on trails, conservation, and education projects at the local level. You can also join as a member-at-large. Either way, all Club activities and benefits are available.

Adirondack **ADK** Mountain Club   Conservation Recreation Education